*The Transfer
and Transformation
of Ideas
and Material Culture*

The Transfer
and Transformation
of Ideas
and Material Culture

Edited by Peter J. Hugill and D. Bruce Dickson

Texas A&M University Press

COLLEGE STATION

The paper used in this book meets the minimum requirements
of the American National Standard for Permanence
of Paper for Printed Library Materials, Z39.48–1984.
Binding materials have been chosen for durability.

∞™

Library of Congress Cataloging-in-Publication Data
The Transfer and transformation of ideas and material
    culture.

    Bibliography: p.
    1. Culture diffusion.   2. Social change.   I. Hugill,
Peter J.   II. Dickson, D. Bruce.
GN365.T73   1988   303.4   87–7115
ISBN 0–89096–364–9 (alk. paper)
ISBN 1-58544-079-5 (pbk.)

To Judy and Mary Ann

_____

Contents

Acknowledgments

The chapters in this volume had their genesis in papers given at an international, multidisciplinary conference held at Texas A&M University in November, 1984. The conference was jointly sponsored by the Colleges of Geosciences and Liberal Arts. Contributors wrote their papers in advance, addressed the issues raised by their research, and modified their papers based on the ensuing discussion.

The authors would like to express their gratitude to all the people who made possible both the diffusion conference and this volume of papers derived from it. Special thanks go to Melvin Friedman, dean of the College of Geosciences, and Daniel Fallon, dean of the College of Liberal Arts, for supporting this endeavor from inception to conclusion with advice, encouragement, and financial aid. Without this unflagging help, neither the conference nor this volume would have been possible. Dean Friedman also invited Professor Torsten Hägerstrand to deliver his conference paper as the Annual Geosciences University Lecture. We would also like to thank Frank E. Vandiver, president of Texas A&M University, for inviting William McNeill to deliver his conference paper to the university community at large as a Presidential Lecture. Our thanks go also to Brian W. Blouet, head of the Department of Geography; Vaughn M. Bryant, Jr., head of the Department of Anthropology; Henry C. Dethloff, head of the Department of History; and Jerry C. Gaston, head of the Department of Sociology—all at Texas A&M. All of these men gave generously of their time in assisting us with the organization of the conference and supported the conference with departmental funds. We would be remiss if we did not thank those scholars who participated in the conference as presenters or discussants. In addition to the authors included in this volume, we are grateful for the participation of James B. Blaut of the University of Illinois; Lawrence A. Brown of Ohio State University; Ernest Easterly of Geoforensics, Inc.; Milton B. Newton, Jr., of Louisiana State University; Mary Lee Nolan of Oregon State University; and Clarissa T. Kimber, Michael B. Levy, W. Alex McIntosh, and Mary Zey-Ferrell of Texas A&M University. Thanks are also due to Miles Richardson, head of the Department of Geography and Anthropology at Louisiana State University, for his critical reading of the conference manuscripts. Finally, we should like to thank Campbell W. Pennington for hosting a particularly pleasant and memorable conference reception.

Introduction

The study of "diffusion" is an undertaking closely associated with cultural geography. Such studies form the centerpiece of the discipline; diffusion, as an explanatory "ism," is often taken as the organizing paradigm of that branch of geography. However, the transfer and transformation of ideas and material culture across space and time is a phenomenon confronted by many other disciplines as well. The study of diffusion has been particularly important in the fields of anthropology and archeology; more recently it has become important in the study of history. Consequently, academic diffusion research is varied and complex, and no comprehensive account of it will be attempted here. Instead, this Introduction provides short overviews of the place of diffusion research in the disciplines of anthropology, geography, and history, and attempts to place in the context of such research the chapters that make up this volume.

Diffusion Research in Anthropology

Sentimentalists find the roots of anthropology in the writings of Herodotus or the Renaissance Humanists. Practically speaking, however, the discipline does not figure significantly in Western thought until the early nineteenth century. Its continental formulation may be found in the writings of Herder, De Signivy, Bachofen and, less certainly, Vico. Anglo-

American anthropology emerged first in the work of McLennan, Maine, Morgan, and Tylor, later in that of Frazer and Boas. Inasmuch as the boundaries of these traditions—like those of the land masses they refer to—were never impervious to external influence, a vigorous intellectual cross-fertilization took place between European and Anglo-American anthropology, as well as between anthropology and related disciplines.

Late nineteenth- and early twentieth-century anthropology, especially that of continental Europe, was strongly influenced by the diffusion theories of the German *Kulturkreis* school of "anthropogeography," and by the historicism and particularism practiced by its members. Foremost in this school were Friedrich Ratzel (1844–1904) and Leo Frobenius (1873–1938). The *Kulturkreis*—literally, "culture circle"—school emerged as part of the reaction to cultural evolutionism, which had dominated the study of culture and society since the mid-1800s.[1] In contrast to the evolutionists, members of this school rejected the notion that human cultures had traversed a single, universal set of developmental stages. Their studies of culture history began with detailed historical analyses and thorough descriptions of the evidence in each particular case rather than with a superficial sorting of all cultures into a priori general categories. The aim of such studies was the reconstruction of the *Urkulturen* or "original cultures" of humankind. In the view of this school, (1) the *Urkulturen* were few in number, (2) the historical configurations of human culture in the world resulted from the diffusion of single traits together with the migration of peoples bearing whole complexes of traits from these *Urkulturen* centers, and (3) diffusion and migration tended to radiate outward from the centers in roughly concentric circles or *kreise* and could thus be traced back to them by means of the careful description and comparison of culture traits.[2]

Despite the systematic and thorough nature of their method, the *Urkulturen* "reconstructed" by members of this school were marred by their excessive reliance on formal similarity between culture traits as proof of historical connection. This led them to the fallacious premise that distance or distributional discontinuity between occurrences of a trait or trait complex were essentially irrelevant to the reconstructions of the historical patterns of diffusion.[3]

Diffusion was recognized as an alternative to evolution in British, as well as continental, anthropology early in this century. Among the most influential exponents of diffusion as an explanation of culture change were the British anatomist G. Elliot Smith (1871–1937) and his disciples W. J. Perry (1887–1949), and W. H. R. Rivers (1864–1922). Smith, Perry, and

Rivers began with the premise that humankind is essentially "uninventive." To them, cultural change was generally due to borrowing rather than independent invention. They coupled this premise with the corollary view that contact between peoples led to diffusion by what Leaf has called "a kind of cultural osmosis."[4] In this volume, Dickson refers to this notion as "epidemic contagion."

These premises remained central to the diffusionist argument in anthropology long after most scholars had rejected Smith, Perry, and Rivers's claim that the bulk of human culture had arisen in Egypt, spread from there throughout the world, and was expressed in only a degenerated form beyond its Nilotic center of origin. Nevertheless, Smith, Perry, and Rivers transformed the study of cultural diffusion from a simple ideographic undertaking into an all-embracing, nomothetic, explanatory "ism."

In American anthropology, the triumph of diffusionism was most evident in the American Indian ethnology of Clark Wissler (1870–1967). Wissler rejected the simplistic view that American Indian culture was essentially static and uniform. He emphasized the geographic diversity of Native American culture and sought to classify its traditions in terms of location and dominant subsistence patterns.[5] What emerged was the distinctly "anthropogeographic" concept of the "culture area." As the term has come to be understood in anthropology, a culture area is:

A part of the world where inhabitants tend to share most of the elements of culture, such as related languages, similar ecological conditions, economic systems, social systems and ideological systems. The separate groups within the area may or may not all be members of the same breeding population.[6]

Wissler originally defined fifteen separate culture areas for the New World.[7] In a later modification, the fifteen anthropogeographic units were reduced to eight.[8] As subsistence became the chief criterion for distinguishing one from another, Wissler referred to these units as the eight major "food areas" of the New World. He concluded that the cultural similarities that existed between the separate peoples within each of these culture areas resulted in large part from diffusion from single "culture centers" within each of them. The culture center was presumed to be the location where all the definitive traits of the culture area were found to coexist; as one moved farther and farther away from the culture center, the number of co-occuring traits began to diminish and their nature began to change. Thus in Wissler's scheme, culture areas were not marked by rigid boundaries. Instead, they were characterized by clinal distributions of traits and graded gently from one to another. Although his scheme was based on ethnographic data, Wissler willingly used archeological evidence to demonstrate that similar complexes of culture traits had persisted within these culture or food areas for long periods of time.

Alfred L. Kroeber (1876–1960) elaborated Wissler's culture areas schema in his classic work, "Cultural and Natural Areas of Native North America."[9] Although he retained Wissler's emphasis on diffusion from a culture center as the primary explanation for the similarity of traits within a given culture area, Kroeber closely related these trait distributions to similarity of environment and material conditions of existence within culture areas, and contrasts in such variables between culture areas.

Anthropological diffusion studies in America were also enriched by the work of Edward Sapir (1884–1939) and Roland B. Dixon (1875–1934). Sapir laid out the logic of diffusion studies in rigorous, if rather one-dimensional, axiomatic fashion.[10] Dixon virtually rejected independent invention as an important element in the genesis of human cultures. He crafted a series of conceptual definitions that received wide currency in anthropology.[11]

The popularity of diffusionist explanations of culture began to decline in mid-twentieth-century anthropology and scholars emphasized: (1) the psychic unity of humankind, (2) the principle of limited possibilities, and (3) the concept of cultural integration. The first of these three doctrines has ancient pedigrees in both geography and anthropology. The admission that humankind consists of a single species presupposes a certain worldwide uniformity in the nature of the human mental process. Such uniformity would presumably lead over time to the independent solution of the same problems by similar means.

The principle of limited possibilities builds on this assumption of human psychic unity. It asserts (1) that human beings have certain primary needs, and (2) that the means whereby these primary needs can be satisfied are limited in number.[12] This principle accounted nicely for the similarities found by anthropologists between kinship systems among widely separated and historically unrelated peoples throughout the world. Anthropologists rejected the view that diffusion accounted for these similarities, as it became apparent that the possible forms that human kinship and family organization can take are determined in large part by the nature of human sexuality and reproduction. For example, the similarity between the system of kinship terminology used by the Eskimo and that of contemporary Americans became understandable in these terms.[13] Hägerstrand discusses this principle in a very original manner in this volume.

A third doctrine that anthropologists tend to counterpoise to diffusionist explanations is the view that cultures are "integrated" entities or systems and therefore resistant to the process of "cultural osmosis" posited by radical diffusionism. This view derives its inspiration from the sociology of Durkheim via the Anglo-American schools of functionalism and structural functionalism. In this view, cultural traits and institutional arrangements persist because they "work." The interconnection among these traits and institutions inhibits change. The diffusionist argument begins with the assumption that human beings are inherently uninventive and consequently are inveterate copiers; the functionalist argument assumes that they are conservative and resistant to change. Although there is truth in each of these assumptions, when carried to extremes both become absurd. In their zealous correction of the errors of radical diffusionism, anthropologists often articulated an equally distorted doctrine that Ammerman and Cavalli-Sforza have christened "indigenism."[14] Scholars of this persuasion invariably see the process of culture change as self-contained and seek the sources of innovation within the local population or cultural tradition that they happen to be studying.

It is safe to say that contemporary anthropologists and archeologists willingly acknowledge that diffusion has occurred throughout prehistory and history. However, they are less likely to agree on the significance of diffusion in a given cultural context and do not regard diffusion*ism* as holding much explanatory power in and of itself. The decline of distribution studies in the discipline testifies to the general view among anthropologists that the "fact" of diffusion explains little; more interesting and significant are contextual or processual questions, like "Why do some things diffuse whereas others do not?" and "Which cultural similarities are due to contact, and which are due to the laws of culture"?

Diffusion Research in Geography

Historically, human geography seeks to answer two major questions: "How do human beings interact with their environment?" and "How is human activity distributed through and expressed in space?" Although these questions have often been viewed as independent of one another, cultural geographers have generally seen them as related and have attempted to answer them both. Both of these questions center on the nature of the relationship between human culture and the environment: Is culture the independent variable and environment the dependent variable, or is it the reverse? Does environment determine culture, or culture the environment?

Although descriptive, empirical writing about lands and peoples began in classical times, the finest expression of this tradition is to be found in the work of the nineteenth-century German scholars Alexander von Humbolt (1769–1859) and Carl Ritter (1779–1859). Ritter's work, however, is marked by a pronounced dualism between geography as the study of "areal differences of spatially associated phenomena" and geography as the science of the earth.[15] These dual perspectives persist in academic geography to the present time. In the first perspective, geography is anthropocentric; the earth is studied as the home of humankind. In the second perspective, human beings can be excluded and only physical geographic features need be studied. In Ritter's anthropocentric work lies the clear origin of the three major trends in human geography: (1) environmentalist theories of the causation of human behavior; (2) a descriptive regional geography of areal differentiation; and (3) a diffusionist theory to account for distributions.

In the later nineteenth century two more German scholars, Ferdinand von Richtofen (1833–1905) and Friedrich Ratzel (1844–1904), attempted to bridge the gap between the human and physical geographic perspectives. Both von Richtofen and Ratzel aimed to integrate environmentalism and the evidence of human transformations of the natural environment. Ratzel's contribution reflected his training as a naturalist and ethnographer, Richtofen's his training as a geologist. Those geographers whose academic background was in geology tended to attribute a causal role to the environment in their interpretations of human behavior.

American geographers, including William Morris Davis (1850–1947), Elsworth Huntington (1876–1947), and Ellen Churchill Semple (1863–1932), also tended to see the environment as the independent variable in human affairs. Of these three, the major contributor to American environmentalist geography was Semple, a Vassar graduate who studied under Ratzel (see chap. 8 in this volume). Semple's environmentalism took a much more sophisticated form than Huntington's reductionist view of human behavior. In her last great work Semple analyzed the development of the Mediterranean as a region naturally facilitating and focusing the movement of peoples and ideas,[16] an idea later elaborated by Fernand Braudel,[17] and ably furthered in this volume by Karl Butzer (chap. 5).

The reaction against environmental determinism in geography is found in the work of a number of scholars at mid-century. However, the most effective opponent of the doctrine was Carl O. Sauer (1889–1975). Sauer preferred the anthropocentric side of Ritter's dualism, viewed the earth as the home of humankind, and was concerned with accounting for the distribution of culture traits. After assuming the chair in geography at Berkeley in 1923, Sauer became strongly influenced by the work of his Berkeley anthropological colleague, Alfred Kroeber.[18] This influence no doubt stemmed in part from Sauer's personal predilections for the communitarian societies of the pre-industrial world; it may also have resulted from the intellectual debt both men owed Ratzel.[19]

In the doctrine of diffusion, Sauer found a way of accounting for the occurrence of culture traits that left humanity in control, yet did not discount the intimate relationship between human beings and their physical environment in preindustrial societies. Sauer and many of his students concentrated on the part of the preindustrial world nearest Berkeley: Central America. These scholars found ample evidence of widespread diffusion of ideas and material culture, facilitated by the topography of the region and not yet destroyed by the centralizing tendencies of industrial society. In a memorable essay, Sauer compared the Caribbean to the Mediterranean as a medium for both facilitating and limiting the diffusion of persons, ideas, and material culture.[20] In Kuhn's terms,[21] Sauer wrought a paradigm shift in human geography that, although strongly questioned in recent years, has yet to be overturned.

In the later 1950s and early 1960s, environmental determinism and descriptive regional geography fell out of intellectual favor. With their passing, the last vestiges of nondiffusionist human geography were swept away by a consciously social scientific and mathematical approach to the problem of explaining both distributions and the location of human activity. This new research direction emerged in large part from the central place theory of the German geographer Walter Christaller (1893–1969).[22] Economic geography as a distinct subdivision of the discipline developed in large measure out of this research stream. Despite attempts of economic geographers to distance themselves from cultural geography, both subdisciplines owe a clear debt to the *Kulturkreis* school of anthropogeography.

The crossover point between the two subdisciplines is found in the work of the Swedish geographer Torsten Hägerstrand (1916–   ) and his students. Mathematical models of diffusion, first generated by Hägerstrand, considerably improved geographers' understanding of the patterns of transmission of ideas and culture traits.[23] Nonetheless, like Sauer, Hägerstrand and his students were concerned with the complex interaction over time between persons, ideas, and the environment. This willingness to consider the effects of this interaction on the morphology of trait distributions distinguished both Hägerstrand and Sauer from the German formal locational theorists such as Christaller and August Lösch.

In addition to the use of mathematics, the diffusionism of Hägerstrand can be distinguished from that of Sauer on another dimension. Sauer and his students generally concentrated their attention on the preindustrial world, but Hägerstrand and his students have been much more concerned with the modern, industrial world. The contrasting nature of their subject matter has important theoretical and practical implications for the work of both. In preindustrial societies, human impact on and control of the physical environment was generally limited. Agriculture was the first and most profound way in which preindustrial peoples altered their environment and, perhaps as a consequence, the Berkeley geographers developed an almost obsessive concern with its worldwide origins and dispersal. The distribution of identical cultivated plants through widely varied physical environments was viewed by Sauer and his students as an obvious indictment of environmental determinism, because such distribution could be accounted for only by reference to human agency. Fred B. Kniffen, as well as other students of Sauer, extended their interests beyond plants to include such other elements of preindustrial agriculture as field patterns and hedge, fence, barn, and house types.[24]

Unfortunately, Sauer and his students were seldom able to formally document the diffusion processes by which they proposed to account for the preindustrial distribution of such traits. Further, they did not feel that their specific analyses of origins and diffusions required a minute accounting for every detail of the processes. They used a method of logical inference from limited data, which often cast them in the role of advocate rather than scientist. Sauer's own *Agricultural Origins and Dispersals* was the model for this genre.[25] Sauer examined the problem of agricultural origins in a logical fashion. He constructed plausible models of the societies likely and unlikely to have developed agriculture dependent upon the nature of the physical environment these societies would have manipulated as hunters and gatherers. His analysis of the dispersal process emphasized the patterns of ocean currents that would have facilitated or impeded the routes open to preindustrial watercraft, as well as the topographic barriers that similarly would have affected human movement overland. In this account, human-kind was pictured as curious, mobile, and an active agency in changing the face of the earth. The existence of identical culture traits in a similar time frame, however far apart, implied the probability of diffusion if the means for that diffusion to have occurred could logically be shown to exist.

Among Sauer's students, George F. Carter (1912–) has been foremost in suggesting a radical diffusionism based on the *Kulturkreis* model. Carter has suggested a single origin of agriculture,[26] and has emphasized the ability of even the earliest of humans to move around the planet relatively easily.[27] Other of Sauer's students, notably Philip L. Wagner (1921–),[28] have been singularly adept at this type of logical, inferential style with its intense concentration on human manipulation of the environment.

In industrial societies, however, technological power and control is so great that the physical environment recedes into the background. The most problematic part of the environment is the social one. The distribution of ideas is shaped by their interaction with the social environment: the complex interaction of cultural, institutional, economic, and political forces. Industrial societies also offer far better data bases from which to study the diffusion of ideas: documentation supercedes the evidence of material culture. Documentation also offers far more opportunity for mathematical analysis.

Diffusion Research in History

The historian William H. McNeill (1917–) makes significant use of documentary, artifactual, and artistic evidence for diffusion in history in his book *The Rise of the West*.[29] McNeill emphasized the substantial debt of the West to diffusion of ideas and material culture, a debt rarely recognized until his writing, except by specialized historians such as Joseph Needham (1900–). Needham's monumental work, *Science and Civilization in China*,[30] indicates strong diffusion from China to the West, a tradition McNeill has done much to confirm in his more recent work.[31] Similar themes have been followed by Lynn White concerning the diffusion of the stirrup from China into medieval Europe via nomadic folk, and the consequent rise of feudalism.[32] As with the cultural geographers, McNeill has a strong sense of interaction between human beings and their environment, although his concern is more global: he is interested in charting the development of the agrarian underpinnings of the "moral-political universe" upon which European civilization rests.

Of all historians, business historians, with their interest in the transmission of the technology of the industrial world, have been most notably diffusionist in outlook. A great deal of attention in this field has been given to the early history of industrialization. Compared with other areas of human endeavor, considerable documentary evidence for the transmission of ideas and material culture exists.[33] Quite naturally, business historians have paid particular attention to the industrialization of early America,[34] Japan,[35] and continental Europe,[36] and to the massive transmission of ideas and material culture occasioned by that industrialization. America and Japan offer competing models of the process of industrial development: America received much of its needed investment monies from abroad, whereas Japan generated most of its internally. Despite the contrasting sources of their investment capital, however, both states imported significant amounts of technology from the industrially more developed nations of Europe. Japanese business historians have been particularly forthright in recognizing the crucial role that diffusion of foreign technology has played in the emergence of Japanese industry.

Many of the recent accounts of the diffusion of technology written by business historians are very much in the style of Carl Sauer. They tend to be nonmathematical accounts of the "origins and dispersals" of particular technologies or technical processes throughout the industrial world. They differ in that the documentation of such industrial diffusion is far more ample than for the preindustrial traits treated by Sauer and his students. In addition, business historians are generally unconcerned with the physical environment and place considerable emphasis on such intangibles as "national character" and "business climate," which diffusionist social scientists avoid.

Summary

Diffusion research has moved away from much of the historicism and particularism that characterized its early history. Although anthropologists have reduced their interest in distribution studies, they are still vitally concerned with the contextual and processual questions that address the issue of what diffuses and why and whether laws of culture may be formulated.

Quantitative human geographers have refined distributional studies to the status of nomothetic laws, in which diffusion paths may be very accurately predicted. Cultural geographers and, to a lesser extent, historians have concerned themselves with qualitative statements about diffusion patterns without losing sight of context or process, but without the rigor of the quantitative human geographers.

We believe that a dialogue among these three groups is a necessary and valuable one, and that the set of essays encompassed by this volume provides the beginnings of that dialogue.

Notes

1. See Robert H. Lowie, *The History of Ethnological Theory* (New York: Holt, Rinehart and Winston, 1937), pp. 157, 177–94.

2. See Annemarie deWaal Malefut, *Images of Man; a History of Anthropological Theory* (New York: Knopf, 1974), pp. 164–71.

3. See Lowie, *History*, p. 158.

4. Murray J. Leaf, *Man, Mind, and Science; A History of Anthropology* (New York: Columbia University Press, 1979), p. 166.

5. See Malefut, *Images*, p. 174.

6. Mary Ann Foley, "Culture Area," in D. E. Hunter and Philip Whitten, eds., *Encyclopedia of Anthropology* (New York: Harper and Row, 1976), p. 104.

7. Clark Wissler, *The American Indian: An Introduction to the Anthropology of the New World* (New York: McMurtrie, 1917).

8. Clark Wissler, *Man and Culture* (New York: Crowell, 1923).

9. Alfred L. Kroeber, "Cultural and Natural Areas of Native North America," *University of California Publications in American Archaeology and Ethnology* 38 (1939): 1–242.

10. Edward Sapir, *Culture, Language and Personality* (Berkeley: University of California Press, 1949).

11. Roland B. Dixon, *The Building of Cultures* (New York: Scribner's, 1928).

12. See Alexander A. Goldenweiser, *Early Civilization* (New York: Knopf, 1922), p. 302.

13. See George Peter Murdock, *Social Structure* (New York: MacMillan, 1949).

14. Albert J. Ammerman and L. L. Cavalli-Sforza, *The Neolithic Transition and the Genetics of Populations in Europe* (Princeton, N.J.: Princeton University Press, 1984), p. xiv.

15. See Robert E. Dickinson, *The Makers of Modern Geography* (London: Routledge & Kegan Paul, 1969), p. 41.

16. Ellen C. Semple, *The Geography of the Mediterranean Region: Its Relation to Ancient History* (New York: Holt, 1931).

17. Fernand Braudel, *The Mediterranean and the Mediterranean World in the Age of Philip II*, 2 vols. (New York: Harper & Row, 1973).

18. See Robert S. Platt, "The Rise of Cultural Geography in America," in Philip L. Wagner and Marvin W. Mikesell, eds., *Readings in Cultural Geography* (Chicago: University of Chicago Press, 1962), p. 39.

19. Friedrich Ratzel, *Anthropogeographie*, 2 vols. (Stuttgart: J. Engelhorn, 1921).

20. Carl O. Sauer, "Middle America as a Culture Historical Location," in Wagner and Mikesell, *Readings*, pp. 195–201.

21. Thomas S. Kuhn, *The Structure of Scientific Revolutions* (Chicago: University of Chicago Press, 1962).

22. Walter Christaller, *Central Places in Southern Germany* (Englewood Cliffs, N.J.: Prentice-Hall, 1966).

23. Torsten Hägerstrand, *Innovation Diffusion as a Spatial Process* (Chicago: University of Chicago Press, 1967).

24. See H. J. Walker and W. G. Haag, eds., *Man and Cultural Heritage: Papers in Honor of Fred B. Kniffen*, vol. 5 of *Geoscience and Man* (Baton Rouge: Louisiana State University, Department of Geography, 1974).

25. Carl O. Sauer, *Agricultural Origins and Dispersals* (New York: American Geographical Society, 1952).

26. George F. Carter, "A Hypothesis Suggesting a Single Origin of Agriculture," in Charles A. Reed, ed., *Origins of Agriculture* (The Hague: Mouton, 1977), pp. 99–109.

27. George F. Carter, *Earlier Than You Think; A Personal View of Man in America* (College Station: Texas A&M University Press, 1980).

28. Philip L. Wagner, *Environments and Peoples* (Englewood Cliffs, N.J.: Prentice-Hall, 1972); *The Human Use of the Earth* (New York: Free Press, 1960).

29. William H. McNeill, *The Rise of the West* (Chicago: University of Chicago Press, 1963).

30. Joseph Needham, *Science and Civilization in China*, vol. 1: *Introductory Orientations* (Cambridge: Cambridge University Press, 1954).

31. William H. McNeill, *The Pursuit of Power: Technology, Armed Force, and Society since A.D. 1000* (Chicago: University of Chicago Press, 1982).

32. Lynn White, Jr., *Medieval Technology and Social Change* (Oxford: Clarendon Press, 1962).

33. See A. G. Kenwood and A. L. Lougheed, *Technological Diffusion and Industrialization before 1914* (New York: St. Martin's, 1982).

34. See David J. Jeremy, *Transatlantic Industrial Revolution: The Diffusion of Textile Technologies between Britain and America, 1790–1830* (Cambridge: MIT Press, 1981).

35. See Akio Okochi and Hoshimi Uchida, eds., *Development and Diffusion of Technology; Electrical and Chemical Industries* (Tokyo: University of Tokyo Press, 1980). This is one of numerous volumes published by the University of Tokyo Press of the annual International Conference on Business History, nearly all of which deal with diffusion. See also A. Okochi and Shin-Ichi Yonekawa, eds., *The Textile Industry and Its Business Climate* (Tokyo: University of Tokyo Press, 1982); A. Okochi and Koichi Shimokawa, eds., *Development of Mass Marketing; The Automobile and Retailing Industries* (Tokyo: University of Tokyo Press, 1981).

36. See Clive Trebilcock, *The Industrialization of the Continental Powers, 1780–1914* (New York: Longman 1981).

PART ONE

Diffusion in Prehistory

CHAPTER ONE

Cultural Historical Diffusion

George F. Carter

The case for diffusion in culture history is most interesting. No one questions the fact that the spread of ideas goes on constantly. Within such limited areas as western Europe, diffusion is assumed, just as it is in limited areas in the Americas. As time and distance increase, the probability of diffusion tends to be viewed more and more negatively and independent invention as an explanation comes more and more to the fore. The hesitation over diffusion within continental areas undergoes a sea change when the great oceans are involved. There have been several humorous phrases coined for this, such as thalasophobia, fear of the sea. The real problem concerns the question of transoceanic contact with the Americas before A.D. 1500. This looms large because of the Americanist school that insists on the independent growth and development of American Indian civilizations. This is the point where I entered the diffusionist controversy some fifty years ago.

I had been granted an A.B. degree in anthropology at the University of California at Berkeley, working mostly under Alfred Kroeber and Robert Lowie. The entire program was ethnological and a splendid introduction to the field of cultural studies. We were flooded with facts, but most studies were of particular peoples in their locales. As students we were warned that such diffusionists as Sir Grafton Elliot Smith and his associates were dangerous radicals, and with that warning it was three decades before I read their work. When I became interested in American Indian portrayals of mammoths, mastodons, and elephants, I finally turned to Smith's *Elephants and Ethnologists* and discovered a witty and very well informed man.[1] He was

quite correct in his claim that MesoAmericans not only portrayed elephants but possessed the southeast Asian elephant mythology. Smith and
his school were half a century ahead of their time and have been most
unfairly lampooned. By this I do not intend a blanket endorsement of everything Smith wrote. I do, however, find that Smith is more often cussed than
discussed, and rarely read.

After graduation I continued work in archeology at the San Diego Museum of Man. A curious train of events thereafter returned me to Berkeley
for graduate study, but in geography under Carl Sauer. While studying under
Sauer, I was not aware of much emphasis on diffusion as a master process. It
was treated as natural. We knew it occurred, and we were aware of the
problem of fitting things into both the physical and the cultural environment, but we were remarkably innocent of trying to formulate laws concerning such processes.

Two Agricultures

When I began my thesis work on American Indian agriculture in the
American Southwest, my interests turned almost at once to crops. I made a
collection of corn, beans, and squash of the entire Southwest and discovered that there were two agricultures present.[2]

This suggested two routes by which crops had come into the area and
two times, or both. One agricultural wave seemed to have come from
Mexico, probably by sea, to the lower Mississippi area and to have spread
thence throughout the East but also across the Plains to the Pueblo region.
The other agriculture had clearly come up the west side of Mexico and was
the basis for the Pima-Papago (Hohokam) agriculture.

My thesis amounted to a huge change in the overview of the problem;
from a single, late agricultural diffusion to very early and plural diffusions.
My suggestion of agricultural beginnings in the Mississippi valley were
then considered five hundred to a thousand years too early. Today they seem
to be five hundred to a thousand years too late!

As a result of my interest in plant geography I was drawn into one of the
great cultural-historical diffusion battles of our time: the question of transoceanic influence on Native American cultures and the origins of these
Indian civilizations. A major theme in my work has been that diffusion is best
proven through biological transfers: plants and animals. Most domesticates

must also fit into a cultural framework of beliefs and usages. These are not easily or rapidly duplicated, so that the time available for duplication becomes an important consideration.

A case in point is that of *Cyprea Moneta*, the money cowry. In 1917 one of Smith's followers, Wilfred Jackson, published a major work on human use of shells. I have since written extensively on the role of this cowry, and Thor Heyerdahl, in *The Maldive Mystery*, has expanded our knowledge on the source of these shells.[3] Money cowries come from the Indian Ocean, but have been found in a burial mound from the Adena culture in Tennessee (500 B.C.–A.D. 500). This money cowry was a most significant find, for it is a biological item not subject to independent invention. Not only was it physically present in America as early as Adena time, but it was found to be currently in use in the most sacred rite of Algonkin tribes along the Great Lakes, the Midewiwin society. As Jackson noted, not only was it the same shell, but the same magical usages were associated with it in West Africa. There is also ample evidence that this rite was transmitted in hieroglyphic writing. This produces a total picture of a very early cultural complex including a biological item that has to be of Old World origin.[4] This association of biological, non-reinventable items with complex beliefs and religious practices forms evidence most difficult for isolationist, independent-inventionists to dispose of.

The best evidence for continued contact between the Old World and the New comes from the evidence of several major plants and the chicken. The plants are the sweet potato, peanut, hibiscus, and maize. Taken together, they form a convincing case for relatively regular contact, mostly across the Pacific. Two other plants, cotton and *cucurbita* (American pumpkins and squashes), introduce the story, for it was through accounts of these that I first seriously investigated the possible diffusion of plants and animals.

Cotton

In 1947 Hutchinson, Silow, and Stephens tackled the cytogenetics of cotton.[5] The taxonomy was confused, for it had grown historically through the chance collections of botanists around the world and lacked any synthesizing base. Looked at cytogenetically, the situation was simple. All Old World cottons had one genome. All New World wild cottons had a different genome. All New World domestic cottons had both genomes. Hutchinson, Silow, and Stephens postulated that continental drift had occurred. The problem was the reunification of the cottons to allow for the hybridization that produced the American domestic cottons. Their solution was to have man carry Old World domestic cotton across the Pacific to the New World, hybridize it (by accident), and so produce the New World domestic cottons.

Increased knowledge of the cotton genomes of the world has changed this picture. A more likely scenario would now invoke an Atlantic crossing to create the American domestic cottons. Hutchinson, Silow, and Stephens not only suggested that cotton had been carried across the Pacific, but listed several other plants that needed investigation. These included an American *cucurbita* in Hawaii and the American sweet potato in Polynesia. My reaction to Stephens's manuscript was utter disbelief.[6] I recall laying it down with shaking hands. But the plant evidence, something that I was accustomed to handling, seemed to say that trans-Pacific diffusion had occurred.

After a few days for reflection and consultation with geneticists, I began to look into the alleged American *cucurbita* (a pumpkin or squash) in Hawaii. In retrospect, I probably began there because my work in the Southwest had made me familiar with a wide range of American *cucurbitas*. I rapidly discovered that the Hawaiian case had been examined by others and that the plant in question was not a *cucurbita* from America but the bottle gourd, *Lagenaria siceraria*, whose probable home is Africa.

Sweet Potato

I then turned to the sweet potato question. Here again I found that the problem had long been under study. The first botanists in the Pacific had recognized that the same plant had the same name all over the Pacific and in a limited area in America. The definitive paper clarifying the historical material is by Donald Brand.[7] Early workers, such as R. B. Dixon, started with a strongly antidiffusionist bias. Dixon investigated the record of Polynesian voyages, however, and concluded that they could and most probably did reach America and return.[8] He then turned to the question of the sweet potato and found that it was clearly pre-Spanish in the Pacific and of American origin.[9] Geneticists and taxonomists have since shown that the sweet potato is American in origin.[10] We have Carbon-14 – dated sweet potato remains from Polynesia that predate European contacts with varied island groups, notably Easter Island and Hawaii. The literature on the sweet potato is extensive and an excellent example of the blinding influence of preconceptions, even when dealing with so hard a piece of evidence as a plant. Many academics persist in a strong antidiffusionist bias despite the evidence.[11] In this case it should be noted that the sweet potato is a very poor candidate for natural dispersal by water, or wind, or birds. It could be carried only by man equipped with seaworthy boats and navigational skills of a high order.

The impact of the sweet potato on my thinking developed slowly. The Polynesians, if they were the bearers of the sweet potato to Polynesia, must have stayed in America long enough to have learned to like the plant. Beyond that, they had to learn how to plant it, propagate it, store it, and cook it. Only cooking it is simple. Sweet potatoes are hard to store, hard to transport, and are normally propagated by cuttings. Such a transfer indicates a considerable learning process. Further, the plant had to fit into Polynesian culture. This it did rather well. The Polynesians were root crop oriented and their earth ovens were quite suitable for roasting sweet potatoes.

Peanut

The case of peanuts was first brought up by Oakes Ames, an economic botanist at Harvard.[12] They are unquestionably New World, with a suggested homeland in southern Brazil, whence they were introduced into Peruvian agriculture. Ames noticed that the peanuts in Boston's Chinatown were not like American commercial peanuts. The Chinese merchants told him they imported them from China, because their Chinese customers preferred them. Ames found that these Chinese peanuts came originally from Peru, although the cultivation of this variety there had ceased long before the Spanish conquest. Within recent decades peanuts have turned up in Chinese archeology in Lungshanoid time, perhaps as early as 3000 B.C. It hardly need be added that peanuts are most unlikely candidates for natural dispersal across the Pacific.

Hibiscus

The hibiscus has a similar story. Just after the turn of the century O. F. Cook argued for the transfer of many plants across the Pacific, mostly from America.[13] Two that he championed were *Hibiscus tiliaceous* and *Hibiscus rosasinensis*. The first can be dispersed by water, but may still be a case of man-borne diffusion for its usages and naming are similar in America and Polynesia. The second is known to most as the red-flowered hibiscus that Polynesian women wear in their hair. As the name indicates, it was thought

7

by botanists, especially Merrill, to be an ancient endemic of Southeast Asia. Merrill was bitterly opposed to the notion that any plant had been carried either way across any ocean in any pre-Columbian time.[14]

I was thus especially alerted to the significance of *Hibiscus rosasinensis* when I found that a Dutch ornithologist working in what was then the Netherlands East Indies noted that this plant was rarely pollinated by natural means in that area.[15] As an ornithologist he saw that this plant required pollination by hovering birds, such as the hummingbird. Hummingbirds are strictly American. His conclusion indicated that the plant was also American. It was not a popular idea, but ongoing research has now established the plant as American and has put the time of its appearance in Asia as before the time of Christ, for the Chinese had gotten this plant from Namviet (today, North Vietnam and southern China) and were exporting it to Persia by the second century B.C. Inhabitants of Namviet stated that they had gotten the plant in the days of their grandfathers "from beyond the eastern horizon," not too inept a way of saying "from America."

Recent work shows that native southeast Asian hovering birds occasionally fertilize the plant. In areas of the world where there are no hovering birds, pollination does not occur. It stands as a clear example of trans-Pacific diffusion. It also contradicts Merrill's claim that economic plants would dominate diffusion. Actually, nonessential plants seem to diffuse fastest: tobacco, chocolate, coffee are obvious examples, and hibiscus is a "useless" ornamental.

Maize

Compound evidence of these complex trans-Pacific movements comes from maize. One of the kinds of maize in Inner Asia is a type known archeologically on the western side of the Andes. Today this rare type of maize is found only in a limited area on the *east* side of the Andes, and in Inner Asia. Presumably it was exported from the coast of South America significantly before A.D. 1500.

Maize in Asia is a complex story that has suffered from the antidiffusionist bias of the anthropologists. Stonor and Anderson pointed out that maize among the hill tribes of Assam plays a major role in ceremony and is claimed by the natives to precede rice in their culture.[16] This assertion was strongly attacked by Oliver and Mangelsdorf,[17] and I replied equally strongly.[18] The picture is complex, but it strongly supports a pre-1500 introduction, if not several introductions, for the kind of maize along the coasts of Asia suggests a post-1500 introduction, whereas in interior Asia there are strange kinds of maize that are difficult to account for as post-1500 introductions.

The great sixteenth-century European herbals studied by Finan clearly portray two kinds of maize.[19] One, a tropical flint maize, of Caribbean type, they label as recently introduced from the newfound Spanish lands. The other is a mid-latitude maize, with a curious resemblance to New England flint maize, although it is more probably an unusual Caribbean variety. Finan also noted that maize was not attributed to America or even called maize for nearly a hundred years after the discovery of America. The great herbals specifically state that the mid-latitude type maize, *Frumentum turcicum*, was introduced to Europe by the Turks in "the days of our grandfathers." The Caribbean-type maize was confidently attributed to the recent Spanish discoveries.

The British scholar Jeffreys began his overseas service in the Arab lands and became an enthusiast for Arabic discoveries. His claims that maize was in use in Africa long before A.D. 1500 were furiously disputed, but he persisted.[20] Jeffreys concentrated on the Portuguese records. The Portuguese claimed they got maize from West Africa well before 1500. They did not use the nearly universal Caribbean word *maize* (*mahiz* and innumerable variations), but a West African word, *zaburro*. Jeffreys eventually was able to demonstrate that the Portuguese were using this word for maize well before Columbus's voyage.

Once interested in maize, Jeffreys pursued it far and wide. He investigated the appearance of maize in the Philippines, and concluded that maize preceded the Spanish. Carl Sauer reached the same conclusion quite independently.[21] Both reviewed the literature, the course of Magellan's voyage, the men involved, the exact words used, and the probability that the men describing maize in the Philippines knew what they were seeing. In West Africa, where Jeffreys's ethnological data suggested the pre-Columbian presence of maize, archeologists failed to carry out C-14 dating of charred maize recovered from respectable depths in village sites. They simply assumed a post-1500 age!

A strong case can also be made for the presence of maize in India before A.D. 1500. In addition to ritual usages and portrayals of maize, there is a claim for maize pollen in northwest India from pre-Columbian levels and Jett has published a probable representation of maize in a temple in India.

The evidence for very early maize in China is interesting on several accounts. By 1540 the Chinese in southwest China were paying their taxes in maize. The time is impossibly early for a Spanish introduction of maize to have reached such a level of acceptance. Not only did the maize have to be taken to China, but it had to be adopted, fitted into the local agriculture, raised to a very high level of production, and then become acceptable as a tax payment. Too many time-consuming processes were involved.

Taken with Anderson's data on maize in inner Asia, one is faced with evidence for some very early trans-Pacific maize transfer. It is this kind of data from China, Assam, and northwest India that increases the probability that the Turks were indeed introducing maize into the Mediterranean well before A.D. 1500.

The plant evidence rules out independent invention. Man cannot invent a plant. Plant homelands are usually well known. When an Old World plant appears in the New World or vice versa, and the plant can be shown to be a poor candidate for transoceanic dispersal by natural means, which is true of most plants, then diffusion is indicated. And this is like Pandora's Box, for when plant exchanges are admitted, it is most likely that ideas were also exchanged.

Chickens

From my ethnology background I knew that American Indians who kept chickens often ate neither them nor their eggs, a specifically Asiatic trait. Sixteenth-century Europeans ate both. Investigation of names for the chicken worldwide turned up the finding that the name for the chicken in the Amazon was very close to the Hindu name for the melanotic silky, commonly a ritual and ceremonial bird in India and Southeast Asia: *karak-nath* in India, *karaka* or *kalaka* in America. Melanotic silkies are widespread in South America, Central America, and Mexico.[22]

On parts of the west coast of Mexico, the name for the chicken is *'otori* or *totori*, and this duplicates the Japanese name for domestic fowl. The Aztec name for the turkey, *totoli*, incorporates this same word. *Totoli* to *totori* is a very simple *r* to *l* shift. The full Aztec word designates the sex of the bird: *huexolotl* and *cihuatotollin*, cock and hen. The modern Mexican word for the turkey, *guacalote*, is of unknown origin.

The next step was an investigation of the biology of the chicken. It is a southeast Asian pheasant, probably domesticated in Burma or thereabouts. Chickens have been domesticated long enough that very distinct strains have emerged. An expert in chickens can identify Chinese, Malay, or Mediterranean chickens with ease, not least by the color of their egg shells.

Mediterranean chickens lay white-shelled eggs. Asiatic chickens lay eggs with brown shells. Even today the chickens used by American Indians are primarily Asiatic, not Mediterranean. Fluffy-feathered Chinese chickens, naked-neck Malay chickens, and other Asiatic strains are prominent. Brown-shelled eggs dominate the American Indian scene except where modern Mediterranean chickens have been introduced.

Most fortunately we have a book on chickens written in Italy a hundred years after the discovery of America.[23] At that time Europeans did not know of or have most of the Asiatic chickens that are so prominent in the hands of the American Indians. Although diffusion from Portuguese introductions on the coast of Brazil might account for the presence of chickens in Peru at the time of the first Spanish contact, the necessary rate of diffusion would be extremely high and we are left with the question of where the Portuguese acquired such Asiatic chickens.

What we lack is published archeological evidence. At Picuris Pueblo in New Mexico, founded about A.D. 1400, chicken bones were deposited at the base of the trash mound for the village. They are present from that time onward. The identification of the bones was by the late Lyndon Hargraves, the expert in the ornithology of the Southwest. The material has never been published, in part because the archeologist, having been embroiled in one furious controversy, had little stomach for getting into another. The site excavation records are impeccable. I have seen Hargraves's identification cards and discussed the findings with him. He stated flatly that there was ample evidence for chickens in America before Columbus, which is the exact opposite of what his letters to me conveyed. He was particularly impressed by Sauer's *In Northern Mists* and assumed a Norse introduction of chickens. So far as I know there is not a shred of evidence for this.

The evidence of these crops and the chicken provides a number of biological items for which independent invention cannot be invoked. Such transfers are rarely rapid: new items must fit into the structure of the culture. Most persons are reluctant adopters of new crops, as is well shown by a Spanish experiment. The Spanish once carried out a demonstration planting of such plants as corn and beans for Polynesians. Subsequent visits showed that the natives adopted none of these plants. From this and other cases I have argued that the appearance of a domestic plant obviously transferred from a distant culture marks a long-term, meaningful contact with a broad learning experience.

The Pacific

It is a historical accident that most discussion has focused on the Pacific. As early as 1800 Alexander von Humboldt saw Asia everywhere in everything in America, except language. Fenollosa, the great expert on oriental art, pointed to just this kind of evidence for Asiatic influences in American art.[24] Covarubius,[25] Heine-Geldern,[26] Ekholm,[27] and most recently Shao[28] have carried studies of Asiatic artistic connections much further. Shang, Chou, and Han dynasty connections are emphasized.

Shang and Chou artistic influence is most apparent on northwest coast American Indian cultures. The great circle sea route from mid-latitude Asia to America passes south of the Aleutian Islands and sweeps down the coast of California to Mexico. This is also the course of the major ocean currents and wind patterns. It is the great highway around the Pacific to Meso-America. Return voyages would be even easier: by the strong, dependable trade winds across the Pacific south of Hawaii, and back to Asia.

The Manila galleons provide models for study of this route. The trip around the north Pacific was long, for the westerlies are intermittent and uncertain. The galleons were often in distress between Manila and Acapulco, but the trip from Acapulco to Guam and on to Manila was easy. As Heyerdahl demonstrated, Pacific crossings can be made even with a slow, sail-equipped, log raft.[29] Following Nishimura, I have shown that the sailing rafts of the west coast of South America are modeled on the sailing rafts of Asia.[30] Inasmuch as the sailing raft may be a precursor of the junk, very early voyages are implied, although sailing rafts are used even today on the east coast of Taiwan.

Such contacts probably reach back to around 3000 B.C. Meggers, Evans, and Estrada read the appearance of pottery on the coast of Ecuador as a result of Asiatic contacts bearing Middle Jomon–style (Japanese) pottery.[31] As with all such claims that controvert the accepted view, this has stimulated a lively controversy. One should consider some of the associated data. American peanuts appear in China about this time, as repeatedly reported by K. C. Chang.[32] The two bits of evidence tend to be mutually supporting.

Meggers, Evans, and Estrada also found in Ecuador an impressive array of traits, clearly Asiatic, and seemingly of Han time.[33] The Chinese annals at this time record an enormous effort expended in trying to rediscover the great land across the ocean to the east. One admiral is recorded as finding the land, returning to China, obtaining a fleet, and setting forth with hundreds of young people and artisans of every sort. He was never heard from again.

The Chinese annals laconically state that he probably found a fertile land and set himself up as a king. It is a curiosity of history that it is at this time that a massive input of Asiatic traits appears on the northwest coast of South America. There is also the brief account of the Buddhist monks from the Turkestan area of southwest Asia who made a voyage to a distant land in the Pacific in A.D. 499, and returned. Obvious garbling has occurred, but a rational treatment indicates a great circle sailing route from China to Mexico. The plant and animal exchanges reviewed, combined with the transfer of Chinese arts and crafts, make such voyages expectable, *not* improbable or impossible.

Drift voyages have been invoked to account for some of this transfer. In the late nineteenth century, records of such voyages accumulated. They showed a considerable frequency of arrivals on the northwest coast of Asiatic seafarers. Asiatic wrecks were even recorded off Baja California and Acapulco. Modern oceanographic research indicates that eighteen months will suffice to complete the circuit of the north Pacific by current drift. A shipwreck, subject to wind-driven forces, should do it in less. A ship handled intelligently would do it in much less.

In fact the whole problem of transoceanic travel has been made to seem vastly more formidable than it actually is. The seas became highways rather than barriers at a very early time in the history of human occupance of the earth, and all distribution and diffusion studies must be adjusted to this fact.

The evidence for the Asiatic connection is now extensive and beyond the scope of a paper such as this. Jett has given us an excellent summary of the material, which I will not duplicate here.[34] Rather I shall highlight materials that I am most familiar with.

Plants are the best evidence for trans-Pacific diffusion, in particular when the plant in question is not a good candidate for natural dispersal. When it can be shown that names and usages accompanied the plants, the evidence is even more conclusive. Despite one suggestion that chickens could have flown across the Pacific (there is seemingly no limit to the resistance to diffusion to America),[35] the insurmountable obstacles remain that after their exhausting flights the chickens had to teach the American Indians not only their names but their ritual usages.

I have repeatedly interspersed cultural evidence among biological evidence. That Asiatic chickens are used by American Indians is significant. This significance is enhanced by the use of Asiatic names, and greatly enhanced when it is learned that specifically Asiatic rites, rituals, and proscriptions are attached to these birds.

13

The Atlantic

The focus on the Pacific has obscured the Atlantic case. If man could cross the Pacific to America with sufficient ease and frequency to influence everything from arts to zodiacs, then the Atlantic should have been equally, if not more, important. The Pacific occupies one half the world. Voyages across it are stupendous undertakings. The Atlantic is smaller, and in the area where early civilizations first reached out into the Atlantic, on the Atlantic faces of Iberia and northwest Africa, the winds and currents are such that quick and reliable delivery to America is assured. One can say with utter confidence that once man was at sea with almost any kind of water craft on the Atlantic face of the Old World, there would soon be arrivals of seaborne people in the Americas, especially in the Caribbean area.

Just when men had seagoing craft is unknown. Archeologists point to probable crossings in the Gibraltar region in the Lower Paleolithic. That means watercraft of some sort a few hundred thousand years ago. Just what watercraft, and just when men began to move outside the Straits of Gibraltar, is unknown. Curiously, some of the evidence may come from America, for when clearly Mediterranean influences are apparent in America, then good watercraft must have existed. Archeological work on the Madeiras and Canaries is in its infancy, but even now some early contacts are evident. Whoever the first settlers were, they certainly were boatborne. At some time people with alphabetical skills arrived, for there are extensive petroglyphic records in the Canaries, and they show unmistakable connections with North Africa. Of immense importance, this same type of alphabetical material also appears in Mexico and elsewhere in America.

Cylinder seals found in Mexico have attracted the notice of a few scholars who have either asked if they did not contain alphabetical writing or concluded that they were indeed sophisticated forms of writing. There are at least two alphabets in the cylinder and stamp seals of Mexico.[36] One of these is clearly related to the Canary Islands and North Africa.

The presence of these alphabetic inscriptions has been overlooked largely because in Mexico the letters were frequently arranged to form pictures. A series of things then prevented the recognition of the alphabetic nature of the material. First, the eye is caught by the picture and deflected from the bits with which the picture is made. Secondly, very few American archeologists are familiar with ancient Old World alphabets. Those who have such familiarity are not Americanist in their orientation and are usually interested in the classic areas of Greece, Rome, Palestine, and Egypt. Thirdly, there is the virtually unshakable notion that there was no alphabetic writing in America. The stage was thus set for scholars to handle thousands of stamp and cylinder seals with no recognition that they bore alphabetical inscriptions.

The mere fact of these being cylinder seals should have triggered some inquiry. Cylinder seals are not common in the world, and from ancient times they bore signatures. Stamp seals are even earlier and are also ownership markers. Stamp and cylinder seals originated in the Near East, and spread east and west. One style of cylinder seal reached America via southeast Asia, focusing on central America.[37] These are stylistically different from the cylinder seals of Mexico and bear designs, not alphabetic inscriptions.

The cylinder seals of Mexico clearly bear alphabetic signs and one set of these letters can equally clearly be related to Libyan. We lack detailed studies of time and place for the numerous stamp and cylinder seals found in Mexico. Until such studies are made, we can do no more than indicate the significance of this alphabetic presence, and must await studies in some depth to find the time, place of introduction, and subsequent course of events.

There is also a burgeoning, yet controversial, field of epigraphic studies. The Americanist dogma has been that the rock art of the Americans was like some modern art, meaningful only to the artist. The opposite view is that there is a fair amount of alphabetic writing among the rock art. Decades ago I had assembled perhaps a dozen examples of what seemed clearly to be alphabetic writing in the American archeological record. Today there are hundreds of such examples.[38] Controversy rages over the reading of the material, and I am no expert in that area, but I should like to focus on a few cases of considerable interest.

To my astonishment the Norse sagas describing the discovery of America have, during my scholarly life, been quite generally deprecated, if not denied. The accounts are quite graphic but, having been written down hundreds of years after the events, cannot be taken as absolute and literal truths. The description of the finding of grapevines is probably factual, and indicates a southern New England location. It is of considerable interest that a Norse coin that dates to about A.D. 1000 has been found in the Penobscot Bay region. Some of the widely publicized finds at the l'Anse au Meadow site in Newfoundland are probably from a Norse site, but most probably not the Hop settlement or Vinland. Most recently the genetic study of cats has shown that the cats in the Boston and New York areas are Norse cats. The geneticists suggest that the Vikings brought them.[39]

The Kensington rune stone has been condemned and resuscitated numerous times. If valid, it would point to Norse exploration deep into America at an astonishingly late (A.D. 1362) date. This inscription has been recently reinvestigated by Hall, a distinguished linguist. He looked at the corpus of Norse writing now available, but *not* available at the time of the discovery of the Kensington stone. Criticism of the Kensington inscription turned on the inclusion of words, letters, and phrases not known to have been used in Norse at the alleged date of the making of the inscription. With the much fuller data now available, the criticisms are seen to be misplaced: the inscription is 99 percent pure Norse of that time. Even the numbering system in the Kensington inscription, once attacked, is now defended.[40]

This case parallels the Parahyba stone found in Brazil. This records the arrival of a storm-driven ship that was part of a flotilla sent out by Hyram of Tyre to circumnavigate Africa. The mariners recorded their numbers, including how many women were aboard, and seemingly sailed on. The stone was attacked as spurious because it contained words and phrases not known in Semitic languages, specifically Canaanite, of that date. Gordon, a noted student of Semitic languages, has recently read a good copy of the inscription and found no unexpected usages.[41] Improved knowledge of early Semitic languages has meant that a case once deemed a fraud is now considered a more likely case of real contact.

How one views such an item as the Parahyba stone depends a great deal on one's background and mental makeup. For a logical positivist this is a very flimsy piece of evidence. The stone has a most obscure history and has long been lost. We have only copies of what is alleged to have been inscribed on the stone. The letters and the language are correct for the period, and at the time that the stone was found the knowledge to make such an inscription did not exist. Therefore, it cannot have been a forgery, and the stone must have actually existed.

As for the matter of the ships and ability to make such voyages, there is no problem, for large ships are much earlier than this. Further, the Phoenicians are believed to have circumnavigated Africa at about this time.[42]

Another interesting trace of Semites in America comes from the Tennessee area. In excavating a mound, the Smithsonian Institution found a set of burials. Associated with one of the skeletons was an inscribed tablet. At the time of excavation it was regarded as an example of Cherokee writing, a writing allegedly invented by Sequoyah. Half a century later it was recognized as Semitic alphabetic writing. Mertz's recognition has been verified by Cyrus Gordon, and the letters indicate that the time is about the second century A.D. The cryptic and incomplete message seems to refer to Bar Kochba, the leader of the second revolt against Rome. The clothing of the Bar Kochba adherents who died in the desert caves of Palestine is said to have been dyed using a red dye (cochineal) made from an insect that lives on cactus. Cactus is strictly American. Absolute identification of this dye requires the analysis of one more side chain of molecules, and I have not found a chemist interested in doing the analysis.

Fell has identified Libyan inscriptions in the United States as well as Mexico.[43] Several tablets are said to carry burial dedications. The famous Grave Creek tablet was found with a skeleton deep inside one of the largest burial mounds in America. Another tablet found on the surface has the same series of letters in the second line. I guessed decades ago that these would prove to be dedicatory tablets and to carry some set phrase similar to our "in sacred memory of." This now seems to be the case.

The great mounds themselves and their associated ceremonial ways and figures are also important. The burial mounds of North America are very similar to those of Bronze Age Europe. The monumental stone structures of the Northeastern United States duplicate the dolmens, menhirs, and passage graves of Europe.[44] Unlike the biological items discussed earlier, such structures may have resulted from independent invention. One might claim that the psychic unity of mankind naturally produces mounds, and even pottery, and that, inasmuch as there are only so many possible kinds of pottery, seeming duplication is bound to result. I consider all of this quite unlikely, based on the fact that such cases are rarely found in isolation from other parts of a cultural complex. The Occasional Publications of the Epigraphic Society present masses of epigraphic evidence that accompany these artifacts.

The gist of all this material is that there were many contacts with America by Europeans. The question is, to what extent these contacts influenced North American cultural growths. The question has not had serious discussion in recent decades, but rather humorous dismissal, such as Wauchope's *Lost Tribes and Sunken Continents*, and so it is difficult to know just what conclusion to come to.[45] Are we to revive the ancient notion that the mound-builders were a non-American people? Or, in a modified form, are we to think of the mound-builders of the Adena Hopewell period as inspired by European contacts? We must ask the same questions for the civilizations in MesoAmerica and South America. There is an enormous field here for studies of contacts in which cases of diffusion and nondiffusion proliferate.

17

Conclusion

It should be clear by now that, although I started as an Americanist with an unquestioning faith in the independence of American Indian cultural growth, both plant and (later) animal geography have steadily driven me into a more and more diffusionist position. Although I have published primarily on the plant and animal evidence, my own studies and those of my students have ranged widely over other fields: writing, stamp and cylinder seals, concrete, blow guns, myths, navigation, watercraft, and so on. The conclusion I have reached is that not only is diffusion the master process within continental limits, but it was very important transoceanically as early as 3000 B.C., and possibly earlier.

The early dates for *Lagenaria*, an Old World plant in America, for allegedly Old World pottery in Ecuador around 3000 B.C., and for the same in the northeastern United States around 1500 B.C. raise the possibility that New World cultural advances occurred under Old World stimulation. I have pointed out that a respectable case for a stimulus diffusion origin of New World agriculture can be made. A "case" is not proof, but it should serve as a caution to those who still think of American Indian civilization as an example of independent human accomplishment. On the contrary, an immense body of evidence indicates that American cultural growths before 1500 were under strong European and Asiatic influences at various times. Such a major scholar as Needham, who began his career assuming there were no trans-Pacific links, later came to see that Mexican culture was very much influenced by Chinese culture.[46]

I must enter here a denial that this is in any way a racist argument, for just such charges have been leveled at the diffusionist position. To deny the American Indians the ability to create civilizations on their own, with no contact with the Old World, is considered to be degrading. I have replied to this objection at some length elsewhere.[47] The gist of my reply is that *if* the American Indians did indeed invent everything on their own, and *if* they did it in the time spans suggested, then this would indeed be a racist argument, for they would be the only people in world history who so rapidly reproduced civilization—a civilization, moreover, that again and again repeated in minute detail the complex inventions of the Old World.

One can give this a humorous twist. If a people that has not made fundamental inventions is racially inferior, then surely the British must be among the most inferior. What did they invent? Not agriculture, not weaving, not metallurgy, not alphabets; nor did they domesticate animals: they borrowed everything. Just to keep the score even, one can sing the same song about the Japanese—or for that matter, about almost any people on the face of the earth. No civilization arose in isolation, as the flowering of the genius of a single people. Great civilizations illustrate that genius lies in the ability of a group of persons to assemble ideas borrowed from far and wide into some new pattern suited to their needs, tastes, and opportunities.

Independent invention can be invoked for some things, and it must occasionally have occurred. However, the claim for total isolation for the New World and its independent redevelopment of virtually everything the Old World invented is a position totally destroyed by the plant and animal evidence. You cannot allow the exchange of plants and animals with their associated ritual and economic ideas, and then deny the possibility of the transfer of other ideas.

A final word on invention (or innovation) and diffusion. They are not antithetical: no invention, no diffusion. There *is* a problem as to the dominance of one over the other. After a lifetime of study of the problem, it is my conclusion that invention is rare, but diffusion is commonplace. Few would dispute that for any limited area. It has been dogma that diffusion did not occur across the great oceans. The gist of this brief review is that transoceanic influences on America resulted from both the relatively easy crossing of the Atlantic and the much longer voyage across the Pacific.

The plant and animal evidence that now approaches the level of absolute proof cannot be dismissed as independent invention.[48] Plants were carried by human agency both ways across the oceans, accompanied by at least one animal, the chicken. Others, such as the turkey and the hairless dog, may have also been transferred. With them went great assemblages of cultural traits and undoubtedly some racial transfers.

The American civilizations can be very profitably studied as classic cases of diffusion, both successful and failed. What exactly happened to the various thrusts of ideas from the Old World? What became of the Roman contact with Mexico? What became of the Bronze Age contact with Northeastern America? And again, what of the obvious, plural Asiatic contacts? What did they accomplish? How far did their ideas spread? How were they adapted, changed, abandoned? Why were the contacts broken off? One has a galaxy of specific studies dealing with the fundamentals of human cultural history. It could fuel a school of thought for a generation or two, and could greatly increase our understanding of cultural history and the nature of man.

Notes

1. G. Elliot Smith, *Elephants and Ethnologists* (London: Kegan Paul, 1924). See also George F. Carter, "Elephants and Ethnologists: Fifty Years Later," *The New Diffusionists* 5/21 (1975): 139–53; George F. Carter, "Some Comments on 'Smith and Perry on Trial,'" *The New Diffusionist* 5/19–20 (1975): 67–74.

2. George F. Carter, *Plant Geography and Culture History in the American Southwest* (New York: Viking Fund Publications in Anthropology 5, 1945).

3. See Thor Heyerdahl, *The Maldive Mystery* (New York: Alder and Alder, 1986).

4. See W. S. Jackson, *Shells as Evidence of the Diffusion of Early Cultures* (Manchester: Manchester University Press, 1917).

5. J. B. Hutchinson, R. A. Silow, and S. G. Stephens, *The Evolution of Gossypium* (Oxford: Oxford University Press, 1947).

6. S. G. Stephens, "Cytogenetics of Gossypium and the Problem of the Origin of New World Cottons," *Advances in Genetics* 1 (1947): 431–42. A later work by Stephens: "Some Problems of Interpreting Transoceanic Dispersal of the New World Cottons," in C. L. Riley et al., eds., *Man Across the Sea* (Austin: University of Texas Press, 1971), pp. 401–15.

7. Donald Brand, "The Sweet Potato: An Exercise in Methodology," in Riley, *Man Across*, pp. 343–65.

8. R. B. Dixon, "The Long Voyages of the Polynesians," *Proceedings of the American Philosophical Society* 74 (1934): 167–75.

9. R. B. Dixon, "The Problem of the Sweet Potato in Polynesia," *American Anthropologist* 34 (1932): 40–66.

10. See R. E. Yen, "Sweet Potato Variation and its Relation to Human Migration in the Pacific," in Jacques Barrau, ed., *Plants and the Migrations of the Pacific Peoples* (Honolulu: Bishop Museum, 1963), pp. 93–117.

11. Curiously I was once viciously attacked at a meeting in Philadelphia by Mangelsdorf and Merrill, who claimed that the sweet potato was of African origin. This claim is found tentatively in E. D. Merrill, "The Botany of Cook's Voyages" *Chronica Botanica* 14/5–6 (1954): 371.

12. Oakes Ames, *Economic Annuals and Human Cultures* (Cambridge: Botanical Museum of Harvard University, 1939). K. C. Chang has repeatedly noted peanuts in China, as has S. Jett: K. C. Chang, *The Archaeology of Ancient China*, Rev. ed. (New Haven: Yale University Press, 1968); Stephen Jett, "Pre-Columbian Transoceanic Contacts," in Jesse D. Jennings, ed., *Ancient Native Americans* (San Francisco: Freeman, 1978). Jett, following Chang, dates the peanut in China between 3300 and 2800 B.C. Jett's study is especially useful for the breadth of data reviewed and for its extensive bibliography.

13. O. F. Cook, *Food Plants of Ancient America*, Annual Report (Washington, D.C.: Smithsonian Institution, 1903), pp. 481–97. See also O. F. Cook, "Quichua Names of Sweet Potatoes," *Journal of the Washington Academy of Science* 6 (1916): 86–90; "Polynesian Names of Sweet Potatoes," ibid. 6 (1916): 339–47.

14. Merrill, *Botany*. This was Merrill's final work on this subject and is rambling, poorly organized, and occasionally self-contradicting. One part of this monograph viciously attacks the major diffusionists, more from a position of authority than from a consideration of the cumulative weight of evidence. In this section of his work, trans-Pacific contact before Columbus is vigorously denied. In other places Merrill

accepts the pre-Columbian transmission of nonagricultural traits "along the northern coasts of Asia to America, thence east and south in America" (p. 273). In a series of postscripts, moreover, Merrill admits the likelihood of pre-Columbian transmission of the sweet potato (p. 371), and the possibility of the transfer of cotton and other species (p. 373).

15. George F. Carter, "Disharmony between Asiatic Flower-Birds and American Bird-Flowers," *American Antiquity* 20 (1954): 176–77; "Hibiscus Rosa Sinensis," *Anthropological Journal of Canada* 15/4 (1977): 26–27.

16. C. R. Stonor and E. Anderson, "Maize among the Hill Peoples of Assam," *Annals of the Missouri Botanical Garden* 36 (1949): 355–404.

17. P. C. Mangelsdorf and D. L. Oliver, "Whence Came Maize to Asia?," *Botanical Museum Leaflets*, Harvard University, 14/10 (1951): 263–91.

18. George F. Carter, "Plants across the Pacific," *American Antiquity* (Memoirs) 18 (1953): 62–71.

19. J. J. Finan, "Maize in the Great Herbals," *Annals of the Missouri Botanical Garden* 35 (1948): 149–91.

20. M. D. W. Jeffreys, "Pre-Columbian Maize in Asia," in Riley, *Man Across*, pp. 376–400. Seven of Jeffreys's papers are located in the consolidated bibliography of this most useful volume.

21. C. O. Sauer, "Maize into Europe," *Akten des 34. Internationalen Amerikanisten-Kongresses*, (Vienna, 1960), pp. 777–88.

22. See George F. Carter, "Pre-Columbian Chickens in America," in Riley, *Man Across*, pp. 178–218. My work on the chicken has been greatly extended by Carl Johannessen and W. and M. C. Fogg. The latest work by Johannessen, "Distribution and Use of the Black-Boned and Black-Meated Chicken in Mexico and Guatemala," summarizes their work to date.

23. Ulisse Aldrovandi, *Aldrovandi on Chickens: The Ornithology of Ulisse Aldrovandi*, vol. 2, bk. 4 (Norman: University of Oklahoma Press, 1963, first published, 1600).

24. E. F. Fenollosa, *Epochs of Chinese and Japanese Art*, 2 vols. (New York: Frederick A. Stokes, 1912).

25. M. Covarubias, *The Eagle, the Jaguar, and the Serpent: Indian Art of the Americas* (New York: Knopf, 1954).

26. R. Heine-Geldern, "Significant Parallels in the Symbolic Arts of Southeastern Asia and Middle America," *Proceedings of the 29th International Congress of Americanists*, 1951, pp. 299–309.

27. G. Ekholm, "Is American Indian Culture Asiatic?," *Natural History* 59/8 (1950): 344–51, 382; "The Archaeological Significance of Mirrors in the New World," *Congresso Internazionale degli Americanisti*, Atti, 40/1 (1973): 133–35. I have listed an early and a late publication as a key to Ekholm's numerous papers.

28. Paul Shao, *The Origin of Ancient American Culture* (Ames: Iowa State University Press, 1983). See also his *Asiatic Influences in Pre-Columbian Art* (Ames: Iowa State University Press, 1976).

29. Thor Heyerdahl's complete works are too numerous to cite, but any serious student of transoceanic movements must consult not only such popular books as his *Kon Tiki* (Chicago: Rand McNally, 1950), but also such scholarly sequels as *American Indians in the Pacific* (Chicago: Rand McNally, 1953), and the important volumes on Easter Island that followed: *Aku Aku, Easter Island*, 2 vols. (Monographs of the School of American Research and the Museum of New Mexico, no. 24, parts 1

and 2, 1961). Thor Heyerdahl, *Early Man and the Ocean* (New York: Doubleday, 1979) is also worth attention. See also Edwin Doran, Jr., "The Sailing Raft as a Great Tradition," in Riley, *Man Across*, pp. 115–38.

30. George F. Carter, "Chinese Contacts with America: Fu Sang Again," *Anthropological Journal of Canada* 14/1 (1976): 10–24.

31. Betty J. Meggers, Clifford Evans, and Emilio Estrada, "Early Formative Period of Coastal Ecuador: The Valdivia and Machalilla Phases," *Smithsonian Contributions to Anthropology*, vol. 1 (Washington, D.C.: Smithsonian Institution, 1965).

32. Chang, *Archaeology*.

33. Meggers, Evans and Estrada, *Formative Period*.

34. Jett, "Pre-Columbian."

35. Michael Wilson, "Cyclones, Coconuts, and Chickens across the Sea," in P. G. Duke et al., eds., *Diffusion and Migration, Their Roles in Cultural Development* (Calgary: University of Calgary, 1978), pp. 65–104, is a full-scale attack on my methods and conclusions.

36. See George F. Carter, "Mexican Sellos: Writing on America, or the Growth of an Idea," in ibid., pp. 186–201.

37. See George F. Carter and Sol Heinemann, "Pre-Columbian Sellos," *Anthropological Journal of Canada* 15/3 (1977): 2–6.

38. See H. B. Fell, *America B.C.: Ancient Settlers in the New World* (New York: Demeter Press, 1976); *Saga, America* (New York: Times Books, 1980); *Bronze Age America* (Boston: Little Brown, 1982). The Epigraphic Society Publications, vols. 1–15, 1974–86, contain a vast amount of material on this subject.

39. S. Adelsteinsson and B. Blumenberg, "Possible Norse Origin for Two Northeastern United States Cat Populations," *Z. Tierzüchtgsbiol.* 100 (1983): 161–74.

40. Robert A. Hall, Jr., *The Kensington Rune Stone Is Genuine* (Columbia, S.C.: Hornbeam Press, 1982); Richard Nielsen, "The Arabic Numbering System on the Kensington Rune Stone," *Epigraphic Society Occasional Papers* 15 (1986): 47–61.

41. Cyrus Gordon, *Before Columbus: Links between the Old World and Ancient America* (New York: Crown Publishers, 1966). One will also find here validation of the Bat Creek inscription, excavated in Tennessee, published by Cyrus Thomas in 1890 and first recognized as a Semitic script by Henrietta Mertz.

42. See M. Cary and E. H. Warmington, *The Ancient Explorers* (London: Methuen, 1929).

43. Fell, *America B.C.*

44. See Salvatore M. Trento, *The Search for Lost America. The Mysteries of the Stone Ruins* (Chicago: Contemporary Books, 1978).

45. Robert Wauchope, *Lost Tribes and Sunken Continents* (Chicago: University of Chicago Press 1962).

46. Joseph Needham, *Science and Civilization in China* (Cambridge: Cambridge University Press). See especially vol. 4, *Nautics*, 1971, for Needham's change of stance regarding Chinese influence in Mexico, pp. 540ff.

47. George F. Carter, "Invention, Diffusion, and Racism," *Anthropological Journal of Canada* 19/1 (1981): 10–12.

48. See George F. Carter, "A Hypothesis Suggesting a Single Origin of Agriculture," in Charles Reed, ed., *Origins of Agriculture* (The Hague: Mouton, 1977), p. 134.

CHAPTER TWO

Limitations of the Diffusionist Approach

EVOLUTIONARY ECOLOGY AND SHELL-TEMPERED CERAMICS

Alan J. Osborn

It is my conviction that the diffusionist approach in both anthropology (including archeology) and geography possesses limited explanatory power. The diffusionist perspective is based on concepts that have limited integrative capabilities or systematic import.[1] My discussion is not to be construed, however, as a condemnation of all diffusionist studies. Instead, the purpose is to suggest that diffusion studies offer analytical techniques for the definition of spatial patterns and for monitoring rates of change that can be utilized to test more inclusive theoretical constructs.

The topic of aboriginal shell-tempered ceramics in eastern North America has traditionally been explained within the context of a diffusionist perspective. This archeological example points out how a broader body of theory—evolutionary ecology—based on natural selection serves to enhance our understanding of human behavior. I believe that this example will reinforce the argument for the severe limitations of the diffusionist perspective; yet, it should also hint at the greater potential of diffusion studies within a broader conceptual framework, which could serve to integrate geography and anthropology.

Anthropology and Geography: Descent with Modification

Charles Darwin spoke of evolutionary developments as "descent with modification."[2] Geographers and anthropologists are well aware of common ancestry—particularly from the work of eighteenth-century social philosophers and historians.[3] During the Enlightenment social scientists placed humans within the natural world and began to delineate patterns of covariance between the physical environment and human behavior.[4] Montesquieu, for example, argued:

Man . . . is regarded as part of nature, and the explanation of historical events is sought in the facts of the natural world. History so conceived would become a kind of natural history of man, or anthropology, where institutions appear not as free inventions of human reasons in the course of its development, but as the necessary effects of natural causes.[5]

Geography and anthropology experienced an epistemological schism during the late 1800s. Wilhelm Dilthey dichotomized the empirical world into *Naturwissenschaften* (physical/biological world) and *Geisteswissenschaften* (human and social world).[6] Dilthey and other neo-Kantian philosophers argued that, unlike the physical/biological world, the human/social realm was "knowable" via personal experience. The physical/biological world could, however, be understood only "from outside"; causal meaning had to be imposed upon it, and it was ultimately a matter for conjecture.[7] This dichotomy has severely hampered our efforts to explain human behavior.[8] Darwin's theory was thus quickly purged from geography and anthropology:

Other ideas which failed to penetrate the discipline [geography] included Huntington's (1924) proposal of "natural selection" as a major conceptual device and Soja's (1971) discussion of concepts from the study of animal behaviour as potential research tools for work on political territoriality. Perhaps geographers' predilections since the 1920s for cultural explanation disposed them against any type of biological argument.[9]

At the same time geography and anthropology developed various related forms of idealism. Porter has suggested that idealism emerged as a result of the "debate centered on whether the task was to seek lawful (nomothetic) generalization and theory, as in the natural sciences, or historical particularistic (ideographic) knowledge and understanding of the objects under study."[10]

The idealist "schools" within the social sciences, which include but are not limited to structuralism, phenomenology, and neo-Marxist anthropology, seek the causes of human behavioral variability within the realms of human thought itself. Johnston states, "All actions, according to the idealist, are the result of rational thought, the parameters of which are constrained by a theory, which in turn is 'any system of ideas that man has invented, imposed, or elicited from the new data of sensation that make connections between the phenomena of the external world.'"[11]

Idealist geographers and anthropologists do not therefore have to concern themselves with the development of nomothetic statements or theory in order to explain variability in human behavior. Anthropology and cultural geography have inherited an idealist tradition via the Kantian superorganicist theories of Kroeber and White, particularly as transmitted to Sauer and Zelinsky:

The superorganic mode of explanation in cultural geography reifies the notion of culture, assigning it ontological status and causative power. . . . In this theory culture is viewed as an entity above man, not reducible to the actions of individuals, mysteriously responding to laws of its own.[12]

Differential adoption, rejection, and "spread" of ideas and material culture are thus explained as follows:

Individuals in a given cultural setting will make their decision to accept, reject, or ignore an innovation on the basis of their image and impression of the new artifact, a decision which will be guided by the beliefs held by themselves and those around them. Thus it is probable that there are cross-cultural differences in environmental cognition which influence innovation, acceptance behavior and migration.[13]

For many archeologists and anthropologists, "culture is an information system, where the messages are accumulated survival information, plus miscellaneous and idiosyncratic noise peculiar to each system."[14] Diffusion, then, like genetic mutation, serves as a source of variety in messages and information:

Why do some cultural systems accept some diffusing innovations and yet reject others? The answer can only be proposed in detail for each specific case but the general syntax is the same. A diffusing communication of new variety will not be accepted if its concomitant dislocation cannot be minimized to a vanishing point—it must be variety which does not contradict and destroy any of the essential attributes concerned with the continuity of the system.[15]

We must ask at this point how such a particularistic approach to diffusion studies can lead to nomothetic explanation? It seems that a more powerful explanation of diffusion is ultimately dependent on the delineation of "essential attributes" or cultural variables, their dynamic interrelationships, and the ranges of tolerance for these interrelationships. How else would we be able to understand degrees of "concomitant dislocation," its minimization, and the adoption/rejection of innovations?

Diffusionism: Unchecked and without Constraints

Temporal and spatial variation in the physical conditions for life often make possible or even actually necessitate variety among organisms.[16]

Charles Darwin understood quite well why fields of red clover thrived only near certain neighboring farms and villages and, in turn, why his flowering orchid (*Lobelia fulgens*) failed to produce seeds. He realized that both these botanical phenomena could be explained as a function of the distribution of domesticated cats.[17] Cats consume field mice and serve as an interspecific check or constraint on rodent densities. Field mice, in turn, depend on bird nests and the honeycomb of bumblebees as a food resource. Bumblebees and red clover flowers interact mutually by providing cross-pollination and nectar, respectively.

Apart from interspecific constraints, Darwin also was aware of a multiplicity of limits (maxima and minima) defined by intraspecific competition, the physical environment, and individual and group life history and population density. His reading of Malthus's essay on human population versus food production capabilities greatly facilitated his theory of natural selection. Darwin came to appreciate the degree to which biological diversity reflected the conformity of organisms (both plants and animals) to a multidimensional environment. Genetic, physiological, and behavioral responses to a set of environmental constraints, which enable an organism to reproduce, constitute an *adaptation*. The successful delineation of these environmental limitations is absolutely essential for explaining the spatial correlates of plant, animal, and human adaptations. The systematic investigation of the spatial correlates of life is biogeography.[18]

Darwin's biological research provided the "natural laboratory experiments" that served to test his hypothetico-deductive arguments regarding evolution.[19] The theory of natural selection offered the conceptual framework for transforming descriptive natural history into a biological science capable of explaining distributional aspects of life both past and present.

Innovation diffusion studies in anthropology and geography exhibit little concern for developing a systematically unified explanatory framework that incorporates checks, limitations, or constraints on diffusion. Frequently, anthropologists and geographers either ignore or hold constant the very factors that serve as constraints or checks on behavioral systems. In many instances, diffusionists cling tenaciously to an idealist perspective that reinforces the mutual exclusion of culture and biology:

The basic tenet of this conceptualization of the spread of innovation across the landscape is that the adoption of an innovation is primarily the outcome of a *learning* or *communication* process. . . . Accordingly, a fundamental step in examining the process of diffusion is identification of factors related to the *effective* flow of information and of the characteristics of information flows, information reception, and resistances to adoption. An important aspect of resistance is an individual's general propensity to adopt innovation, or his *innovativeness*. Another important aspect of resistance is the congruence between the innovation and the social, economic, and psychological characteristics of the potential adopter.[20]

Given this idealist perspective of diffusion, how do we anticipate the factors that affect or constrain information transmission? How do we anticipate the degree of innovativeness of an individual or group? And, when we speak of congruity between innovation(s) and the "social, economic, and psychological characteristics" of adopters, are we not ultimately concerned with adaptation? "Idealists [have] focused on individual actors [and] omitted any reference to the environmental constraints and influences on his actions."[21]

Archeological Patterns and Their Explanation

Traditionally, archeologists have subscribed to a normative view of culture, which assumes that material remains reflect one variable—"fossilized ideas"—once shared by members of a past society or culture. Deetz describes such a view and states, "artifacts are man-made objects; they are also fossilized ideas. In every clay pot, stone ax, wooden doll, or bone needle, we see preserved what someone once thought pots, axes, dolls, and needles should look like."[22] Variation through space and time reflects both the geographical distribution of different cultures and change in ideology through time. Factors that contribute to or cause variation in artifacts and the material remains of the past were thought to include innovation, diffusion, migration, and miscegenation.

Given this cultural perspective, traditional archeologists have focused primarily on archeological variation along two dimensions—time and space. Little seems to separate normative archeology and much human geography; both have been preoccupied with the recognition of regularities and patterns in material culture and ideology throughout space and time. Most frequently, however, pattern recognition has been regarded as an end in itself. Binford states that "the recognition of patterning and its interpretation has been the basis of archeological *explication* of the past" (italics added).[23]

As in geography, archeology experienced a dramatic change in orientation involving both theoretical perspective(s) and associated methodologies during the "positivist" reorientation of the 1960s and 1970s. Archeologists adopted a systemic view of cultural behavior and began to consider culture as an "extrasomatic means of adaptation to both biophysical and social environments."[24] Cultural adaptation was considered to represent a series of behavioral responses to environmental constraints ultimately determined by the process of natural selection.[25] Cultural systems were perceived as a number of interrelated subsystems or components—for example, technology, subsistence, and ideology—that served to meet the security demands of a population/group.

Given these basic conceptual tools, "processual" archeology could then proceed to investigate the causal, dynamic linkages between any aspect of past human behavior and the archeological material record. In fact, processual archeology was now capable of subjecting behavioral explanations, both past and present, to evaluative, empirical test. In this regard, Binford states:

> It is suggested that if archeologists are to be successful in understanding the organization of past cultural systems, they must understand the organizational relationships among places which are differentially used during the operation of past systems. . . . The association among different things "falling out" of a system during an occupation may inform about the organization of the human action which occurred at the site. . . . The accuracy with which we are able to give meaning to the record is dependent upon our understanding of the processes which operated in the past to bring into being the observed patterning.[26]

With these theoretical arguments and assumptions in mind, let us now turn to an examination of one specific archeological example. This example was chosen to illustrate the manner in which a systemic approach may enable us to maximize the potential of the archeological record and to illustrate the essential nature of behavioral theory for interpreting spatial, temporal, and material patterns in that record. This explanatory effort is designed to integrate much of what anthropologists currently understand about human behavior and its causes. This effort is meant to go beyond the current limitations of innovation diffusion.

Systemic Implications of Shell-tempered Ceramics

Shell-tempered ceramics have long been utilized as a diagnostic "trait" of late prehistoric cultures of the middle and lower Mississippi Valley. Archeological occurrences of shell-tempered ceramics throughout the eastern United States have been viewed primarily as a result of innovation or trait diffusion and/or human migration from the American Bottoms or "Mississippian culture heartland" centering on Cahokia in East St. Louis. Hall states, for example: "Some ideas like shell-tempering diffused outward from the middle Mississippi Valley and were accepted or rejected locally for reasons we are only beginning to discover. . . . Oneota pottery (eastern Great Plains area) probably spread in some directions by migration and in others by diffusion."[27]

"Mississippian culture complexes" have generally been viewed from a normative archeological perspective. Mississippian cultural manifestations are perceived as clusters of characteristic traits including maize farming, village life, monumental earth platforms, Southern Cult politico-religious iconography, warfare, and a ceramic assemblage composed of shell-tempered globular vessels, seed jars, bowls, plates, effigy handles, and ceramic "trowels."[28] Archeologists have generally regarded observed variability (temporal, spatial, and formal/content) to reflect only one "cultural" process: the differential adoption or rejection of Mississippian ideology.

If it is possible, however, to account for the variability in distribution of shell-tempered ceramics in terms of evolutionary ecology, archeologists will be equipped to explain better the differential adoption/rejection of ceramic technology, as well as associated aspects of Mississippian culture complexes. Obviously, technological, economic, social, and political information was transmitted between human groups. Human "migrations" and population adjustments no doubt occurred during late prehistoric periods. However, diffusion and migration as cultural processes do not possess explanatory power, nor do they enable us to discuss the differential distribution and persistence of so-called cultural traits once diffusion or migration has occurred.

Recent archeological studies have called for relatively extensive revision and reformulation of our ideas regarding the nature of Mississippian cultural complexes throughout eastern North America.[29] Smith has proposed that the "Mississippian" phenomenon (A.D. 800–1500) be viewed as an adaptive system that tapped unearned energy and nutrients from floodplain habitats using maize horticulture and hunting along ecotones to sustain high population densities.[30] Similar behavior responses to environmental change and/or population growth between A.D. 800–1400 are observable in the archeological record in the Midwest, the lower Great Lakes, and the Mississippi-Ohio River drainages. These adaptive behavioral responses include intensification of maize horticulture; adoption of a food storage strategy; increased socio-cultural complexity; appearance of large population aggregates; settlement systems mapped onto productive farm land and ecotonal boundaries; intensive exploitation of the white-tailed deer, turkey, and raccoon; and expansion of hunting niche breadth to include aquatic resources.

A number of recent paleodemographic and paleonutritional studies demonstrate that human populations were exposed to increased variety and intensity of nutritional and physiological stresses throughout the Midwest coinciding with periods of population growth and increased dependence on maize.[31] Heavy dependence on maize and low animal protein intake produced high infant mortality, iron deficiency anemia, porotic hyperostosis, reduction in stature, enamel hypoplasia, increased caries, and arrested periods of growth.[32]

Ceramic vessels containing crushed mollusc shell were manufactured during the historic period by a number of aboriginal groups including the Osage, Fort Walton groups, Burial Urn groups (A.D. 1500–1700) in Alabama, the Monongahela culture of Pennsylvania (ca. A.D. 1740), the Caborn-Welborn phase (A.D. 1400–1700) of the Ohio River settlement, the Fort Ancient Tradition (A.D. 1400–1750) of the Ohio River Valley, and the Pamunkey Indians (ca. A.D. 1878) of Virginia.

Little if any shell-tempered ceramic is observed north of 46 degrees north latitude or west of 99 degrees west longitude in North America. Environmental constraints on maize cultivation coincide quite well with observed northern and western limits of shell-tempered ceramics. Yarnell, for example, describes the northern limits of aboriginal maize cultivation:

We have found no early historic reports of corn growing north of 47.5 degrees nor of corn growing in an area with an average frostless season of less than 120 days. In addition to this we find prehistoric archeological sites producing the remains of crop plants are all located south of 47.6 degrees and within the 120-day limit. This strongly indicates that one of the effective limits of prehistoric Indian agriculture is the line marking the limits of the 120-day average frost-free period, even though the Indians had corn that could mature in 60 to 70 days.[33]

Shell-tempered ceramics occur in archeological assemblages through-out much of eastern North America. Their temporal range spans the Mississippian culture period (A.D. 800–1500) and extends well into the historic period in eastern North America. Early dates for shell-tempered pottery include the Steed-Kisker components (A.D. 860 ± 110 to A.D. 1290 ± 80) near Kansas City, the Moingona phase (A.D. 690–960) in central Iowa, and the Jefferson phase (A.D. 900–1000) in the Pickwick Basin, Alabama.

The northern limit for the distribution of both shell-tempered ceramics and maize also approximates the isotherms for mean summer and mean summer night temperatures of 66° F and 55° F, respectively.[34] Jenkins further points out that the largest corn yields are produced in areas where the mean summer temperature for June, July, and August ranges from 68° F to 72° F.[35]

The limit for the distribution of shell-tempered ceramics also coincides with precipitation and humidity thresholds for maize production.[36] Jenkins states, "In the United States the western limit of production coincides approximately with the line of mean summer (June, July, and August) precipitation of 8 inches."[37] Rainfall during the growing season must be evenly distributed and average from 3 to 6 inches during the months of June, July, and August.

The westernmost occurrences of shell-tempered ceramics cluster around 98 degrees west longitude, which coincides with the westernmost limits of maize cultivation defined by summer moisture availability.[38]

Nutritional Considerations for Maize-based Diets

Aboriginal maize production provided considerable quantities of food energy per unit area of crop land. Prehistoric maize farming in Mexico probably did not achieve significance until maize varieties were developed that yielded a minimum of 200–250 kg/hectare, or 81–101 kg/acre.[39] With respect to food energy yield(s), we find that a kilogram of yellow maize (dry basis) contains approximately 4,040 kcal;[40] prehistoric minimum yields would, therefore, equal some 808,000–1,000,000 kcal/hectare. Ethno-historic peoples of the middle Missouri subarea in the Plains produced an estimated 4.7 million kilocalories per hectare. Contemporary maize subsistence farming in Mexico, Central America, and Africa produces almost 12.5 times as much energy.[41]

Despite these relatively high returns for aboriginal energy production, maize horticulture—like cereal farming in general—poses a number of potential health problems.[42] Many of these health threats involve the synergistic relationships between diet and disease. Like many cereals, maize is deficient in such essentials as the amino acids tryptophan and lysine; the metals iron and zinc; calcium, vitamin C, and niacin. Pellagra has traditionally been linked to heavy dependence on maize and associated deficiencies in tryptophan and niacin.[43] This disease was first described by Casal in northern Spain in 1730 after the introduction of maize from the New World. Since that time pellagra has been observed in maize-producing regions throughout the world.

Three major symptoms of pellagra are dermatitis, diarrhea (ulceration of the intestines affecting nutrient absorption), and dementia, although there are numerous additional problems.[44] Nutritional research involving pellagra has revealed that dietary imbalances in other amino acids might affect the metabolic pathway between tryptophan and niacin within the liver. Some investigators suggested that excessive levels of leucine and the resulting imbalance in the leucine/isoleucine ratio leads to the onset of pellagra.[45] Others have concluded that pellagra is caused by a vitamin B-6 deficiency.[46]

Pellagra has also been identified among societies dependent on sorghum in India. Sorghum, unlike maize, is relatively rich in both tryptophan and niacin. Here pellagra has been linked to fungi-contaminated grain, which causes mycotoxicosis due to the presence of the trichothecene compound, T-2 toxin.[47] Other investigators have argued that pellagra is causally related to elevated levels of leucine in maize, which results in the depletion of serotonin in the human brain.[48] Serotonin depletion, in turn, is associated with mental disorders characteristic of pellagra. Administration of isoleucine restores the imbalanced leucine/isoleucine ratio. Isoleucine supplementation apparently blocks the tryptophan-niacin metabolic pathway in the liver thus making more tryptophan available for serotonin synthesis.

Although the specific nature of the causal links between heavy dependence on maize and the incidence of pellagra has not yet been identified, a specialized maize diet exacerbated by animal protein deficiency results in a number of physiological and psychological problems. For the purposes of this discussion, it is important to point out that pellagra may decrease female fertility: such pellagra symptoms as vaginitis and amenorrhea probably affect female reproductive success. Several investigators have pointed out that estrogen inhibits tryptophan metabolism and may ultimately account for the disparity in pellagra occurrence among adult males and females.[49] The debilitating effects of pellagra impair child care. Inflammation of the gastrointestinal tract caused by pellagra threatens both mother and infant viability. Diarrhea and parasite infection within the small intestine impairs iron, zinc, and amino acid absorption.

Increased dependence on maize and associated decrease in animal protein frequently lead to iron-deficiency anemia. Maize, like many other cereals, inhibits iron absorption.[50] Iron absorption is impaired by the high concentration of phytic acid and the low concentration of the counteracting enzyme, phytase. Iron-deficiency anemia is exacerbated in adolescent females during initial menses and in adult females during menstruation, pregnancy, and childbirth.[51] Premature or multiple-birth infants suffer from iron-deficiency anemia due to insufficient iron stores at birth; this deficiency is further exaggerated by subsequent periods of accelerated growth and iron intake.

The weaning period constitutes a particularly critical threat to infants—especially if the child is weaned early and is shifted abruptly from breast milk to low animal protein, high carbohydrate diets of solid food. Infant diets based on cereal crops such as maize greatly increase health risks during the early stages of life:

The absorption of dietary iron in infants can be impaired by episodes of acute and chronic diarrhea. . . . Diarrhea promotes malabsorption by increasing intestinal motility and thereby reducing the amount of time that dietary iron is exposed to the absorption surfaces of the intestines. In addition, episodes of diarrhea are accompanied by hydration, loss of appetite, and substitution of solids by starchy gruels which are lower in nutritional quality.[52]

Nutritional deficiencies and weanling diarrhea establish conditions particularly well-suited for parasite infections. Iron-poor diets, increased intestinal motility, and parasites greatly amplify the process of nutrient malabsorption in recently weaned infants. Prolonged periods of breastfeeding may also lead to iron-deficiency anemia due to insufficient dietary iron and diminished iron stores in the older infant. We might expect to observe increased incidence of iron-deficiency anemia and greater risks for infants in those societies where the mother is required to work away from the household, as in the more extensive maize horticultural systems:

Among the Gusii of Kenya, for example, women are responsible for corn and millet cultivation upon which the society primarily depends, and they put young child nurses in charge of younger children and infants. The responsibilities of these child nurses cannot be described as casual and include feeding [supplemental feeding including solid foods], cleaning, and long hours of carrying.[53]

As agricultural intensification occurs, however, we find that women spend greater amounts of time within or near the domestic household and less time tending crops. With increased agricultural intensification, subsistence production shifts from root crops to seed crops, which require more processing time; furthermore, greater amounts of time are required for household chores, females have more children, and child-care costs increase markedly.[54]

Maize Consumption and Shell-tempered Ceramics: Systemic Interrelationships

More than a century ago Mexican physician Ismael Salas described in detail the maize preparation and cooking methods of MesoAmericans, which he thought were responsible for the absence of pellagra in Mexico and Central America.[55] Since the publication of Salas's thesis, a number of investigators have examined the interrelationships between alkali treatment of maize and its improved nutritional content. A similar treatment of maize using lime or wood ashes is described for various aboriginal groups throughout North America.[56]

Alkali maize processing serves to soften the tough outer kernel and more importantly to free lysine and tryptophan, which are chemically bound within the gluten fraction of maize protein. Furthermore, treatment of maize with slaked lime or wood ashes improves the amino acid balance between leucine and isoleucine, adds needed potassium, magnesium, copper, and zinc, and gives "a 2,010 percent increase in calcium, 37 percent increase in iron, and a 15 percent increase in phosphorus."[57]

Katz, Heidger, and Valleroy investigated aboriginal diet and food processing techniques involving maize throughout the New World.[58] They found that among the fifty-one societies examined there was a "highly significant relationship [which] strongly supports the associated concepts that alkali is necessary for high consumption and, by correlation, for high production of maize."[59] This study also describes additional aboriginal maize processing methods including the use of wood ash or lye, green roasting, burned gastropod or mollusc shells, and ash roasting.[60] Nations suggests that the Lacandon Maya in the southern Maya lowlands added slaked freshwater gastropods to water for boiling maize in order to enhance the nutritional value of tortillas and gruels.[61]

Prehistoric shell-tempered ceramics used throughout much of the eastern deciduous forest of North America may have served the same function. Burned freshwater mollusc shells in this case were added directly into the paste of prehistoric ceramic cooking vessels during the "Mississippian" period(s). This technological feature of "Mississippian" peoples had very definite implications for prehistoric nutrition. This nutritional link between heavy maize consumption and alkali processing might also account for the use of calcite temper in the manufacture of cooking vessels by the Yucatecan Maya and the Uinta Fremont culture in Utah.

Stimmell suggests that shell-tempered ceramics were manufactured because they were light in weight and could withstand greater amounts of thermal shock. She emphasizes that shell-tempered vessels could tolerate a greater range of firing temperature and exhibited fewer firing failures if sodium chloride was also added to the paste.[62] Plog suggests that "different raw materials may be used for functionally different types of vessels."[63] DeAtley posits that raw materials would be incorporated into the paste of cooking vessels to increase the wall porosity of the vessel and its resistance to thermal shock.[64]

Stimmell's materialist interpretation does not help us understand under what adaptive contexts we might expect to observe increased use of ceramic vessels with these characteristics. Perhaps the initial incorporation of burned and crushed mollusc shells into the paste as temper was a time-efficiency response to the increased labor demands required by maize production and processing. Such food by-products as bulk-processed freshwater mollusc shell valves were thus recycled. Such ceramic vessels might be produced more efficiently, because firing failure rates were lower and increased porosity made cooking vessels more resilient to thermal shock during repeated episodes of heating and cooling.

There is an additional and very important consideration with regard to aboriginal alkali processing. Stored maize frequently becomes contaminated by fungi with debilitating and potentially lethal mycotoxins—particularly aflatoxins,[65] a danger "increased with warmth, moisture, and damage to the product."[66] Schoental presents a provocative counterargument to the amino acid-niacin etiology of pellagra; mycotoxins produced by fungus on stored maize are causally linked to "gastrointestinal disorders, haemorrhage, skin lesions, neurological disturbance and 'septic angina.'"[67] Some fungi are "thermotolerant and could survive a few years."[68]

Schoental further suggests a link between maize mycotoxins, alkali processing, and antipellagenic effects:

How can the absence of pellagra among the tortilla-eating people be explained? The locally grown maize may have been mostly sound; moreover the treatment with slaked lime would hydrolyze the ester groups present in T-2 toxin and other trichothecenes: the respective hydroxl derivatives are known to be less toxic by a factor of 10 or more.[69]

Finally, it is known that nutritionally stressed, vitamin B-deficient populations are especially susceptible to mycotoxicosis.[70] If alkali processing does, in fact, enhance the conversion of tryptophan to niacin, we find that vitamin B deficiencies would be rectified. At the same time alkali processing would serve to detoxify the fungal-derived aflatoxins in stored ripened maize. Such a set of interdependent relationships between maize horticulture, ripened maize storage, and alkali processing can also be linked to specific varieties of aboriginal maize. Hall states that the higher protein, resilient, more storable flint varieties of maize were those best suited for alkali processing.[71]

The widespread utilization of shell-tempered ceramics throughout the deciduous forests of eastern North America can be understood as an integral part of "Mississippian" adaptations, which evolved in this region between A.D. 800 and A.D. 1500. We might expect that initial use of maize appeared as a response to energy stress during the growing season in temperate environments. Temperate deciduous environments might be food-poor during the summer season, especially for aboriginal populations that depended heavily on white-tailed deer during the winter.[72] If aboriginal population densities remained below a threshold imposed by white-tailed deer availability, their overwintering problem was solved and there was no need to adopt more labor-intensive food storage responses.[73] Yet, increased seasonal reliance on carbohydrate-rich maize and associated shifts in female labor during the horticulture season might have served as the impetus for increased fertility and further population growth. Increased population growth rates and increasing dependence on maize may also have led to decreased home range size(s), reduced mobility, and regional packing. Higher population densities and resulting depression of local animal resources would also have led to the exploitation of lower-ranked food resources including freshwater molluscs and other aquatic foods. One method for decreasing the handling or processing time for shellfish includes "bulk firing," which steams and opens the molluscs simultaneously.[74]

This systemic causal argument possesses considerable utility. We find that ceramic technology involving the manufacture and use of shell-tempered ceramic culinary and storage vessels is systematically linked to aboriginal demography, nutrition, storage technology, and labor organization (Fig. 2.1). It will enable us to gain a better understanding of the underlying processes that led to maize horticulture in eastern North America. Such systemic relationships can be used to account for the geographical and temporal distribution of "Mississippian culture." Furthermore, such an explanatory argument will enable us to explain variation in prehistoric and historic ceramics including intrasite and intersite differences in the composition of ceramic assemblages.

It should be pointed out that these aspects of prehistoric life in eastern North America have been of interest to idealist archeologists for many decades. Yet the explanations of these archeological questions about "Mississippian culture(s)" have focused primarily on an ideographic approach to innovation diffusion. Shell-tempered ceramics may have emerged and diffused within an aboriginal system of communication. However, innovation diffusion theory does not possess sufficient explanatory power to enable us to account for the distributional and compositional patterns for shell-tempered ceramics in the archeological record. Variability in prehistoric/historic shell-tempered ceramics can be explained primarily in terms of natural selection—that is, variable environmental constraints imposed on past feeding and reproductive behavior. Given this evolutionary ecological perspective, archeologists must view the appearance and persistence of shell-tempered ceramics as a technological/behavioral response to stress instead of a cultural innovation based on cognition.

Conclusions

"More than four decades have passed since Carl Sauer called attention to the overlapping interests of geographers and anthropologists and suggested that a gradual coalescence might represent the first series of fusions into a larger science of man."[75] The purpose of this chapter has been to emphasize the complexity of systematic interelationships that link human individuals and groups to the "web of life." The archeological study dis-

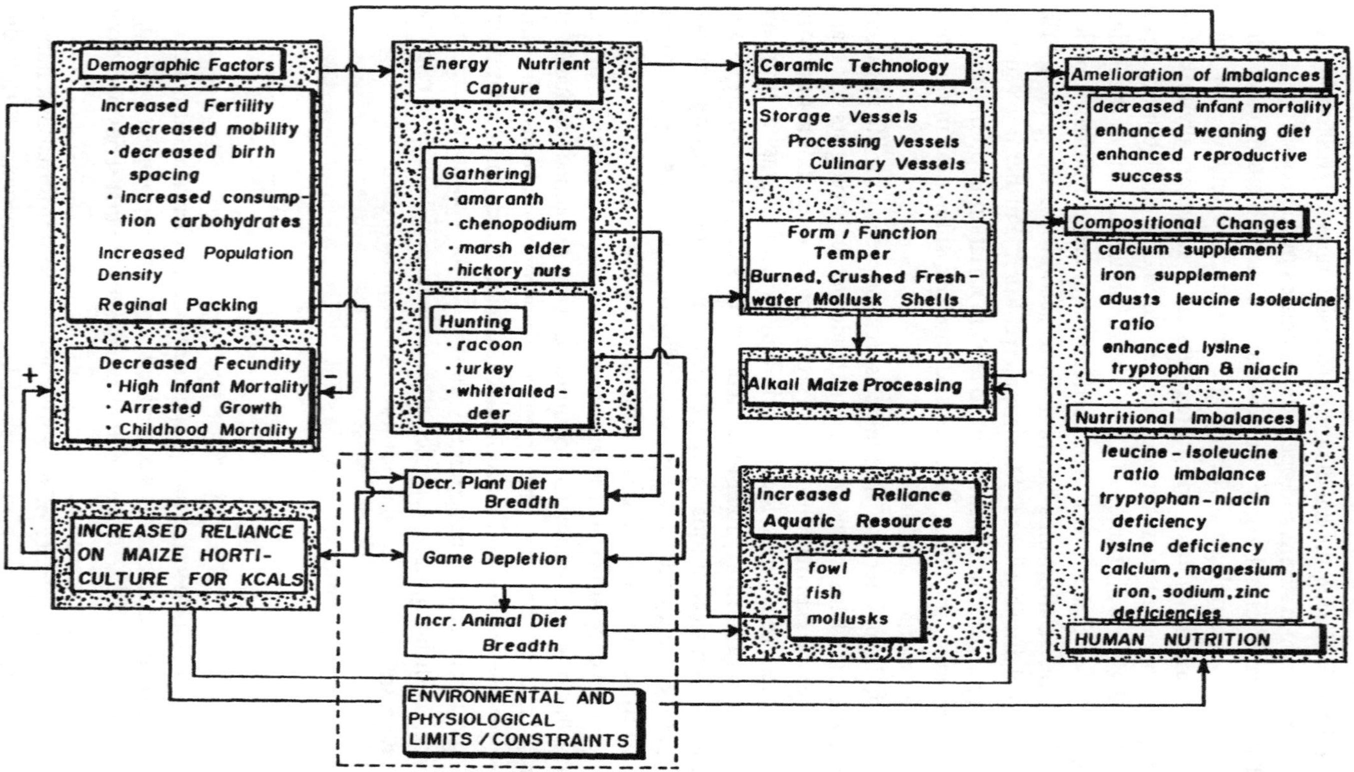

Figure 2.1. Interrelationships between shell-tempered ceramics, ecological constraints, maize horticulture, nutrition, and demography.

cussed here involves ecological, physiological, nutritional, technological, and social variables, which are integrated in order to assign meaning to the static material record of the past. Unlike the idealists who supposedly possess "empathetic talents" for "knowing" the causes of human action, archeologists, anthropologists, and geographers must focus attention on human behavior and its explanation from "outside" the system. Although it has not been formalized, a body of human behavioral theory does exist; but, in order to appreciate its explanatory power, we must leave the insularity and comfort of our own discipline(s). Many of us believe that scientific theory must be expressed in terms of a calculus or in the metalanguage of mathematics before we can "do science." Yet what form of mathematics did Darwin utilize to integrate and to systematize much of what we know about variability in life forms? Ghiselin comments in this regard:

A theory is valued because it provides a clue as to where to look for discoveries that have yet to be made; it has heuristic function. Viewed from without, science appears to be a body of answers; from within, it is a way of asking questions. For this reason, the crudest approximation, if it provides hints for the solution of a broad range of problems, has every advantage over the most elegant mathematical law which asserts nothing of interest.[76]

The archeologically based study offered here illustrates the complex nature of human behavior. Prehistoric garbage and debris possess no meaning awaiting discovery. Our understanding of the past is not a direct function of the quantity of archeological material that lies scattered about the landscape or buried deep within the earth. As scientists, we impart significance to this static record. It consists of the material correlates of past human behavior that directly or indirectly reflects all aspects of previous adaptive responses to the limitation and constraints of the environment. The existence and variable nature of such environmental contraints are then causally linked via our behavioral theory to observed variations in the archeological record. Our behavioral theory consists of a set of patterns or regularities and they, in turn, are used to bring "order to chaos" in the real world. A more determined interest in the development of a theory of human behavior will enable social scientists not only to dissect the world, but also to put all the pieces back together again.

Notes

1. See Carl G. Hempel, *The Philosophy of Natural Science* (Englewood Cliffs, N.J.: Prentice-Hall, 1966), p. 83.

2. Charles Darwin, *The Origin of Species* (New York: Washington Square, 1963), pp. 142–43.

3. See Marvin Harris, *The Rise of Anthropological Theory* (New York: Crowell, 1968); F. W. Voget, *A History of Ethnology* (New York: Holt, Rinehart and Winston, 1975); P. W. Porter, "The Kinship of Anthropology and Geography," in E. A. Hoebel, R. Currier, and S. Kaiser, eds., *Crisis in Anthropology: View from Spring Hill, 1980* (New York: Garland, 1982), pp. 223–43.

4. See Harris, *Rise*, pp. 649–50.

5. Quoted in R. G. Collingwood, *The Idea of History* (Oxford: Oxford University Press, 1946), pp. 78–79.

6. In Harris, *Rise*, p. 268; Leonard Guelke, "Geography and Logical Positivism," in D. Herbert and R. Johnston, eds., *Geography and the Urban Environment* (London: Wiley, 1978), vol. 1, pp. 35–60.

7. In Harris, *Rise*, pp. 267–69.

8. See William H. Durham, "The Adaptive Significance of Cultural Behavior," *Human Ecology* 4 (1976): 89–121; R. Brook Thomas et al., "An Anthropological Approach to Human Ecology and Adaptive Dynamics," *Yearbook of Physical Anthropology* 22 (1979): 1–46; William M. Denevan, "Adaptation, Variation, and Cultural Geography," *Professional Geographer* 35 (1983): 399–407.

9. John A. Agnew and James S. Duncan, "The Transfer of Ideas into Anglo-American Human Geography," *Progress in Human Geography* 5 (1981): 42–57; see also E. Huntington, "Geography and Natural Selection," *Annals*, Association of American Geographers, 14 (1924): 1–16; E. Soja, *The Political Organization of Space* (Washington, D.C.: Association of American Geographers, Commission on College Geography, 1971).

10. Porter, "Kinship," p. 25.

11. R. J. Johnston, *Geography and Geographers: Anglo-American Human Geography since 1945* (New York: Wiley, 1979), p. 132.

12. James S. Duncan, "The Superorganic in American Cultural Geography," *Annals*, Association of American Geographers, 70 (1980): 181–98, 131.

13. A. C. Kershaw, "Diffusion and Migration Studies in Geography," in P. G. Duke et al., eds., *Diffusion and Migration: Their Roles in Cultural Development* (Calgary: University of Calgary Press, 1978), pp. 6–13. See also Amos Rapoport, "Environmental Cognition in Cross-Cultural Perspective," in G. T. Moore and R. G. Golledge, eds., *Environmental Knowing* (Stroudsburg, Pa.: Dowden, Hutchinson, and Ross, 1976), pp. 220–34.

14. David L. Clarke, *Analytical Archeology* (London: Methuen, 1968), p. 89.

15. Ibid., pp. 97–98.

16. Eric Pianka, *Evolutionary Ecology*, 3rd ed. (New York: Harper and Row, 1983), p. 20

17. Darwin, *Origin*, pp. 58–59.

18. See Pianka, *Evolutionary*, p. 324.

19. See Michael T. Ghiselin, *The Triumph of the Darwinian Method* (Berkeley: University of California Press, 1969), pp. 32–45, 63.

20. Lawrence A. Brown, *Innovation Diffusion: A New Perspective* (London: Methuen, 1981), pp. 5–6.

21. Johnston, *Geography*, p. 132.

22. James Deetz, *Invitation to Archaeology* (Garden City, N.Y.: Natural History Press, 1967), p. 45.

23. Lewis R. Binford, *An Archaeological Perspective* (New York: Academic Press, 1972), p. 193.

24. See Leslie A. White, *The Evolution of Culture* (New York: McGraw-Hill, 1959); Lewis R. Binford, "Archaeology as Anthropology," *American Antiquity* 28 (1962): 217–25; "An Archaeological Perspective," in Lewis R. Binford and Sally R. Binford, eds., *New Perspectives in Archaeology* (Chicago: Aldine, 1968).

25. See Lewis R. Binford, "Willow Smoke and Dog's Tails: Hunter-Gatherer Settlement Systems and Archaeological Site Formation," *American Antiquity* 45 (1980): 4–20.

26. Lewis R. Binford, "The Archaeology of Place," *Journal of Anthropological Archaeology* 1 (1982): 5–31.

27. Robert L. Hall, "The Mississippian Heartland and Its Plains Relationship," *Plains Anthropologist* 12 (1967): 175–83.

28. See Dale R. Henning, "Mississippian Influences on the Eastern Plains Border," *Plains Anthropologist* 12 (1967): 184–94.

29. See L. H. Larson, Jr. "Functional Considerations of Warfare in the Southeast during the Mississippi Period," *American Antiquity* 37 (1972): 383–92; Christopher S. Peebles and Susan M. Kus, "Some Archaeological Correlates of Ranked Society," *American Antiquity* 42 (1977): 421–48; Bruce D. Smith, "Variation in Mississippian Settlement Patterns," in Bruce D. Smith, ed., *Mississippian Settlement Patterns* (New York: Academic Press, 1978), pp. 479–504.

30. See Smith, "Variation," p. 486.

31. See John W. Lallo, "The Skeletal Biology of Three Prehistoric Indian Societies from Dickson Mounds," Ph.D. dissertation, Department of Anthropology, University of Massachusetts, 1973; John W. Lallo et al., "The Role of Diet, Disease and Physiology in the Origin of Porotic Hyperostosis," *Human Biology* 49 (1977): 471–83; John W. Lallo et al., "Paleoepidemiology of Infectious Disease in the Dickson Mounds Population," *Medical College of Virginia Quarterly* 14 (1978): 17–23; Della C. Cook, "Subsistence Base and Health in the Prehistoric Illinois Valley: Evidence from the Human Skeleton," *Medical Anthropology* 3 (1979): 109–24.

32. See Mark N. Cohen and George J. Armelagos, *Paleopathology at the Origins of Agriculture* (New York: Academic Press, 1984).

33. Richard A. Yarnell, "Aboriginal Relationships between Culture and Plant Life in the Upper Great Lakes Region," *Anthropological Papers, Museum of Anthropology*, University of Michigan, vol. 23, 1964.

34. See Merle T. Jenkins, "Influence of Climate and Weather on Growth of Corn," in USDA, ed., *Climate and Man: 1941 Yearbook of Agriculture* (Washington, D.C.: U.S. Government Printing Office, 1941), pp. 308–20, 340.

35. Ibid.

36. See W. A. Mattice, "Weather and Corn Yields," *U.S. Department of Agriculture Monthly Weather Review* 59 (1931): 105–12.

37. Jenkins, "Influence," p. 312.

38. See Waldo R. Wedel, "An Introduction to Kansas Archaeology," *Bureau of American Ethnology*, Bulletin no. 174, 1959.

39. See Anne V. T. Kirkby, "The Use of Land and Water Resources in the Past and Present Valley of Oaxaca," *Memoirs of the Museum of Anthropology, University of*

Michigan, no. 5, 1973; J. R. K. Robson et al., "The Nutritional Significance of Maize and Teosinte," *Ecology of Food and Nutrition* 4 (1976): 243–49.

40. A kilocalorie (kcal) is the amount of heat energy required to raise the temperature of one kilogram of water 1° centigrade.

41. See David Pimentel and Marcia Pimentel, *Food, Energy, and Society* (London: Edward Arnold, 1979).

42. See A. Alland, "Discussion, Part V," in R. B. Lee and I. DeVore, eds., *Man the Hunter* (Chicago: Aldine, 1968), p. 244; M. T. Newman, "Nutritional Adaptation in Man," in A. Damon, ed., *Physiological Anthropology* (New York: Oxford University Press, 1975), pp. 210–59; J. L. Abrams, Jr., "The Relevance of Paleolithic Diet in Determining Contemporary Nutritional Needs," *Journal of Applied Nutrition* 31 (1979): 43–59.

43. See J. Goldberger, "The Etiology of Pellagra: The Significance of Certain Epidemiological Observations with Respect Thereto," *Public Health Reports* 29 (1914): 1683–86; J. Goldberger et al., "The Prevention of Pellagra: A Test of Diet among Institutional Inmates," *Public Health Reports* 30 (1915): 3117–31; FAO, "Maize and Maize Diets: A Nutritional Survey," *F.A.O. Report*, no. 9, 1953; G. A. Goldsmith, "The B Vitamins: Thiamine, Riboflavin, Niacin," in G. H. Beaton and E. S. McHenry, eds., *Nutrition: A Comprehensive Treatise* (New York: Academic Press, 1964), pp. 110–207; Daphne A. Roe, *A Plague of Corn: The Social History of Pellagra* (Ithaca: Cornell University Press, 1973); Solomon H. Katz et al., "The Anthropological and Nutritional Significance of Traditional Maize Processing Techniques in the New World," in E. S. Watts et al., eds., *Biosocial Interrelations in Population Adaptation* (The Hague: Mouton, 1975), pp. 195–232; Robson et al., "Nutritional Significance," pp. 234–49; W. H. Sebrell, Jr., "History of Pellagra," *Federation Proceedings* 40 (1981): 1520–22.

44. See Goldsmith, "B Vitamins"; Roe, *Plague*; Sebrell, "History."

45. See C. Gopalan and S. G. Srikantia, "Leucine and Pellagra," *Lancet* 1 (1960): 954–57; C. Gopalan, "Possible Role for Dietary Leucine in the Pathogenesis of Pellagra," *Lancet* 1 (1969): 197–99; B. S. N. Rao, "Effects of Leucine on Enzymes of Tryptophan Metabolism," *American Journal of Clinical Nutrition* 25 (1972): 6; C. Gopalan and K. S. J. Rao, "Pellagra and Amino Acid Imbalance," *Vitamins and Hormones* 33 (1975): 505–29.

46. See C. Gopalan and K. Krishnaswamy, "Effect of Excess Leucine on Tryptophan Niacin Pathway and Pyridoxine," *Nutrition Review* 34 (1976): 318–19.

47. See R. Schoental, "Mouldy Grain and the Aetiology of Pellagra: The Role of Toxic Metabolites of *Fusarium*," *Transactions of the Bio-chemical Society* 8 (1980): 147–50.

48. See K. Krishnaswamy and T. Raghuram, "Effects of Leucine and Isoleucine on Brain Serotonin Concentration in Rats," *Life Science* 11 (1972): 1191–97.

49. See David. A. Bender, "Effects of Oestradiol and Vitamin B on Tryptophan Metabolism in the Rat: Implications for the Interpretation of the Tryptophan Load Test for Vitamin B Nutritional Status," *British Journal of Nutrition* 50 (1983): 33–42; David A. Bender and Lena Totoe, "Inhibition of Tryptophan Metabolism by Oestrogens in the Rat: A Factor in the Aetiology of Pellagra," *British Journal of Nutrition* 51 (1984): 219–24.

50. See M. Y. El-Najjar, "Maize, Malaria and the Anemias in the Pre-Columbian New World," *Yearbook of Physical Anthropology* 20 (1976): 329–37; M. Y. El-Najjar et al., "The Etiology of Porotic Hyperostosis among the Prehistoric and Historic Anasazi Indians of the Southwestern United States," *American Journal of Physical*

Anthropology 44 (1976): 477–88; Robert P. Mensforth et al., "The Role of Constitutional Factors, Diet, and Infectious Disease in the Etiology of Porotic Hyperostosis and Periosteal Reactions in Prehistoric Infants and Children," *Medical Anthropology* 2 (1978): 1–59.

52. Ibid., p. 18.
53. Sara B. Nerlove, "Women's Workload and Infant Feeding Practices: A Relationship with Demographic Implications," *Ethnology* 13 (1974): 207.
54. See Carol R. Ember, "The Relative Decline in Women's Contribution to Agriculture with Intensification," *American Anthropologist* 85 (1983): 285–304.
55. Ismael Salas, "Etiologie et Prophylaxie de la Pellagre," Thesis, University of Paris, 1863.
56. See T. Rousell, *Traité de la Pellagre et des Psuedo-Pellagres* (Paris: Baillière, 1866); O. Y. Cravioto et al., "Nutritive Value of the Mexican Tortilla," *Science* 102 (1945): 91–93; R. Bressani and N. S. Scrimshaw, "Effect of Lime Treatment on *In Vitro* Availability of Essential Amino Acids and Solubility of Protein Fractions in Corn," *Journal of Agriculture and Food Chemistry* 16 (1958): 774–78; E. Kodicek and P. W. Wilson, "The Availability of Bound Nicotinic Acid to the Rat: Part I, The Effect of Limewater Treatment of Maize and Subsequent Baking into Tortillas," *British Journal of Nutrition* 13 (1959): 418–30; M. Behar, "Food and Nutrition of the Maya Before the Conquest and at the Present Time," in *Biomedical Challenges of the American Indian*, Pan American Health Organization Publication no. 165, 1968; Solomon H. Katz et al., "The Anthropological and Nutritional Significance of Traditional Maize Processing Techniques in the New World," in E. S. Watts et al., *Biosocial Interrelations in Population Adaptation* (The Hague: Mouton, 1975), pp. 195–232; K. L. Carpenter, "Effects of Different Methods of Processing Maize on Its Pellagragenic Activity," *Federation Proceedings* 40 (1981): 1531–35.
57. FAO, "Maize," p. 22.
58. Katz, "Anthropological."
59. Ibid., p. 216.
60. Ibid., pp. 217–20.
61. James D. Nations, "Snail Shells and Maize Preparation: A Lacandon Maya Analogy," *American Antiquity* 44 (1974): 568–71.
62. Carol Stimmell, "A Preliminary Report on the Use of Salt in Shell-Tempered Pottery of the Upper Mississippi Valley," *Wisconsin Archaeologist* 59 (1978): 266–74.
63. Stephen Plog, *Stylistic Variation in Prehistoric Ceramics: Design Analysis in the American Southwest* (Cambridge: Cambridge University Press, 1980), p. 87.
64. See S. P. DeAtley, "A Preliminary Analysis of Patterns of Raw Material Use in Plainware Ceramics from Chevelon, Arizona," Master's thesis, Department of Anthropology, University of California, 1973.
65. See Schoental, "Mouldy Grain."
66. Robert C. Patten, "Aflatoxins and Disease," *American Journal of Tropical Medicine* 30 (1981): 422–25.
67. Schoental, "Mouldy Grain," p. 147.
68. Ibid., p. 148.
69. Ibid., p. 149.
70. Ibid., p. 150.
71. Robert L. Hall, "An Interpretation of the Two-Climax Model of Illinois Prehistory," in David L. Browman, ed., *Early Native Americans: Prehistory, Demography, Economy, and Technology* (The Hague: Mouton, 1980), pp. 401–62.

72. See Alan J. Osborn, "Fire Ecology, Whitetailed Deer, and Prehistoric Central Plains Adaptations," paper presented at the 95th annual meeting of the Nebraska Academy of Sciences, Lincoln, Nebraska, 1985.

73. See Binford, "Willow Smoke," p. 4–20.

74. See Alan J. Osborn, "Aboriginal Utilization of Marine Food Resources," Ph.D. dissertation, Michigan State University, 1977; "Amazing Paste How Sweet the Taste! Mississippian Influence, Maize Horticulture, and Shell-Tempered Ceramics in the Eastern Plains," paper presented at the 39th annual meeting of the Plains Anthropological Conference, Bismarck, North Dakota, 1981.

75. Marvin W. Mikesell, "Review Article: Geographical Perspectives in Anthropology," *Annals*, Association of American Geographers, 57 (1967): 617–34.

76. Michael T. Ghiselin, *The Triumph of the Darwinian Method* (Berkeley: University of California Press, 1969), p. 236.

CHAPTER THREE

Anthropological Utopias and Geographical Epidemics

COMPETING MODELS OF SOCIAL CHANGE AND THE PROBLEM OF THE ORIGINS OF AGRICULTURE

D. Bruce Dickson

The earliest definite hominid remains appear in Africa around 4 million years ago. The earliest evidence for the domestication of plants and animals appears in various places in the Old and New Worlds sometime around or after ten thousand years ago. By the time of Christ, agriculture was the most common form of subsistence. Thus, for roughly 99.75 percent of its time on earth, the human being has been a gatherer or hunter rather than a farmer. Yet, it is this fundamental subsistence transformation from food collecting to food producing that has made possible the emergence of urban life, civilization, the state, complex technology, and the Malthusian population nightmare that we find ourselves living today. Small wonder, given the global impact and rapid occurrence of this metamorphosis, that prehistorians have been preoccupied with explaining it and isolating its causes. Explanations have taken many forms and have invoked a wide variety of causes. No attempt will be made to review them all here.[1] Instead, I should like to focus on two particular *classes* of explanation for the rise of agriculture, which counterpoise one another as polar opposites. I have christened these "utopian" and "epidemic" explanations.

"Epidemic" theories appear mostly in the tool kits of cultural geographers and culture historians. Such explanations emphasize the distribution of culture traits, culture complexes, or domesticated species. Continuous distributions of these phenomena are taken as prima facie evidence of contact between cultures. As in an epidemic disease, *contact* is regarded as a universal historical process that, in itself, accounts for culture change.

Such theories emphasize the cumulative, even "accumulative," nature of cultures and their susceptibility to novelty and to change.

Utopian theories tend to be the work of anthropologically trained prehistorians. They are heavily influenced by functionalism or structural functionalism, general systems theory and, perhaps, neoclassical economics. Thus, although these theories are social scientific in intent, they find their ultimate inspiration and intellectual origin in the works of such classic utopian writers and philosophers as Plato and Sir Thomas More. Utopian explanations tend to focus on the holistic, interdependent, and intercommunicating nature of cultures and to see them as closed, self-maintaining systems that tend toward equilibrium. They emphasize cultural conservatism and resistance to change.

Speaking of ideology in social science generally, Paul Diesing says: "The strength of a perspective consists of its ability to bring certain aspects of society into clear focus thereby making their empirical study possible; the weakness of a perspective consists of the way it distorts or hides other aspects of society."[2]

Diesing suggests that, in appraising social scientific explanations, we must first identify these strengths and weaknesses, and then develop an "organization of perspectives" that maximizes the former and minimizes the latter. This chapter describes the problems in each of these classes of theories, and sketches an "organization of perspectives" that accounts more usefully for the origins of agriculture than either the utopian or the epidemic approach.

"Epidemic" Explanations

The word "epidemic" is derived from the Greek *epi*, upon or among, and *demos*, people. Its etymology conveys its meaning: an epidemic "comes upon a people" suddenly and at once. The use of the term in medicine denotes a widespread outbreak of an infectious disease that affects many persons due to the rapid and contagious mode of its dispersal. Such dispersal often occurs in discrete waves, or pulses, separated from one another by periods of low infection. In epidemiological theory, the spread of an epidemic disease is brought about through the mixing of infected and uninfected persons.[3] In the process, an epidemic may be transmitted to large numbers of persons. The dispersal of epidemic infection does not occur evenly, like the outward spread of ripples from a rock thrown into a placid garden pond. Instead, the epidemic waves spread in conformity with physical geography, with the more subtle geography of population, and with the hierarchy of social and economic life.[4]

The epidemic model of cultural diffusion is the view that culture "traits" and "complexes" also spread through contact. Ideas or traits are thought to be engendered, like epidemic diseases, in "hearths" from which they emerge and spread in waves. In epidemic accounts of culture change, contact between the possessors of a trait and those who lack it is considered sufficient explanation for diffusion. Patterns of continuous distribution or similarities of style or function found in different areas are taken as prima facie evidence that contact and diffusion have in fact occurred. The model has wide currency in cultural geography and, earlier in this century, was popular in anthropology and archeology as well. In various formulations, the model is at the heart of most diffusionist accounts of the development of cultures. Its proponents regard epidemic diffusion as the most common source of cultural change. As Carl Sauer puts it: "In the history of man, unless I misread it greatly, diffusion of ideas from a few hearths has been the rule; independent, parallel invention the exception."[5]

Carl Sauer's Epidemic Theory of Agriculture

The most influential application of the epidemic model is found in Carl Sauer's *Agricultural Origins and Dispersals*. Sauer began his now-classic formulation of the problem with a list of six preconditions for the original transformation of food collecting into food production within a hearth:

1. A strong economic base, because "needy and miserable societies are not inventive, for they lack the leisure for reflection, experimentation, and discussion."
2. A subsistence system oriented toward plant gathering rather than hunting in order that they be predisposed toward agricultural experimentation.
3. A largely sedentary settlement system that would allow time to tend crops.
4. A woodland location rather than one on plains or grasslands where tough sod would resist primitive agricultural tools.
5. A location off the floodplain of large rivers where the practice of agriculture would demand drainage and irrigation.

6. Access to a wide variety of plants and animals in the surrounding environment.

According to Sauer, these essential preconditions were most likely to have been met by fishing peoples situated close to the great rivers of tropical southeastern Asia. The rich mixture of available lake, river, and forest resources would have enabled these southeastern Asian fisherfolk to develop a semisedentary or even sedentary settlement pattern based on food collecting. The requirements of fishing would have led them to gather plants whose fibers could be processed into fishing or nets or from which fish poisons, drugs, or medicines could be obtained. Perhaps only secondarily would they have sought plants for food. In any case, the gathering of plants eventually led them to experiment with the vegetative reproduction of certain root crops. Sauer concludes that a domestication process resulted from this manipulation and experimentation with the plants within the optimal economic and environmental setting of the southeastern Asian tropical lowlands.[6]

Once he had advanced his theory of domestication, Sauer was not much concerned about testing it. In fact, the theory might best be regarded as what Kuhn calls a "thought experiment"—that is, a logical construction of which the experimental consequences are never meant to be strictly realizable in nature.[7] When Sauer's theory was published in the early 1950s, little archeology had been undertaken in southeastern Asia and virtually none of that work had been done in tropical lowland riverine zones. Sauer was not convinced that archeological work there would meet with much success anyway: "At the time the ice caps were melting away, sea levels were rising markedly and hence rivers were filling their valley floors so that only chance locations not buried beneath sea or alluvium may be found."[8]

Sauer then turns to the other thrust of his book: the account of the spread or "dispersal" of agriculture in accord with the epidemic model of cultural diffusion. In his view, early agriculture spread widely throughout the Old World in company with domesticated geese, dogs, ducks, and pigs. Sauer attends very little to the impediments to the adoption of agriculture complexes or to why hunter-gatherers living in environments very different from the tropical lowland riverine zone would find such practices useful within, or conformable to, their subsistence systems. Sauer believed the advantages of food production would have been self-evident to hunters and gatherers. Exposure to the idea of agriculture, like exposure to a contagious disease, was thus explanation enough for its spread.

For Sauer, the presumed epidemic spread of the southeastern Asian agriculture complex had other implications as well. In the process of its diffusion, he saw agriculture as stimulating the domestication of other plants and animals in a series of "secondary" hearths in the Old World, including southwestern Asia, Ethiopia, western Africa, western India, and northern China. The spread of the southeastern Asian complex to these areas led to the domestication of local plants. These local plants were initially reproduced vegetatively. However, in southwestern Asia and elsewhere, seed cropping eventually developed as well.

Sauer suggested that a similar—probably independent—developmental sequence occurred in the New World. He saw the lowland tropical region that rings the Caribbean Sea as the most likely hearth for a New World agriculture complex and assumed that it diffused in epidemic fashion from that region to the remainder of the hemisphere. As in the Old World, Sauer saw New World seed cropping developing later in response to the introduction of the idea of cultivation along with tropical lowland root crops.

A Critique of Sauer's Agriculture Epidemic

Sauer's explanation for the rise of agriculture consists essentially of five hypotheses:

1. The fact that plants could be domesticated through vegetative reproduction was an "idea" that could be "discovered."
2. This discovery took place independently perhaps only twice, once in the Old and once in the New World.
3. Both times the discovery occurred in a limited historical, geographical, and cultural "hearth" among lowland tropical fishing peoples.
4. Once discovered, the idea of agriculture spread in epidemic fashion beyond both its Old and New World hearths.
5. The subsequent discovery that seed crops could also be domesticated was stimulated by the arrival of the idea of vegetative reproduction; subsequently the idea of seed cropping also spread in epidemic fashion outside its secondary hearths.

In his first hypothesis, Sauer gave primacy to cognition in the origins of agriculture—although he saw the material circumstances of the transformation as important. Although this hypothesis appears immune to empirical testing, it has been attacked on logical grounds by a number of scholars including White,[9] Flannery,[10] and Cohen.[11] In their view it is absurd to suggest that only in the Holocene did hunter-gatherers "discover" that plants, upon which their very existence depended, were produced from roots or seeds. Rather than assuming such naïveté, Flannery preferred to see these hunter-gatherers as "practiced and ingenious . . . lay botanists" whose survival during the Pleistocene was predicated in large measure upon their ability to translate practical understanding of the natural world into successful strategies for survival within it.[12] To suggest that Pleistocene peoples were unaware of the links in the seasonal botanical chain that leads from root or seed to fruit is as illogical as suggesting that they were ignorant of the connection between human intercourse and human conception. To conclude that the "discovery" of this linkage took place only twice, once in the Old and once in the New World, compounds the error.

Logical objections can also be raised to Sauer's second unverifiable hypothesis that, once discovered, agriculture spread like an epidemic simply because it was a better idea than food collecting. Rindos calls theories such as Sauer's "intentionalist" because they necessarily assume that the "ultimate benefits of agriculture for a society would have been observable in the early stages . . . [and that] a society aware of these benefits would act to take advantage of them."[13] He then adduces a series of arguments suggesting such assumptions are unwarranted. His most telling criticism, however, is his observation that although ants and termites have domesticated certain plant and animal species, we do not attribute this to their invention and diffusion of the idea of agriculture.

Clearly, other factors are operating here and, by extension, in the human sphere as well. Sauer recognized this when he specified six preconditions for the initial discovery of the idea of agriculture. If the original development of agriculture demanded a specific material and systemic context among fisherfolk in tropical lowlands, we might ask why it is logical to conclude that the resulting agriculture complex could diffuse so far outside its original hearth simply through contact and the epidemic transmission of an idea. Must not material and systemic causes be invoked to explain the worldwide spread of agriculture as well as its initial emergence?

Sauer's third, fourth, and fifth hypotheses may be empirically tested. If Sauer was correct, the earliest archeological evidence of plant domestication should (1) consist of root crops or other plants that are vegetatively reproduced and (2) be recovered in the tropical lowlands of southeastern Asia and the Caribbean. Outside these two regions, the earliest evidence of domestication should consistently (1) prove to be more recent than the tropical evidence, (2) demonstrate that vegetatively reproduced plants preceded the appearance of domesticated seed crops, and (3) exhibit a homogeneous repertoire of domesticated species rather than diverse, regionally specific ones.

Our ability to test empirically whether or not Sauer was correct in selecting tropical lowland fishing peoples as the lead actors in his drama is still quite limited.[14] Despite increasing archeological activity in tropical regions, particularly those of Thailand and the New World, poor preservation of plant macrofossils and pollen in lowland sites renders the recovery of direct evidence of plant domestication an unusual event. Nonetheless, recent archeological work by Gorman at Spirit, Banyan Valley, and Tham Pa caves in northwestern Thailand has produced a limited quantity of very early Holocene plant materials, including shell fragments, seeds, nuts, and plant parts.[15] According to Yen, three classes of plants are represented in these collections:

1. Trees or perennial plants which grow wild today in the surrounding primary or secondary forests.
2. Annual or perennial plants represented in the region today as cultigens, including rice (*Oryza*) at Banyan Valley Cave.
3. Possible annual crop plants, including some poorly preserved specimens tentatively identified as either *Phaseolus* or *Vicia*.[16]

The significance of the plant material from these caves was its recovery in the context of the Hoabinhian, a southeast Asian Mesolithic technological complex dated at the site to between 12,000 and 5600 B.C.[17] This early date, the presumed cultivated or domesticated status of some of the plant species, and the presence of seeds originally identified as possible members of either the genus *phaseolus* (common bean) or *vicia* (broad bean) has led some scholars to conclude that (1) southeastern Asia experienced an agricultural revolution earlier than either southwestern Asia or the New World, and that (2) Sauer's theory of agricultural origins had been partially vindicated.[18]

Subsequent ethnobotanical work in northwestern Thailand, combined with a closer physical and taxonomic examination of the plant remains, has called these initial conclusions into question.[19] The tentative identification of some of the seeds as either *phaseolus* or *vicia* remains inconclusive, but it now appears that the plants in the earliest assemblages from the cave sites were probably not domesticated. It seems likely that the plants from these assemblages were wild rather than domestic, but it is important to note that virtually every plant specimen in them represents a species that ultimately was domesticated.[20] Harris suggests that these assemblages very likely reflect the first stages of the domestication process in the region.[21] If this interpretation is correct, it makes the absence of any evidence of vegetatively reproduced plants within the assemblages particularly damaging to Sauer's theory. In fact, this absence has lead Gorman to conclude that we should abandon the notion that vegetatively reproduced plants were necessarily the first plants to be domesticated in southeastern Asia.[22]

Outside the lowland tropics, the archeological record, as it is understood at present, does not support the primacy of vegetatively reproduced plants. They are neither the earliest known cultivars worldwide, nor do they invariably predate the appearance of seed crops in the nontropical regions. The failure of the archeological evidence thus far to support Sauer's hypothesis about the primacy of root crops may be because it is incorrect to assume that plants that can be reproduced vegetatively are necessarily the simplest to domesticate.

Zohary's work with wild wheat and barley has demonstrated that such wild cereal grains are genetically highly plastic and thus susceptible to rapid change under conditions of human manipulation.[23] The genetic plasticity of such wild cereal grains, combined with the emergence in the terminal Pleistocene of hunting and gathering economies that focused on wild grain exploitation, points to the temperate and semiarid regions of the Old and New Worlds as more likely loci for the earliest "hearths" for domestication.

At the same time, a variety of biological and biogeographical research casts doubt on the notion that agriculture emerged in only one or two centers, tropical or otherwise. Harlan,[24] Harlan, de Wet, and Stemler,[25] and others point to the decidedly *noncentric* quality of the origin of many of the world's most important domesticated plants. They argue for widespread, and in large measure independent, domestication processes occurring in many regions during the early Holocene epoch.

Another aspect of this lack of centricity in the origins of cultivated species undercuts the final testable hypothesis in Sauer's theory. If epidemic diffusion from a single hearth explains the spread of agriculture in the Old World during the early Holocene, we would expect to find an essential similarity between the plant and animal assemblages in Asia, Africa, and Europe prior to the fifteenth or sixteenth centuries. However, instead of a worldwide sharing of basic cultigens, the agricultural assemblages of those great regions consisted of unique repertoires of plants and animals markedly contrastive to one another prior to European expansion.

The distinct agricultural complexes cannot be explained away as due simply to the differing environments of the three macroregions: in the century following the discovery of the New World, a profound mixing of the species that made up these discrete complexes occurred between the Americas and Asia and Europe. This sixteenth-century mixing, called by Crosby the "Columbian Exchange," was a dramatic process of genuine epidemic diffusion, when agriculturalists on opposite sides of the world exchanged and adopted each other's cultivated plants.[26] The resulting relative homogeneity of the domesticated animal and plant repertories in the world today is testimony to both the speed and intensity of this exchange. It is also evidence that epidemic diffusion did not cause the worldwide emergence of agriculture in the early Holocene.

Sauer's model of agricultural origins and dispersals is an example of what Karl Hempel calls an "explanation sketch" rather than a formal theory— this because, in addition to the interacting variables that it posits, it includes a model of history. Speaking of such explanation sketches, Binford notes:

All the imagined events must be accurate (something theories do not demand). Where variables are combined with events, there is the danger of attack on both fronts: your historical facts may be proven to be wrong, or it may be argued that your variables were inappropriate. Frequently, by showing one of these two elements to be ill-conceived, the other is also rejected.[27]

Both sorts of attacks have been successfully launched against Sauer's explanation sketch. In my judgment, the logical interrelationship of his major variables has been found inadequate. At the same time, the particular historical sequence that he outlines has been plausibly tested using archeological, geographical, and biological data and found wanting.

"Utopian" Explanations

"Utopia," which means literally "no place" in slightly fractured Greek, was the name coined by Sir Thomas More for the imaginary ideal polity he described in 1516. The term has since come into general use in reference to any social or political system envisioned by its designer as perfect. As Kateb puts it, utopian writers have "employed the imaginary to project the ideal."[28] But in a provocative paper on utopianism in sociology, Dahrendorf also includes "perfectly bad" societies, such as the totalitarian state in Orwell's *1984*, under the utopian rubric. In his view, the systems described by Orwell and Plato, More and Huxley, have one element in common:

"They are all societies from which change is absent. Whether conceived as a final state and climax of historical development, as an intellectual's nightmare, or as a romantic dream, the social fabric of utopias does not, and perhaps cannot, recognize the unending flow of the historical process."[29]

Dahrendorf also notes that utopias tend to be seen by their creators as characterized by isolation, uniformity or consensus in values, social stability or immobility, and the absence of structurally generated conflict. The contrast between such utopian visions and actual social life is great indeed, but in Dahrendorf's view it is just such visions that condition much of the theoretical discourse in modern sociology. Structural functionalism, with its concepts of equilibrium or homeostasis and its view of individuals who depart from institutionalized normative patterns as deviants, is clearly a utopian vision according to Dahrendorf.[30] The emphasis on social immobility in these approaches is a particular departure from the experience of familiar social reality.

The substance of Dahrendorf's critique applies equally well to much contemporary theory in anthropology and archeology. Here too the static notions of "equilibrium states" and "functional interdependence" have taken deep root. The view that societies tend toward immobility, unless disturbed by powerful and generally external forces, has been widely accepted.

Binford and Flannery's Hunter-Gatherer Utopia

An example of the impact of utopianism in archeology is the so-called Binford-Flannery model of the post-Pleistocene transformation of human economies from food collection to food production.[31] Earlier models of this transformation, most notably that of Braidwood, assume that human culture continually evolves toward greater specialization and differentiation.[32] In such a view, the domestication of plants and animals is a natural and inevitable result of this evolutionary or developmental process. Binford regarded this notion as a retreat into vitalism or orthogenesis. He rejected the idea that progressive change is inherent in culture on the grounds that such a hypothesis cannot be tested and therefore cannot contribute to a scientific understanding of culture. In his view, culture is the human extrasomatic means of adapting or accommodating oneself to one's environment. Progressive cultural change is not inevitable in such a model; it occurs only in response to changes in the adaptive situation.[33]

Using analogies drawn from ethnographic studies of modern hunter-gatherers, Binford rejected the view that peoples were experiencing continuous cultural differentiation and specialization toward the end of the Pleistocene. Instead he assumed they had reached equilibrium with their environments. That is, that they were able to maintain their population at or below the human carrying capacities of the environments to which they were adapting and thus had little impetus to change their cultural system, let alone to transform its subsistence base from food collection to food production.

Yet it is precisely this sort of dramatic metamorphosis that did occur in a number of societies shortly after the close of the Pleistocene epoch. According to Binford only two testable factors could have caused this upset in the presumed state of equilibrium and cultural immobility of terminal Pleistocene society and led to the establishment of sedentary agricultural life.[34] These factors would be either:

1. A change in the *physical environment* of a population, which reduced the biotic mass of the region and decreased the amount of wild plants and animals. Environmental change would disrupt the equilibrium previously established between the population and available foodstuffs and would favor the development of more efficient means of food collection and extraction.

2. A change in the *demographic structure* of a region, which led one group to infringe upon the territory of another. Such a change would upset the established equilibrium. By increasing the population density in a region, such infringement would reduce the amount of wild food available per capita and favor the development of more efficient extractive methods.

Traditional explanations, such as invention or increasing cultural complexity, might be brought in at this point, but to Binford the actual trigger of domestication was neither human genius nor the inherent tendency of cultures to evolve to higher stages. Rather it was the changing material conditions of human existence, which jarred socio-cultural systems out of their natural states of equilibrium and forced them to adapt.

In the case of the southwestern Asian agricultural transformation, Binford concluded that late Pleistocene environmental changes in the region were too minor to have been very disruptive.[35] The transformation was brought about by external or internal demographic disequilibrium or stress. Internal stress is caused by population growth within a region; external stress results from migration from one region to another. But if equilibrium between population and resources was assumed by Binford to be the natural state in hunter-gatherer societies, how was demographic stress initiated? Binford found his answer in the manner in which these equilibria are maintained. Hunter-gatherer societies may be either "open" or "closed" with regard to their population policy. Closed systems maintain population below the carrying capacity of their environments by cultural means: infanticide, abortion, sexual abstinence, or periodic migration. Open systems do not use these means of control. Instead, such systems grow until they approach the carrying capacities of their environments. A segment of the group "buds off" to form an independent social unit in adjacent territory, a process repeatable until the adjacent territory was full. After this point, expansion of the open system would occur only into already populated areas. Binford envisioned two results of such a process:

1. If the arriving peoples differed culturally from the receptors, natural selection would favor either the group with the better population control methods or the one able to increase its productive efficiency.

2. If the arriving peoples possessed subsistence patterns that were not completely translatable into the new circumstances, these new conditions, coupled with the demographic imbalance set off by the new group's arrival, might provide the impetus for both the foreign and the indigenous groups to develop new subsistence patterns and techniques.[36]

Binford argued that in optimal habitats the abundance of natural resources would have resulted in the development of sedentary or semisedentary subsistence systems. This, in turn, would have resulted in population growth in such habitats. Populations from open systems in these optimal zones would eventually spread beyond their boundaries.

Binford hypothesized that surplus population from the groups living in the centers of the optimal zones would thus periodically disrupt the population equilibrium established by groups living on the margins. The resulting demographic stress would create an adaptive or selective advantage for those groups able to deal with this stress either through better population control (by developing closed population policies) or by increasing their productivity through manipulating the wild plants and animals on which they depend. When such demographic stress occurred in marginal zones that contained domesticable plants and animals, this manipulation began the process of their transformation.

The selective advantage that such manipulation or tending would confer in terms of increased productivity of certain wild species would be reinforced by favorable genetic changes in the wild species as a consequence of human selection. Binford suggests that the intersection of the ranges of the wild ancestors of domesticated species with zones of externally derived demographic stress occurred independently at least four times in at least four areas including southwestern Asia, MesoAmerica, South America, and southeastern Asia. He further suggests that such intersection probably occurred inland, but adjacent to coastal or estuarine environments in all four localities. He reached this conclusion because (1) in estuarine and coastal environments, mollusk collecting, waterfowling, fishing—some of the most productive forms of hunting and gathering known—can all be practiced within concentrated areas, and because (2) in southwestern Asia, MesoAmerica, South America, and southeastern Asia, highly productive coastal zones are commonly found adjacent to semiarid inland regions of markedly lower biotic mass. If the societies located in these coastal optimal zones were open with regard to population growth policy, groups that budded off from them could have moved only to adjacent zones of markedly lower carrying capacity.

Kent Flannery's contribution to the Binford-Flannery model also rejected climate change in favor of demographic stress as the major cause of the rise of agriculture in southwestern Asia.[37] Flannery supplemented Binford's model by emphasizing key changes he believed must have occurred in the ecological relationships between terminal Pleistocene hunter-gatherers and the wild plants they were harvesting. Flannery used ethnographic studies of modern hunter-gatherers in combination with general systems theory to construct a general model of food-collecting subsistence. He noted that wild plants and animals were neither uniformly distributed in a territory, nor uniformly available throughout the year. Instead, they varied—often dramatically—in their concentration and accessibility over space and time. Flannery suggested that hunter-gatherers developed procurement systems built around this spatial and temporal variability. Such systems involved seasonal changes in location that followed a temporal order or schedule within a territory.

Careful scheduling of seasonal movement and activity contributed to the survival of the social group year after year by assuring the steady and continuous collection of wild foodstuffs and by preventing their overexploitation. Optimal combinations of resources exploited in terms of tight seasonal schedules also inhibited change. In stable environmental settings such systems were characterized by immobile equilibrium relationships between resources and populations. In other words, they became conservative, fixed, unchanging. Like Binford, Flannery had a utopian vision of hunting and gathering societies as balanced and immobile in their natural states.[38]

Flannery applied his equilibrium model of hunter-gatherer subsistence to the archeological record in Mesopotamia and the Levant, and to the epi-Paleolithic period culture complexes there known respectively as the Karim Shahirian and the Natufian. Analysis of faunal and floral remains recovered from southwest Asian sites indicates that the Natufians practiced a broad-spectrum form of subsistence in which the hunting of antelope and the gathering of various wild cereal grains played prominent parts. The apparent success of the Natufian adaptation led Flannery to hypothesize that they had developed an optimal seasonal schedule and that their populations were in equilibrium with their terminal Pleistocene environments.

Had all things remained equal, Flannery believed, this equilibrium state would have continued indefinitely. However, not all things remained equal and the Natufians were forced to leave utopia. Flannery suggested that the trigger of change was a "genetic kick" that occurred within the wild cereal grain populations they were collecting. Building on the work of Harlan and Zohary,[39] Flannery noted that wild grasses and cereal grains are genetically highly plastic. Although wild plant species all have excellent mechanisms for seed dispersal, genetic mutations that retard natural seed dispersal occur continuously within their populations. Such mutations are fatal to progeny of the individual plants that carry them; natural selection acting on wild populations assures that only the genetic makeup of plants with efficient dispersal mechanisms will be transmitted to succeeding generations. Yet plants with retarded seed dispersal mechanisms are easier for humans to collect and would unconsciously be selected by seed gatherers like the Natufians. As soon as the collectors began to *reseed* the grain intentionally, a greater percentage of these mutations would become concentrated in the resulting grain populations than would be present in them naturally. As a consequence of human selection, the grain populations would be altered genetically over the generations. Further, these alternations would result in an increase in the productivity of the cereal grain plants per unit of labor invested in their collection.[40]

In the terminology of general systems theory, such increasing returns create a "positive feedback loop"—that is, more returns per unit of labor in an activity lead to greater investment of labor in that activity in the future. This leads to still greater increases in productivity, then to still greater investment, and so on. Eventually this positive feedback would have meant that the Natufians had to alter their seasonal schedule to allow more time for grain collection and manipulation. Flannery considered that the shift from hunting and gathering to sedentary agriculture had been a gradual one that came about with the reduction in the number and spatial distribution of exploited resources and the creation of greatly altered seasonal schedules arranged around the requirements of the nascent cereal grain cultivation.

Flannery suggests that the specific cause of the reseeding that led to this "genetic kick" was the introduction of wild cereal grains into habitats outside their natural range. This would also have resulted in hybridization with local races of grasses, a further source of increased productivity. At this point, Flannery's and Binford's models coalesce, suggesting that the seeding of wild grains in areas beyond their natural ranges may have occurred earliest in southwestern Asia on the margins of the primary resource zones. Flannery saw this seeding as a consequence of the population pressures described by Binford resulting from the disturbance of adaptive equilibrium by externally induced demographic stress. The efforts of the inhabitants of these less favored localities to, in Flannery's words, "produce artificially, around the *margins* of the 'optimum' zone, stands of cereals as dense as those in the *heart* of the 'optimum' zone,"[41] may have led them to attempt to introduce and manipulate wild cereal grains there.

Flannery suggested that these events must have taken place sometime between 10,000 and 8000 B.C. among southwest Asian hunters and gatherers like the Natufians. Eventually, the continued rescheduling of their nomadic subsistence round in response to the increasing productivity of cereals led to sedentary dry farming and to caprine domestication sometime before about 5500 B.C. and to advanced farming after that date.[42]

Of course, in the Binford and Flannery scenario, equilibrium is never recaptured. The population genie is out of the bottle, and man enters history as we know him today. He has been cast out of stable, unchanging, immobile utopia as irrevocably as Adam and Eve from the garden. Yet, that eponymous pair had only their own willfulness to blame for their expulsion; the Natufians, it would seem, were victims of the hidden forces of plant genetics, human reproduction, and the unintended consequences of their own most innocent behavior.

A Critique of the Binford-Flannery Utopia

Like Sauer's theory, the Binford-Flannery model can be reduced to a limited set of hypotheses:

1. Hunting and gathering societies are open systems that adapt or accommodate human populations to their physical environments.
2. Over time, such systems come into static equilibrium with their

environments—that is, their outputs in terms of population do not exceed their inputs in terms of natural resources.

3. Hunting and gathering systems remain in static equilibrium unless they are disturbed by changes in either their physical environment or demographic structure.

4. In general, the hunting and gathering systems of the late Pleistocene epoch were in equilibrium with their environments.

5. Post-Pleistocene changes in the physical environment of southwestern Asia were insufficient to disturb significantly the equilibrium of the hunting and gathering systems located there.

6. Changes in demographic structure caused the transformation from hunting and gathering to agriculture in southwestern Asia. Specifically, surplus human population was periodically "donated" by open societies in zones of optimum resource productivity to "receptor" societies located on their margins in zones of lower resource productivity. These "donations" upset the equilibrium established between population and natural resources in the marginal zones and created demographic stress there.

7. The transformation of subsistence from food collecting to food producing occurred earliest in societies that were: (a) located in marginal zones, (b) within the natural ranges of easily domesticable species of plants or animals, (c) hunting and gathering these domesticable animal and plant species, and (d) experiencing demographic stress.

8. Population stress in the marginal zones favored those societies able to either (a) regulate or reduce their populations or (b) increase the productivity of their territories by manipulating the plant and/or animal species that they had hitherto merely been harvesting or hunting.

9. The human manipulation of certain wild cereal grains led to favorable genetic changes in those species that increased their productivity. Increased productivity led to increased manipulation, thence to the rescheduling of seasonal activities and finally to full domestication.

10. The spread of this innovation was not through epidemic diffusion. Rather it followed population stress or spread as agricultural societies expanded and replaced hunting and gathering groups. Of course the archeological record left by such population expansion might give the appearance of epidemic diffusion from the source of the stress.

These hypotheses are perhaps even more difficult to test empirically than Sauer's. The first hypothesis, that static equilibrium is the natural state of hunting and gathering societies, is a utopian vision with little empirical basis or connection to social reality. Hypotheses two, three, and four are clearly related to hypothesis one. Because, however, the equilibrium assumption is the essential premise from which the Binford-Flannery model is logically deduced, let us grant them temporary immunity and examine hypotheses five through ten.

In contrast to Sauer, Binford and Flannery seek the causes of the agricultural transformation entirely in the changing interrelationship of human social organization, demography, and the natural environment rather than in the discovery and the spread of ideas. Unlike the Sauer approach, this model consistently dismisses the intentions and reasons of human agents— what Giddens calls the "rationalization of action—as irrelevant to the explanation of social change.[43] The Binford-Flannery model is one of long run equilibrium in which independent material forces—population growth and the production of natural resources—oppose one another and eventually achieve static balance. This balance is upset only by a disturbance in one of the forces; human cognition has little to do with it.

Although both models are "explanation sketches" in Hempel's terms, Sauer's account is almost entirely a historical reconstruction, whereas the Binford-Flannery account is, at its heart, an attempt at formulating a nomothetic law of cultural development setting forth the relationship of specific variables under certain conditions in hunting and gathering societies. If the relationship is a "law," its workings must be universal—that it, independent of time and place.

If the Binford-Flannery model is correct we should expect to find, ceteris paribus, archeological and historical evidence that domestication occurred wherever and whenever the specific conditions of the model were met—that is, wherever hunting and gathering societies (1) located in areas marginal to optimal resource zones, (2) exploited the wild ancestors of domesticated plant and animal species, and (3) experienced subsistence stress due either to population increase or environmental change, so that either (a) domestication of one or more of these wild species can be shown to have followed, or (b) the reasons for its failure to occur can be accounted for within the terms of the law.

The test implications of this supposed law are virtually the reverse of those for Sauer's model. First, domestication would not have been limited to only one or two centers of "hearths." We would instead expect the archeological evidence for the origins of agriculture to be decidedly "noncentric" in character. Rather than seeking the earliest evidence of agriculture in a single environmental zone, such as tropical riverine lowlands, we should instead plot the former worldwide ranges of the wild ancestors of domesticated plants and animals, note the points where such ranges intersect zones of optimum resource productivity, and then look on the "margins" of those intersections for evidence of domestication.

Binford concludes that habitats with aquatic and/or marine resources possess such optimum exploitive potential worldwide. Without so much as a nod to Carl Sauer, he suggests that "fisher-foragers" adapted to these zones would consistently "donate" surplus population into semiarid zones on their margins and thus produce domesticated plants and animals. He suggests that rivers draining into the Black Sea in European Russia and south-central Europe may have contained such marginal "tension zones" and thus be logical places for early domestication to have occurred.[44] As noted earlier, the "noncentric" character of early domestication is becoming increasingly apparent and is clearly more consistent with the expectations of the Binford-Flannery model than with Sauer's theory. It remains to be seen whether or not these multiple centers may be regarded as having been in productively marginal, tension zones.

A second, related implication of the presumed universality of the Binford-Flannery model is that domestication could not be limited in *time*. Inasmuch as it must occur in hunting and gathering societies whenever the requisite conditions are met, there is no reason to assume that domestication is strictly a post-Pleistocene phenomenon. Rather, as George Carter has observed, if the emergence of agriculture was a natural, mechanistic process, we should expect to find it appearing early in human prehistory among virtually all cultures.[45] If domestication proves to be limited in its occurrence in time, then we must conclude that an unrecognized variable causes or modifies the process and that the Binford-Flannery model is at best incomplete.

Flannery suggested that the subsistence practices that eventually led to domestication were worked out between 38,000 and 8000 B.C.[46] Other scholars, such as Reed, hypothesized that the domestication of plants and animals actually began during the Pleistocene.[47] The evidence for this is ambiguous and inferential. The strongest case in recent years has been made by Bahn, who contended that upper Paleolithic period peoples in southwestern Europe had begun to domesticate the horse and reindeer,[48] and by Wendorf and Schild who, until recently, claimed to have discovered evidence of possibly domesticated emmer wheat and barley in archeological contexts in Upper Egypt dating to before 16,000 B.C..[49]

Reviving a much earlier view of the upper Paleolithic period economy, Bahn denies the common assumption that the large quantities of horse bones found at Solutre and other sites of the period in southwestern Europe were due to mass game drives.[50] He favored the view that these bone middens accumulated gradually and asserted that the horses at Solutre were tended in semidomesticated herds rather than hunted. Animals so tended would be available for slaughter as needed. Bahn suggested similarly that reindeer were semidomesticated and that "reindeer nomadism" (as formerly practiced by the Lapps of northern Scandinavia) developed during the upper Paleolithic period.[51] Human selection largely replaces natural selection in herds of domesticated animals. As a consequence, the demography of domestic herds contrasts markedly with that of wild herds.

However, Spiess found no significant differences between age and sex proportions in reindeer remains from the various components at the French upper Paleolithic site of Abri Pataud and proportions in the wild modern Nechina herd in Alaska.[52] Similarly, Levine observed that age proportions of horse remains from selected upper Paleolithic period middens in France and Germany essentially duplicated the age proportions in fossil sites from the same areas where man was not the agent of collection. Thus, Bahn's hypothesis must be rejected.[53]

Wendorf and Schild, unlike Bahn, reported direct evidence for the late Pleistocene beginnings of domestication. They recovered charred emmer wheat and two-rowed barley grains from a single, firmly dated, upper Paleolithic archeological context in Upper Egypt near the Sudanese border. Inasmuch as this region is outside the known range of the wild ancestors of emmer wheat and barley, Wendorf and Schild at first concluded that the charred grains were, at the very least, "candidates for the oldest-known, humanly-nurtured grain in the world."[54] Yet systematic and persistent efforts by the excavators did not discover additional contexts containing such grains in their upper Paleolithic sites. Further, when the grain specimens themselves were radiocarbon dated by spectrographic analysis, the dates were late Holocene. The excavators concluded that the apparent evidence of Pleistocene domestication was, in fact, due to recent contamination.[55]

In sum, if the Binford-Flannery model is correct, the process of domestication would not be limited to the Holocene but must also have occurred when the requisite conditions were met in the Pleistocene. At present, however, the only reasonably certain evidence of domestication that we have is of post-Pleistocene age.

Some Alternatives to Epidemics and Utopias

Why have these two theories—one utopian and the other epidemic in character—failed to provide us with comprehensive explanations of the worldwide, post-Pleistocene transformation from food collection to food production? Perhaps because both are based on inappropriate analogies, which lead to unrealistic views of human behavior and culture process. I suggest that the explanation of the initial origins of agriculture must begin with the recognition that the problem entails at least four dimensions:

1. *Domestication was not simply a historical "discovery" or "invention," which then spread as an "idea" by epidemic diffusion.*[56] As noted earlier, species of ants maintain domesticated plants and animals; whence came the great geniuses that made these necessary discoveries or inventions for them? Hominids have been plant gatherers for four million years or more; anatomically modern human beings have been on earth for forty thousand to a hundred thousand years. Can we accept the notion that the knowledge that forms the basis of domestication was really a "discovery" made only during the last ten thousand years?[57]

Are we not better served by regarding discoveries of this kind to be behavioral changes, which, like genetic mutations, occur commonly within human societies but become of practical importance only in the right material circumstances? In this view, manipulation and experimentation with plants and animals has often—perhaps always—been a feature of hunting and gathering subsistence, but only during the Holocene did new material conditions of life favor or select for such practices. The explanation of the emergence of agriculture then becomes a matter of identifying these unique Holocene material circumstances.

2. *The subsistence systems of hunting and gathering societies are not transformed simply through the epidemic transmission and adoption of new ideas any more than are the subsistence systems of other human societal forms.* To contend that early domestication diffused in a primarily cognitive and epidemic fashion is to ignore the very real social, environmental, and ideological impediments facing both the adoption of such an idea by hunter-gatherers and its implementation in their subsistence systems. The historical record of culture change among Native American hunter-gatherers provides some instructive examples in this regard. For instance, the Numa or Shoshonean-speaking peoples of the Great Basin persistently resisted all efforts at inducing them to abandon broad-spectrum food collecting in favor of settled farming. However, late in the nineteenth century, subsistence

agricultural practices did indeed diffuse widely among them in a rapid, epidemic fashion. This epidemic diffusion did not follow the introduction of the "idea" of agriculture, which after all had been known to the Shoshoneans for a long time. Rather, it spread among them only after the native plant ecology of the Great Basin, upon which their food collection system was based, was profoundly modified by the arrival of large herds of domestic cattle and sheep in the company of Anglo settlers.[58]

The record of Native and Euro-American culture contact and diffusion in the New World provides insight into the nature of the dispersal of agriculture during the early millennia of the Holocene. It suggests that:

1. The early diffusion of agriculture was most commonly "relocation diffusion"[59] rather than epidemic diffusion—that is, diffusion brought about by the intrusion and expansion of agricultural populations into new areas, rather than the communication and spread of the idea to indigenous hunting and gathering peoples.

2. Where the epidemic diffusion of agriculture occurred among hunting and gathering peoples, it was probably only *after* the material conditions of the food collecting subsistence of the adopting group had been altered substantially by post-Pleistocene climate change, mammalian extinctions, sea level change, or the intrusion of agricultural peoples.

Finally, in the *absence* of either intrusive agricultural peoples or fundamental changes in the material environment, I can envision only one circumstance in which agriculture could diffuse in epidemic fashion among early Holocene hunter-gatherers. Such diffusion might occur among food collecting groups possessed of what Woodburn has called "delayed return" subsistence systems. Woodburn distinguished these from "immediate return" subsistence systems, whose members reject the notion of surplus accumulation. Citing ethnographic examples, Woodburn stated:

[Immediate-return societies are] nomadic and positively value movement. They do not accumulate property but consume it, give it away, gamble it away or throw it away. Most of them have knowledge of techniques for storing food but use them only occasionally to prevent food from going rotten rather than to save it for some future occasion.[60]

In contrast to the rapid use or consumption of resources characteristic of immediate-return systems, in delayed-return economies there is always a period of weeks, months, or even years between the initial application of labor and its productive return. Further, once obtained, "this yield, or some part of it, is then allocated in some way or other to provide for the requirements of the participant or participants."[61] Woodburn's dichotomy between delayed- and immediate-return subsistence systems cuts across the more well known distinctions between societies based on technology or modes of production. Woodburn's key variables are the willingness or reluctance to accumulate surplus and to invest current efforts for future returns. All other things being equal, the epidemic diffusion of agriculture could occur only among those hunting and gathering societies whose ideology and practice already predisposed them to the delayed-return form of subsistence necessary in food production.

3. *Hunting and gathering societies as a rule do not establish "equilibrium" relationships with their environments any more than do other human societal forms. Such states of immobility when they occur are exceptions to be explained, not conditions to be assumed.* As noted at the outset of this chapter, the utopian assumption that prehistoric hunting and gathering societies established equilibrium relationships between their populations and their environments has been borrowed from recent ethnographic studies of modern, non-Western societies. However, as Salisbury has pointed out, such studies have of necessity relied "on data from only relatively short time periods. The multitude of variables measured for any one society have not been fully demonstrated to be causally related, but most have rather been *assumed* to be functionally related."[62]

Salisbury suggested that the duration of these studies has simply been far too brief to allow them to demonstrate that equilibrium was actually ever sought or achieved by members of the societies under study. Societies thus maintain not quantitative *equilibrium* between their population and resources, but qualitative *continuity* within the stream of successive generations of their members.

In a similar, if somewhat more systematic, vein, Giddens has suggested we dispense with the view that human social structures are fixed patterns of social relationships and see them instead as generative "rules and resources" arranged in coordinated systems.[63] These rules and resources are used by members of societies as guidelines for acting and for evaluating action in the various changing circumstances of life. They are used much as players use rules in playing a game.

These sets of semantic or generative rules govern what Giddens has called the "production and reproduction of systems of social interaction."[64] The resulting action may tend toward equilibrium or immobility in some circumstances, but that is neither the overt nor latent "function" of the rules. Rules are merely guidelines for conduct and foster the qualitative continuity in social life over time that Salisbury has emphasized. In situations characterized by markedly changing material conditions, cultural game playing, using systems of generative rules, must always lead away from immobility or equilibrium toward what Salisbury calls "cultural extrapolation." Perhaps the profound alteration of material circumstances that occurred at the beginning of the Holocene, as well as the cultural transformation from food collecting to food production that followed these alterations, can best be interpreted using generative models of this type rather than those emphasizing either equilibrium states or change brought about through contact and epidemic diffusion.

4. *Domestication was not the inevitable result of the mechanistic interaction of a limited set of variables governed by fixed laws of cultural development.* Many prehistorians still labor under the burden of the Enlightenment. They quest for "laws of society and culture," which they see as extensions of the "laws of nature." Such laws must describe dependable sequences of events in society and the conditions under which, ceteris paribus, these events invariably occur. The problem with this quest is that it has thus far failed to isolate any such laws. Perhaps the specific difficulty in explaining the origins of agriculture in a nomothetic manner stems from the fact that the transformation was not in reality an orderly sequence of causal events that followed from the interaction of a limited set of material variables.

It is becoming increasingly clear in the archeological record that the domestication of plants and animals was a process initiated no earlier than the terminal Pleistocene or early Holocene epochs in a large, but by no means unlimited, number of locations on earth. We should therefore regard the transformation to be a particular historical process rather than a universal or nomothetic one. Its explanation must begin with the detailed accounting of circumstances surrounding its emergence in each area. But lest such circumstantial descriptions lead simply to ad hoc accounts, it must be recalled that the agricultural transformaton appears to have coincided worldwide with varying combinations and intensities of (1) climate change, (2) mammalian extinctions, (3) sea-level changes, and (4) human population increase.

Thus, reconstruction of local sequences of events preceding and surrounding agricultural transformation in various parts of the world must also account for the effects that these general events had on local circumstances. It is my hope that the reconstructions of the specific chains of circumstance that surrounded the rise of agriculture in the various regions of its emergence will be based on conceptual models that are in spirit neither "utopian" nor "epidemic."

Notes

1. See Peter J. Ucko and G. W. Dimbleby, eds., *The Domestication and Exploitation of Plants and Animals* (London: Gerald Duckworth, 1969); G. A. Wright, "Origins of Food Production in Southwestern Asia: A Survey of Ideas," *Current Anthropology* 12/4–5 (1971): 447–77; Charles A. Reed, "The Pattern of Animal Domestication in the Prehistoric Near East," in Ucko and Dimbleby, *Domestication*, pp. 361–80; Charles A. Reed, "Origins of Agriculture: Discussion and Some Conclusions," in his *Origins of Agriculture* (The Hague: Mouton, 1977), pp. 879–953.

2. Paul Diesing, *Science and Ideology in the Policy Sciences* (New York: Aldine, 1982), p. 12.

3. See Andrew Cliff and Peter Haggett, "Island Epidemics," *Scientific American* 250/5 (1984): 144.

4. Ibid.

5. Carl O. Sauer, *Agricultural Origins and Dispersals* (New York: American Geographical Society, 1952), p. 23.

6. Ibid., p. 27.

7. Thomas S. Kuhn, "A Function for Thought Experiments," in his *The Essential Tension: Selected Studies in Scientific Tradition and Change* (Chicago: University of Chicago Press, 1977), pp. 240–65.

8. Sauer, *Agricultural Origins*, p. 23.

9. Leslie A. White, *The Evolution of Culture* (New York: McGraw-Hill, 1959), p. 283.

10. Kent V. Flannery, "Archaeological Systems Theory and Early MesoAmerica," in Betty G. Meggers, ed., *Anthropological Archaeology in the Americas* (Washington, D.C.: Anthropological Society of Washington, 1968), pp. 67–68.

11. Mark N. Cohen, *The Food Crisis in Prehistory: Overpopulation and the Origins of Agriculture* (New Haven: Yale University Press, 1977), pp. 22–23.

12. Flannery, "Systems Theory," p. 67.

13. David Rindos, *The Origins of Agriculture: An Evolutionary Perspective* (New York: Academic Press, 1984), p. 11.

14. Paul C. Mangelsdorf observes that "if one sought, as an exercise in imagination, to design a completely untestable theory of agricultural origins and dispersals, it would be difficult to improve on this one" ("Review of *Agricultural Origins and Dispersals* by Carl O. Sauer," *American Antiquity* 19 [1953]: 87–90). Mangelsdorf rather overstated the case, but barriers to its testing remain. Unfortunately, he leaves readers with the impression that he believed that agriculture could not have begun in the lowland tropics, because if it did, we could never prove it scientifically. Such reasoning is reminiscent of that of the divine fool of the Sufis, Mulla Nasrudian, who, upon losing his key in the darkened alley behind his house, goes out to the street lamp in front to look for it because the light is better there.

15. See four studies by C. F. Gorman: "Hoabinhian: Pebble-tool Complex with Early Plant Associations in Southeast Asia," *Science* 163 (1969): 671–73; "Excavations at Spirit Cave, North Thailand: Some Interim Interpretations," *Asian Perspectives* 13 (1970): 79–108; "The Hoabinhian and After—Subsistence Patterns in Southeast Asia during the Late Pleistocene and Early Recent Periods," *World Archaeology* 2/3 (1971): 300–19; "*A Priori* Models and Thai Prehistory: A Reconsideration of the Beginnings of Agriculture in Southeastern Asia," in Reed, *Origins of Agriculture*, pp. 321–55.

16. Douglas E. Yen, "Hoabinhian Horticulture: the Evidence and Questions from Northwest Thailand," in J. Allen, J. Golson, and Philip Jones, eds., *From Sunda to Sahel* (New York: Academic Press, 1977), p. 571.

17. Gorman, "Hoabinhian and After," pp. 301–303.

18. See W. G. Solheim, "Northern Thailand, Southeast Asia and World Prehistory," *Asian Perspectives* 13 (1970): 145–62; "An Earlier Agricultural Revolution," *Scientific American* 226 (1972): 34–41.

19. See Jack R. Harlan and J. M. J. de Wet, "On the Quality of Evidence for Origin and Dispersal of Cultivated Plants," *Current Anthropology* 14/1–2 (1973): 52; Yen, "Horticulture."

20. See I. C. Glover, "The Hoabinhian: Hunter-gatherers or Early Agriculturalists in Southeast Asia?" in J. V. S. Meagan, ed., *Hunters, Gatherers and First Farmers Beyond Europe* (Leicester: Leicester University Press, 1977), p. 158.

21. D. R. Harris, "The Prehistory of Tropical Agriculture: an Ethnoecological Model," in Colin Renfrew, ed., *The Explanation of Culture Change* (London: Duckworth, 1977), p. 410.

22. Gorman, "*A Priori* Models," pp. 338–39; Yen, "Horticulture," pp. 590–93.

23. See five studies by Daniel Zohary: "Studies on the Origin of Cultivated Barley," *Bulletin of the Research Council of Israel* D9 (1960): 21–42; "Spontaneous Brittle Six-row Barleys, Their Nature and Origin," *Proceedings of the First International Barley Genetics Symposium*, Wageningen, 1963, pp. 27–31; "The Progenitors of Wheat and Barley in Relation to Domestication and Agricultural Dispersal in the Old World," in Ucko and Dimbleby, *Domestication*, pp. 47–66; "Origin of Southwest Asia Cereals: Wheats, Barleys, Oats and Rye," in P. H. Davis, Peter C. Harper, and I. C. Hedge, eds., *Plant Life of Southwest Asia* (Edinburgh: Royal Botanic Garden, 1971), pp. 235–63; "The Origin of Cultivated Cereals and Pulses in the Near East," *Chromosomes Today* 4 (1973): 307–20.

24. Jack R. Harlan, "Agricultural Origins: Centers and Noncenters," *Science* 174 (1971): 468–74; "The Origins of Cereal Agriculture in the Old World," in Reed, *Origins of Agriculture*, pp. 357–83.

25. Jack R. Harlan, J. M. J. de Wet, and Ann B. L. Stemler, "Plant Domestication and Indigenous African Agriculture," in *Origins of African Plant Domestication* (The Hague: Mouton, 1976), pp. 3–19; but see George F. Carter, "A Hypothesis Suggesting a Single Origin of Agriculture," in Reed, *Origins of Agriculture*, pp. 99–109.

26. Alfred W. Crosby, *The Columbian Exchange* (Westport, Conn.: Greenwood, 1972).

27. Lewis R. Binford, *In Pursuit of the Past* (New York: Thames and Hudson, 1983), p. 197.

28. George Kateb, "Utopias and Utopianism," *The Encyclopedia of Philosophy* vol. 8 (New York: MacMillan, 1967), p. 212.

29. Ralf Dahrendorf, "Out of Utopia: Toward a Reorientation of Sociological Analysis," *American Journal of Sociology* 64/2 (1958): 115. Chad Walsh calls such "perfectly bad" societies "dystopias" in his provocative book, *From Utopia to Nightmare* (Westport, Conn.: Greenwood, 1972).

30. Dahrendorf, "Out of Utopia," pp. 118–21.

31. The so-called Binford-Flannery model is a synthesis of the explanations of the agricultural transformation presented separately by Lewis R. Binford ("Post-Pleistocene Adaptations," in Sally R. and Lewis R. Binford, eds., *New Perspectives in Archaeology* [New York: Aldine, 1968], pp. 313–41) and Kent V. Flannery ("The

Ecology of Early Food Production in Mesopotamia," *Science* 147 [1965]: 1247–56; "Archaeological Systems Theory"; "Origins and Ecological Effects of Early Domestication in Iran and the Near East," in Ucko and Dimbleby, *Domestication*, pp. 73–100; "The Origins of Agriculture," *Annual Review of Anthropology* 2 [1973]: 271–310). The hybrid version was developed by Wright ("Origins of Food Production," and tested against southwest Asian archeological data by him and, more recently, by H. J. Pomerantz ("Prelude to Domestication in the Levant: Kebaran and Natufian Ecology," Ph.D. dissertation, Brandeis University, 1979). The model has never been wholly accepted either by Binford or Flannery, and parts of it have been specifically repudiated by both: Binford, *Pursuit*, pp. 198–213; Flannery, "Archaeology with a Capital S," in C. L. Redman, ed., *Research and Theory in Current Archaeology* (New York: Wiley, 1973), pp. 47–53.

32. Robert J. Braidwood, "The Agricultural Revolution," *Scientific American* 203/3 (1960): 130–48.

33. Binford, "Adaptations."

34. Ibid., p. 328.

35. Were the environmental changes that occurred at the end of the Pleistocene in the Near East really of little moment to the hunting and gathering societies living there? Current evidence from the Levant and Mesopotamia summarized by Karl W. Butzer certainly indicates that the massive dessication once thought to have occurred there at the end of the Pleistocene simply did not happen: "Patterns of Environmental Change in the Near East during Late Pleistocene and Holocene Times," in Fred Wendorf and A. E. Marks, eds., *Problems in Prehistory: North Africa and the Levant* (Dallas: Southern Methodist University Press, 1975), pp. 389–410; "The Late Prehistoric Environmental History of the Near East," in W. C. Brice, ed., *The Environmental History of the Near and Middle East since the Last Ice Age* (New York: Academic Press, 1978), pp. 5–12. This is not to say that the current environments in those areas today duplicate past conditions. Of course they do not, but this difference may be due in large part to poor land management, overgrazing, deforestation, and salinization. Taken together, these anthropogenic changes appear to be more significant than climatically induced environmental alterations at the end of the Pleistocene epoch. However, for a summary of the evidence favoring significant climate change at that time, see H. E. Wright, Jr., "Environmental Changes and the Origin of Agriculture in the Near East," *Bioscience* 20/4 (1970): 210–12, 217; "Environmental Change and the Origin of Agriculture in the Old and New Worlds," in Reed, *Origins of Agriculture*, pp. 281–318.

36. Binford, "Adaptations," p. 331.

37. Flannery, "Ecology"; "Systems Theory"; "Origins."

38. In fact, Flannery's reliance on the concept of homeostasis appears to place him in what he himself refers to as the "Ex-Lax" school of archeological theory: "Archaeology with a Capital S." The single condition of membership in this school is a willingness to emphasize "natural regularity" in one's explanation of sociocultural process.

39. Zohary, "Studies"; "Spontaneous"; "Progenitors"; J. R. Harlan and D. Zohary, "The Distribution of Wild Wheats and Barley," *Science* 153 (1966): 1074–80.

40. Harlan, de Wet, and Stemler, "Plant Domestication," pp. 8–9, discuss other "automatic" modifications in plant genetics in addition to changes in seed dispersal mechanism that occur as soon as humans begin to sow seeds rather than merely gathering and consuming those produced in the wild. The authors note that these mutations would also ordinarily be eliminated by natural selection in wild popula-

tions. They are unconsciously favored within the cultivator's field because they enhance a seed's harvestability and therefore the likelihood that it will be gathered and planted in the following season. These automatic changes include selection toward uniform maturity rate, larger seed size, and the elimination of prolonged seed dormancy. Of course the authors also note that numerous other changes in taste, color, and plant morphology are brought about by the cultivator's *conscious* selective efforts.

41. Flannery, "Systems Theory," p. 81.

42. Ibid., p. 74.

43. Anthony Giddens, "Functionalism: *après la lutte*," in his *Studies in Social and Political Theory* (London: Hutchinson, 1977), p. 121.

44. Binford, "Adaptations."

45. Carter, "Hypothesis," pp. 92, 94, 96.

46. Flannery, "Ecology," p. 1251.

47. Reed, "Origins," p. 884.

48. Paul G. Bahn, "The 'Unacceptable Face' of the West European Upper Paleolithic," *Antiquity* 52/206 (1978): 183–92.

49. Fred Wendorf and R. Schild, "The Earliest Food Producers," *Archaeology* 34/5 (1981): 30–36.

50. Bahn, "Face," p. 185.

51. Ibid., p. 189.

52. Arthur E. Spiess, *Reindeer and Caribou Hunters: An Archaeological Study* (New York: Academic Press, 1979), p. 185.

53. See Marsha Levine, "Mortality Models and the Interpretation of Horse Population Structure," in Geoff Bailey, ed., *Hunter-Gatherer Economy in Prehistory* (Cambridge: Cambridge University Press, 1983), pp. 23–46; see also G. Smolla, "Neolithische Kulturerscheinungen: Studien zur Frage ihrer Herausbildungen," *Antiquitas*, series 2, vol. 3 (1960): 1–180.

54. Wendorf and Schild, "Producers," p. 31.

55. Wendorf, personal communication.

56. Much has been written on this point and little that is new can be added here. The reader is invited to consult Edgar Anderson, "Man as a Maker of New Plant Communities," in W. L. Thomas, ed., *Man's Role in Changing the Face of the Earth* (Chicago: University of Chicago Press, 1956), p. 766; Flannery, "Origins of Agriculture," pp. 307–308; Donald R. Lathrap, "Our Father the Cayman, Our Mother the Gourd: Spinden Revisited, or a Unitary Model for the Emergence of Agriculture in the New World," in Reed, *Origins of Agriculture*, p. 714.

57. See Carter, "Hypothesis," p. 98.

58. See Jack S. Harris, "The White Knife Shoshoni of Nevada," in Ralph Linton, ed., *Acculturation in Seven American Indian Tribes* (New York: Appleton-Century, 1940), pp. 39–118; Julian H. Steward, "Basin-Plateau Aboriginal Sociopolitical Groups," *Smithsonian Institution, Bureau of American Ethnology, Bulletin* 120 (1938); Joseph C. Winter, "The Process of Farming Diffusion in the Southwest and Great Basin," *American Antiquity* 41/4 (1976): 421–29. Marek Zvelebil, "Postglacial Foraging in the Forests of Europe," *Scientific American* 254/5 (1986): 104–15, finds evidence of a similar resistance to the adoption of agriculture by indigenous hunting and gathering peoples. According to Zvelebil, the archeological record of the early Holocene epoch in northwestern Europe indicates that foragers there adopted agriculture only after their environment was substantially altered by the forest-clearance practices of intruding Early Neolithic–period agricultural peoples.

59. Peter Haggett, *Geography: A Modern Synthesis* (New York: Harper and Row, 1975), p. 348.

60. James Woodburn, "Hunters and Gatherers Today and Reconstruction of the Past," in Ernest Gellner, ed., *Soviet and Western Anthropology* (London: Duckworth, 1980), p. 99.

61. Ibid., p. 97.

62. Richard F. Salisbury, "Non-equilibrium Models in New Guinea Ecology: Possibilities of Cultural Extrapolation," *Anthropologica* 17/2 (1975): 128.

63. Giddens, "Functionalism," p. 131.

64. Ibid., pp. 132–33.

PART TWO

Diffusion in History

CHAPTER FOUR

Diffusion in History

William H. McNeill

Diffusion of skill and knowledge from one community to its neighbors and neighbors' neighbors constitutes the central process of human history. Ever since significant differences in skills arose among separate human groups, borrowing back and forth has taken place whenever someone saw a real or apparent advantage in doing so. Borrowing nearly always involved modifying what was borrowed to make it fit smoothly into a different set of skills and customs. Sometimes, too, negative borrowing took place. By this I mean that when one community felt itself threatened by contact with strangers, the perceived danger might provoke special efforts at strengthening local defenses. Outright invention mingled with disguised borrowing in such circumstances more often than not. And in real situations the attraction of the new nearly always competed with fear and distrust of what was strange and unfamiliar in the minds of both parties to an encounter.

It is easy to support these propositions on abstract grounds. Most persons will agree that it is intrinsically easier to borrow than to invent, if only because when one borrows there is tangible reason for thinking the thing will work. Moreover, it is pretty clear that ever since our species arose, venturesome roving has been part of the repertoire of human behavior. Roving may be especially characteristic of young males; but entire communities, too, have often found it necessary or advantageous to trek toward new ground, taking their chances with whatever they might encounter along the way.

This meant that strangers showed up from time to time in even the most isolated communities. As soon as skills differentiated, so that some human groups knew things and could do things that others could not, these recurrent encounters with strangers offered an opportunity for the diffusion of new skills. With the rise of civilizations, high skills concentrated in a few metropolitan centers. Peoples in touch with such centers were able to upgrade their own capacities, and regularly did so within limits set by geographical and social conditions. The historical record therefore attests to a sporadic but persistent spread of civilized skills onto new ground. And as skills spread, they had to be altered and adjusted to fit the social and geographical climate prevailing in the regions where borrowing took place. That, I submit, is the warp and woof of human history abstractly stated.

Concretely, diffusion of skills is far more difficult to follow in detail than my general propositions suggest. In the first place, much occurred at an everyday artisan level and was never recorded or even noticed by the small clique of scribes and literati who monopolized writing in ancient and medieval times. Often, too, skilled artisans kept their secrets deliberately, not wishing to allow outsiders to find out how they plied their trade and earned their living. Sometimes, too, ideological principles required borrowers to deny that they had imitated strangers. Christian monks of late antiquity, for example, may have learned techniques of mysticism from Indian holy men—techniques of breath control, for example, which when carried to an extreme produce a sensation of shooting lights when brain functions stagger under the influence of oxygen shortages. Christian mystics began to see God, whereas older prophets and holy men of the Near East had only heard God. But no Christian monk could or would admit that he had learned anything important from a pagan, and if techniques of mysticism were borrowed from India, one can be perfectly certain that no written record attesting to that fact was ever made.

Whether or not Christian monks learned anything important from itinerant Indian experts in the supernatural is uncertain; indeed most scholars who have studied early Christianity disregard the possibility and look only to antecedents within the Mediterranean and Near Eastern heritage for new forms of monkish behavior. This is, perhaps, as much due to expert myopia as to the state of the evidence, but it makes diffusion from India a risky explanation for what happened among the monks of Egypt and Syria.

Even in far more recent times, religious contagion across faiths is hard to demonstrate. The participants, on principle, repudiated the notion that they could learn anything from unbelievers. Yet, in the mid-seventeenth century, an agent for the English Levant Company, a Fifth Monarchy man, who believed that the Book of Revelation was about to be fulfilled, hired a Jewish dragoman in Smyrna to help him with his business. The Jew's son, Sabbatai Sevi, presently announced that he was the Messiah and convinced a fair number of his fellows in the Ottoman empire of the truth of his claim. He was soon arrested; to save his life he became a Muslim, as did some of his followers. This rather inglorious retreat did not end the wave of religious excitement Sabbatai Sevi's messianic claims had stirred up. Jewish communities in Poland were aroused, and some began to believe in the imminent end of the world. Soon excitement communicated itself to Orthodox Christians of Russia, where, again, many so-called Old Believers began to prophesy that the end of the world was at hand. All this took place at a time when literacy was widespread and when religious controversy provoked a vast propaganda literature.

No scholar really doubts that in this case the millenarianism of a sect of English Puritans triggered the extraordinary upheaval that took place in east European Jewry and Orthodox Christendom. But there is no written evidence to that effect. Whatever it was that actually happened took place on an oral, face-to-face basis among humble folk who had all sorts of personal reasons for believing that the wickedness of the world was so great that its end must indeed be close. Nevertheless, historians have been willing to go beyond the available texts by recognizing that the wave of millenarian hope was a single wave, crossing the three faiths secretly, so to speak, and without leaving direct written traces.

These examples perhaps suffice to show how inadequate literary records are as evidence of borrowing and diffusion of skills and knowledge. Historians, however, are professionally text-bound and feel uneasy in the absence of written evidence. Consequently, the profession has systematically underestimated the range and role of diffusion in history. This tendency has been reinforced by the parochialism that concentration on a single literary tradition is bound to induce. A scholar who has mastered Greek, Latin, and the modern languages needed for classical studies is likely to pay no attention to what was happening in India or China when Greece and Rome were in full career. Sanskritists and sinologists have the same tendency to concentrate within their respective provinces of learning and not think very much about borrowings, if any, across language lines. Those who wrote in ancient languages, and whose texts have survived to our day, were likewise limited by their literary erudition and sensibilities and were inclined to suppose that nothing of value or importance could possibly come from a place where their own skills, knowledge, and belief were unknown.

The literary record therefore tends to divide humankind into separate and more or less watertight compartments. Everyone who depends on texts for evidence will be impelled to overlook or minimize the borrowings across cultural and literary boundaries that did, in fact, occur. Only when art history and the material remains uncovered by archeology are made to supplement literary testimony can a juster estimation of the role of borrowing in times past be hoped for, and even that leaves many gaps. The sort of religious changes already referred to left little or no material traces, and many other borrowings in the realm of ideas remain similarly difficult or impossible to prove. Consequently a full and accurate account of cultural diffusion will never be written. All we can hope for is history written with a keen sensitivity to the possibility and probability of borrowings, material and immaterial alike.

Transport and Communication, Overseas and Overland

Due attention to the findings of archeology certainly shows that even in prehistoric times, before writing had been invented, material goods circulated over fairly long distances. Obsidian from volcanic sites in Asia Minor traveled several hundreds of miles in the fourth millennium B.C., presumably because the cutting edges that obsidian flakes provided were superior to any alternatives then available. Later, when the first cities had arisen in the land of Sumer, a long-range search for metals and timber carried at least as far as modern Rumania, where the Carpathian Mountains presumably supplied silver or other valued metals. A few mutilated Sumerian clay tablets, pierced and perhaps worn as amulets by the local inhabitants, are the silent and isolated evidence of this distant contact. Sea travel was a good deal easier, and ancient Sumer sent ships south to the Indus valley and, directly or indirectly, other vessels seem to have reached the Red Sea and opened up contacts between Sumer and the Nile valley at the time when Egyptian civilization was first taking shape.

From this beginning, transport and communication overseas and overland carried strangers and their goods far and wide within the Old World. Similar movements no doubt occurred in the Americas, though evidences of long-distance contacts among American Indians are less well known than those of ancient Near Eastern lands and the Mediterranean shores. Seafaring in the Indian Ocean is also almost entirely unknown. Only isolated occurrences, such as the migration of Malay-speakers from Borneo or some nearby island to Madagascar at about the beginning of the Christian era, show what sailors of the southern seas were capable of in early times.

In the Mediterranean we are far better informed. The dispersal of megalith builders from Malta to the Atlantic and Baltic shores of Europe and Africa is well known. That occurred before 3000 B.C. Thereafter, Minoans, Phoenicians, and Greeks paved the way for a united Mediterranean world, finally achieved by the Roman conquest, but prepared for by trade relations and the consequent diffusion of civilized skills along the seaways from 1500 B.C. onward.

Land communication was always more costly and carrying capacity was smaller, because animal and human backs can carry far less than even a simple dugout canoe. Still, a person can walk across Asia in less than a year. Once horses had been domesticated, movement across the Eurasian steppe became comparatively easy. Horses could feed themselves en route by grazing for a few hours each day, and in case of need their human masters could feed on their blood by tapping a vein in the horse's side. But a warlike, nomadic way of life defined itself on the steppe about 2000 B.C. soon after domesticated horses appeared on the scene, and it was a long time before conventional understandings among rival tribesmen and urban merchants became firm enough to permit regular caravan trade through either the steppe or the desert lands lying south of the Eurasian grasslands. Thereafter, interpenetration of steppe and urban cultures accelerated, so that in the course of the first millennium of the Christian era steppe warriors became more formidable and better organized. The great conqueror Ghengis Khan and his heirs succeeded in uniting almost all the steppe and most of civilized Asia under a single political roof in the course of the thirteenth century.

Two centuries later came an even more dramatic breakthrough of barriers—this time oceans—when European seamen discovered America and soon after circumnavigated the globe, thus making the Ocean Sea into a single medium, connecting Europe with all the other coastlands of the earth.

Thus we recognize, across the centuries of recorded history, a process of sporadic improvement in communications by both land and sea. The process was unidirectional, though intermittent, and it is perhaps worth

trying to pick out the critical thresholds in the history of human communications since every change in the patterns of circulation of persons and
goods created new opportunities for cultural diffusion.

Sea Transport

Rafts, coracles, and other simple flotation devices date from very early
times, but anything we would recognize as a ship is not much older than the
beginnings of civilization itself, late in the fourth millennium B.C. Not until
ships suitable for navigation on calm seas had been around for a long time did
the social nexus arise within the Mediterranean that made long-distance
trading and raiding a viable way of life. This was achieved about 1500 B.C.
The relatively long delay between technical and social development is not
really surprising, for until local inhabitants learned to dig ores, cut timbers,
raise grain, or prepare some other kind of trade goods of interest to strangers
coming from the civilized parts of the Mediterranean shores, seafaring
could not become really profitable. And distant peoples learned to do such
things only through contagion—usually when local magnates discovered
the delights of possessing goods manufactured in civilized workshops,
which they could not get hold of except by making their dependents work
to prepare trade goods for exchange with strangers come from afar.

This low-grade diffusion of civilized tastes and attitudes, as well as the
emergence of new forms of social differentiation, tended to thicken up,
generation after generation. By the time the Roman empire arose, the
coastlands of the Mediterranean had therefore achieved a more nearly
equal level of development, though the western provinces always remained less skilled and less urbanized than the more anciently civilized east.
Navigation was only seasonal. Ships were hauled ashore in bad weather, and
in winter months no one dared to sail.

It may seem unlikely that ships unable to brave the perils of Mediterranean winter storms could cross oceanic spaces. Indeed, deliberate voyaging out of sight of land for days on end was always unusual in the ancient
Mediterranean. But in the Indian Ocean, at some unknown date before 200
B.C., sailors learned to rely on the monsoon winds to carry them very long
distances and far from any shore. The Polynesians, using even simpler ves-
sels than those of the ancient Mediterranean and Indian oceans, crossed the
Pacific vastness all the way to Easter Island and Hawaii, beginning about
A.D. 600. And then there is Herodotus' account of the circumnavigation of
Africa by Phoenicians in the sixth century B.C., which gets its credibility

from Herodotus' incredulity at their report of seeing the sun in the northern sky!

In general, I suggest that from the time sailors began to cross the seas, occasional drift voyages of altogether unusual length must have occurred when some storm drove a boat into unknown waters. Crossing either the Atlantic or the Pacific under such circumstances was likely to be fatal for those on board, but winds and currents at appropriate latitudes are such that drift voyaging across the ocean is entirely possible. All a vessel needs to do is to stay afloat and, after the lapse of a few weeks or months, an American coast will heave over the horizon.

How often such misadventures happened is impossible to say, but in the 1840s, soon after whites first settled on the Oregon coast, a Japanese fishing boat came ashore with one crew member, a young boy, still alive. He was rescued and in due course sent to Dartmouth for an education, with the odd result that when Japan opened its doors to foreigners in 1854 the one Japanese who knew English was the young fisherman! Similar accidental voyaging must have occurred before, probably repeatedly. But whether any of the boats that fetched up on American shores carried culturally meaningful messages to the American Indians is another question. Cultural diffusion across ocean spaces must have been exceptional indeed as long as ships were unmanageable in stormy weather.

All-weather navigation depended on improvements in ship design. Junks capable of sailing the high seas in rough weather developed among the Chinese soon after A.D. 1000. That is about the horizon point for the appearance of relatively large quantities of porcelain shards on the east coast of Africa and at other ports of the Indian Ocean. Overseas trade on the south China coast became a significant source of income for the southern Sung dynasty (A.D. 1127 to 1279), but until more archeological work has been done in southeastern Asia and throughout the coastlands of the Indian Ocean, the timing and scale of change in Chinese oceanic navigation will remain unclear.

For Europe and the Mediterranean we are far better informed. The development to all-weather shipping in that part of the world occurred toward the close of the thirteenth century. Stern post rudders, covered decks, multiple sails and masts, and new rigging all contributed. Chinese and European shipbuilding methods had nothing in common; only the use of the compass to assist navigation under clouded skies seems to have been a shared technique, diffusing, as is well known, from the Far East to Europe along the seaways.

The consequences of all-weather sailing for the world were very great. Ships capable of surviving the storms and tides of the Atlantic coasts of Europe had little to fear elsewhere. This made the explorations of the six-teenth century comparatively easy, but not automatic as is shown by the fact that the Chinese, who had been in a position to cross the high seas safely at least a century before Europeans did so, chose instead to back away from overseas ventures. They dispatched a series of imperial fleets of im-posing magnitude into the Indian Ocean between 1405 and 1433, but then withdrew and utterly abandoned long-distance voyaging. Imperial policy preferred to concentrate resources on defense of the land frontier against the nomads. Construction of sea-going ships was therefore prohibited and the seaways were abandoned to Japanese "pirates" and other outlaws. But what the Chinese decided against, Europeans embraced. As a result the world soon became a far more closely interacting whole. Previously iso-lated, or nearly isolated, peoples found themselves exposed to cultural and epidemiological disasters when European and African strangers carried unfamiliar infections across the seas along with new goods, skills, and appe-tites.

Land Transport

Sea transport was always superior to land transport, being cheaper, safer, and capable of carrying far larger cargoes. Horizon points in overland trans-port, indeed, are inextricably intermingled with military technology and conquest. The earliest harnessing of horseflesh to human purposes, for example, precipitated a far-ranging reorganization of political and social structures across Eurasia. Between about 1800 and 1500 B.C. conquerors in horse-drawn chariots overran the civilized lands of the ancient Near East, India, and China. Chariot aristocracies also arose through most of barbarian Europe. For the first time, cultural influences (at least those connected with the arts of chariotry and horse taming) ran all across Eurasia, from the Atlantic to the Pacific coast. The Eurasian ecumene, linking China, India, the Middle East, and Europe together into an interacting whole, had come unambiguously into existence for the first time, although earlier migratory movements had carried wheat and barley from their locus of initial domesti-cation throughout almost the same area that the charioteers were able to conquer.

What linked the Eurasian ecumene together for a full three millennia, from the chariot age to after A.D. 1500, was the vast sea of grass that extended from Hungary in the west to Manchuria in the east. Across this almost unbroken stretch of steppelands, horsemen could move with ease, and often did. Except for Japan and the westernmost part of Europe, the civilized world to the south of the steppe was perpetually exposed to nomad warriors' raids. Indeed, most of Eurasian political history is no more than the record of incursions from the steppe, followed in due course by a decay of tribal cohesion among the conquerors. Then, either a fresh nomadic invasion or a native reaction against the alien intruders initiated a new political cycle.

From about 800 B.C. the formidability of steppe peoples increased considerably when they began to ride directly on the backs of their horses. This meant greater mobility than chariots had allowed and a far cheaper, yet no less effective, means of showering arrows on an enemy. Defense against the steppe raiders became the principal military problem for all civilized lands thereafter, a problem never completely solved until the seventeenth century, when infantry firearms finally became efficient enough to break up a cavalry charge by even the most skilled mounted bowmen.

Throughout the long centuries when steppe warriors enjoyed superior mobility and striking power, their military confrontation with civilized peoples was gradually modified by the infiltration of civilized goods, ideas, and skills among the tribesmen. An important landmark in this process was the regularization of caravan trade. Exact stages are irrecoverable. Elements of caravan management may be discerned as early as the second millennium B.C. The lucky find of a collection of merchant correspondence in Asia Minor, dating from about 1900 B.C. and written in Akkadian script, allows scholars to discern a surprisingly well organized transport of goods from the city of Ashur on the upper Tigris westward to Cappadocia, where connection was made with traders coming from still farther away. Donkeys carried cloth and other civilized manufacturers in one direction and came back with metals. Rules for calculating costs and arrangements with local peoples assuring safe passage were all in place; information as well as goods circulated, as the existence of the Akkadian correspondence proves.

When horses were domesticated, they provided stronger pack animals, but in semiarid Middle Eastern landscapes, feeding them was often expensive. Horses therefore never became a very widely used means of transport in the ancient Middle East. Mules were cheaper to feed and just as strong, but the domestication of camels in the course of the first millennium B.C. provided an even better solution for the overland portage of goods. Camels were able to carry larger loads than horses or mules. They fed on dry scrub that could not sustain a horse and were so efficient that wheeled vehicles were superceded in all good camel country: Arabia, the Middle East, northern Africa, and central Asia. Wheeled vehicles date back to early Sumerian times, but wagons were clumsy and slow. For many centuries, only horned oxen could be effectively harnessed and a pair of oxen moved more slowly than a camel, yet in the absence of hard-surfaced roads could carry only a little more weight. No wonder, under the circumstances, that wheeled transport withered wherever camels were easy to maintain.

Seafaring became a viable way of life in Mediterranean and Indian ocean waters only after about 1500 B.C. as appropriate social institutions and attitudes developed among coastal dwellers. In the same way overland caravans could become an important element in human affairs only after appropriate arrangements became customary among the peoples of the Eurasian ecumene, and in particular among the steppe peoples whose way of life and geographical location allowed them to intercept or endanger long-distance overland trade.

This was achieved by about 100 B.C. when caravan connections between China and Middle Eastern cities became more or less reliable. From about then until the seventeenth century, a caravan world continued to flourish and expand from its initial heartland in the Middle East northward onto the steppe and southward into India and Africa. Arrangements and practices were as complex and well defined as those that sustained the ancient and medieval sea trading network of the Mediterranean Sea and the Indian Ocean. Standard packaging for commodities to be carried on camels or mules, and standard seals, made safe delivery of a known quantity and quality of goods possible at a distance and without the owner necessarily going along. Insurance was even available, at least by the seventeenth century. Caravanserais, often located a day's travel apart, provided safe accommodation along the way.

Protection costs were defined by custom and, of course, had to be kept within limits that made trade profitable. This was undoubtedly the trickiest aspect of caravan life, for local strong men and robbers were perpetually tempted to confiscate everything, and only experience could show that taking a small portion from passing merchants could, in the long run, yield more income than short-range seizure. This lesson had to be learned time and again, and many a trader must have lost his goods and his life when the principle was forgotten by some greedy, short-sighted marauder along the way.

Relatively little is known about details. Caravan personnel were nearly always illiterate and private contracts between merchants of the kind that illuminate medieval seafaring practice have not been unearthed by scholars. Still, it is worth realizing that conversions to Islam in Africa and central Asia registered the presence and sporadic expansion of this caravan network with considerable accuracy. At least until the seventeenth century, and in Africa until the mid–nineteenth century, the caravan network was a serious rival to seafaring networks in carrying goods and ideas, techniques and information, across cultural and political lines. Historians accustomed to European conditions of travel find it hard to appreciate the efficiency of caravan portage for valuable goods. The secret was that the animals fed themselves en route wherever natural vegetation allowed, so propulsion came almost as free as the wind that drove sailing ships. Carrying capacity was always less than the capacity of ships, but costs were not so much intrinsic to the mode of transport as political, in the form of protection payments.

Two locally restricted forms of overland transport were also important. Deliberately constructed roads, wide enough and smooth enough to carry wheeled vehicles, date back to the Assyrians in the eighth century B.C. The Persian and Roman empires continued and expanded such road networks, but with the domestication of camels and the rise of caravans roads became quite unnecessary in the Middle East. After the collapse of the Roman empire in western Europe, road maintenance ceased for centuries and Roman networks decayed drastically. Still, the idea of roads and wheeled transport lingered in Europe where, largely for climatic reasons, camels were never at home. Hence, road building and wheeled transport retained their viability in Europe, and Europeans even learned in the thirteenth century how to harness horses to wagons so as not to choke their windpipes when they pulled. Eventually, cheaper ways of making all-weather roads were discovered, mainly in the eighteenth century, and from there the path to the invention of the railroad was clear. The remoteness of Europe from the native habitat of the camel, and the cool, moist European climate, combined to preserve what elsewhere had become an inefficient form of overland transport until persistent efforts to improve the efficiency of wagons began to pay off in quite unexpected ways from the eighteenth century onward.

A second localized form of inland transport was the use of canal boats. Canals constructed for irrigation purposes could also serve as arteries of transport, and no doubt did so from the beginning of large-scale arterial irrigation works. In Mesopotamia, however, seasonal variations in water supply probably deprived canals of most of their importance as carriers of goods. The landscape where canals and river transport worked best was in China. There, as rice culture spread, the valleys of the Huang ho and Yang-tse came to be irrigated by a dense network of canals. Their value for the movement of goods was much increased in the seventh century A.D. when the construction of the Grand Canal connected the two great agricultural regions with each other. Thereafter, canal boats, pulled from the banks by animals or men, provided China with a capacious and very cheap internal transport system and allowed exchange of bulk products across long land distances on a scale no other part of the earth could begin to match before the railroad age. China, like Europe, retained its own peculiar form of transport into modern times.

Europeans imported the technology of canal locks from China as early as the fifteenth century, when successful canal building began in northern Italy; but the main era of canal construction in Europe was reserved for the eighteenth century when France, Germany, and England all invested heavily in canals to connect existing river systems and cheapen heavy transport. The railroad age of the nineteenth century eclipsed canals in Europe and America, however, and canals therefore never gained the long-range importance they had and continue to have in China.

Patterns of Cultural Diffusion

Within this rough scheme of the history of transport, it is easy to pick out some highlights of cultural diffusion flowing along pathways defined by the prevailing modes of transport. Around B.C. 2500, the Sumerian pantheon of gods and a design of battle axe developed by Sumerian bronze casters spread northward to Indo-European speakers on the Eurasian steppe. This nicely illustrates the communicability of both ideas and material techniques. The fact is, I believe, that a new idea as powerful and persuasive as the Sumerian view—namely, that what occurred in the world depended on the will of a handful of gods who personified natural forces like sun, moon, earth, air, and water—is just as attractive as a new axe or more powerful bow. At any rate it is a striking fact that all the diverse Indo-European tribesmen, when they emerged into the light of recorded history, worshiped gods who were recognizably related to the great gods of the Sumerian pantheon, whereas the battle axe soon disappeared from their repertory of weapons.

Later patterns of diffusion support the notion that ideas are highly contagious. Missionary religions have spread as fast and far as any of the gadgets of civilization, and have sometimes made a good deal more difference. First Buddhism, then Christianity, Manichaeanism, and Zoroastrianism moved east along the caravan routes of central Asia. Later, Islam took over primacy and reduced all its rivals to marginality. Art accompanied the higher religions throughout their pilgrimage. Thus, for example, Buddhist statues carried an art style into China and Japan that originated from a merger of Greek or Greco-Roman art with Indian ideas. Thus here, too, material skills and manifestations accompanied the spread of ideas. Indeed our best evidence for the propagation of Buddhism and of other missionary religions is the diffusion of their respective art forms.

All-weather seamanship, when it came along to cheapen and increase the flow of porcelain and other goods across the southern seas, carried with it not merely the compass but also the practice of reckoning in Arabic numerals, which propagated an abstract, mathematical idea about place-value notation. The improved ease of calculation that the new system of notation allowed is difficult to exaggerate and is comparable to the cheapening of literacy that the invention of the alphabet had permitted some two thousand years earlier. The alphabet was propagated along Mediterranean sea routes and through the southern seas, beginning in the thirteenth century B.C. when the first alphabets were invented. It may therefore appropriately be associated with the seasonal navigation of early times, just as place-value numeration should be associated with the intensified commerce and larger-scale transactions inaugurated by all-weather navigation.

The Mongol unification of most of Eurasia was followed by the diffusion from China to Europe and the Muslim world of two capital inventions: gunpowder and printing. Improved designs for wind and water mills and the whole notion of a blast furnace may also have reached the west from China, thanks to the new frequency of movement to and fro that Mongol suzerainty of the whole stretch of land from Russia to China provoked.

Once we come to modern times, new patterns of cultural diffusion that followed upon the European opening of the oceans are more familiar. Europe took much from overseas. American food crops such as maize, potatoes, tomatoes, sweet potatoes, and peanuts added to the European food supply very significantly. China profited enormously from these same crops, as did Africa. Porcelains, calicoes, and other luxury goods imported into Europe from India and China for centuries were eventually imitated successfully by European craftsmen and, in the case of calicoes, new mass-production methods of manufacture were eventually developed by European entrepreneurs who could not compete with the skilled labor of India on any other basis.

The export of skills from Europe to Asia went slowly at first, because in most respects the civilized peoples of Asia were equal or superior to Europeans. In the Americas and Africa that was not the case, and both these continents experienced a massive influx of European skills, trade goods, and ideas. There was, nonetheless, a fundamental contrast. American Indians were radically vulnerable to European and African diseases and could not resist European conquest. Settlers from across the ocean took possession of the land in most of the Americas, bringing with them European ways of life. Africa, on the other hand, was lethal to European intruders, who had little resistance to a variety of endemic tropical diseases. Consequently, even though the slave trade ravaged African societies and profoundly changed military and economic relationships among African peoples, the continent remained immune from the sort of colonization that transformed the ethnic character of American populations so drastically.

Until the nineteenth century, Africans were more or less free to choose what to borrow and what to disregard from the array of novelties European ships brought to their attention. Then the discovery of effective prophylaxis against the most prevalent tropical diseases allowed European missionaries, traders, and soldiers to penetrate the interior and fasten political control over nearly all the continent. But even at the height of the age of imperialism, most African land remained in African hands, unlike the situation in the Americas.

By the middle decades of the nineteenth century, European technology and other skills had clearly outstripped anything Asians knew. This resulted mainly from the use of power machinery in Europe and the changes in production we commonly describe as the Industrial Revolution. New political ideas and organization also undergirded European power; so did natural science and other aspects of European literary and intellectual culture. For about a century, Europeans, and persons of European descent overseas, found it easy to suppose that the pattern of history had always been like the situation they themselves were experiencing. Europe and European antecedents in the ancient Mediterranean and Near East were assumed always to have been the center of historical progress; other peoples either had no history or had always lagged behind.

This frame of mind made it hard for scholars to believe that anything so important in European development as gunpowder or printing had come from China. Given the lack of written evidence, why should one not assume independent invention? Recently, as a juster appreciation of the range of Chinese technical accomplishments in medieval times has been made possible through the writings of Joseph Needham and others, opinion has shifted toward the diffusionist point of view. Still, careful study of how printing and gunpowder began and started to flourish in Europe makes it entirely clear that the techniques, even if borrowed, developed along very different lines and played different roles in Europe from the Chinese experience. Gunpowder, combined with a European mining and metallurgy that assured a comparatively abundant supply of metal, proved far more explosive than it ever was in China.

Alphabetic printing with movable type was technically quite unlike Chinese wood block printing and, interestingly, had completely different consequences for European society. In China, cheaper books consolidated the mandarin class by making accession to the privileged circle of literati easier than before. Cultural stabilization, simultaneously promoted by other circumstances, resulted. In Europe, printing propagated a variety of radical new ideas more widely than ever before. European culture split apart into Protestant and Catholic camps, and long-standing discrepancies between Christian and pagan elements of the European heritage were emphasized.

Anthropologists and others have argued that because borrowed skills and ideas play such different roles in different societies, borrowing is not really important. They prefer to emphasize the unique use each community makes of whatever it may share with others. Borrowing, followed by adaptation to make things unique again, is rather like the chicken and the egg. It is pointless to debate which comes first or is the more important. In real situations, borrowing provokes invention, when the new does not quite fit what was on the spot already; and invention provokes borrowing, whenever what has been invented proves attractive or threatening to others. Thus we have a powerful feedback loop that has kept human society in motion throughout its history.

In our own time, and perhaps from the time when civilizations first arose, processes of social change have become autocatalytic. Invention has even been institutionalized in research labs and elsewhere, though only in the last century. With the development of electromagnetic communications and air transport, human beings find themselves sharing the surface of a closely interconnected globe. Far larger numbers of persons than ever before are in a position to know more and more about what is done and how it is done in distant places. With information comes the ability to imitate, altering local practices within limits set by the social and geographical context. Cultural diffusion can be expected to accelerate under these circumstances, without, however, erasing local differences, inasmuch as borrowings, as always, still have to be fitted to local conditions and can therefore never be entirely the same as in their place of origin.

CHAPTER FIVE

Diffusion, Adaptation, and Evolution of the Spanish Agrosystem

Karl W. Butzer

Diffusion and Culture Change

Using the cybernetic analog, Clarke has compared culture with an information system in which the messages represent accumulated survival and reproductive information.[1] Such "information" is expressed in particular dietary and organizational strategies that can be productively examined within the framework of cultural adaptation—namely, long-term, non-genetic adjustments of cultures to their environment.[2] In a more specific framework that stresses the reciprocal influences between cultural habits and selective environmental pressures, adaptive strategies have been described as sets of behaviors that reflect cognitive mapping of the environment, by means of which a population adjusts to both "environmental" and socio-demographic challenges.[3] Such adjustments most commonly involve feedback mechanisms, which function within the existing behavioral and technological spectrum and often serve to maintain a steady state equilibrium of basic activities and values. Less frequently they may require more substantial technological or behavioral accommodations or both, as a consequence of which new culture traits may be adopted or old ones discarded. Occasionally, more fundamental changes are called for and ac-

I am indebted to B. Martí Oliver (Valencia) and John Peterson (Austin) for discussion, and to Gregory Knapp (Austin) for critical reading of a semifinal draft.

companied by changes in social behavior, technology, and resource utilization.[4]

In addressing the process of diffusion we are only marginally concerned with the constant interplay of the small-scale adjustments within the existing behavioral and technological spectrum that are integral to equilibrium maintenance. At the other end of the scale, fundamental cultural transformations are amenable to the analysis of diffusion patterns, but tend to be too complex or obscure for effective understanding of the critical, underlying processes. It is at the intermediate scale that we are best equipped to first establish the spatial and temporal coordinates that define the dispersal of ideas, behavior, technology, or artifacts—ideally in a regional context—and subsequently to examine the circumstances and processes of change. The various contributions in this volume amply illustrate the scope of diffusion studies, ranging from prehistoric times to the present, and from culture trait substitutions to ideational receptivity. Hägerstrand[5] and Gould[6] have provided theoretical frameworks for the study of diffusion that identify patterns and regularities, but that have only limited explanatory power to relate such changes to cultural systems and their adaptive dynamics.

A critical variable in the crystalization and change of cultures is adaptive response to stress or to new information. Such information may derive from exogenous innovation and be introduced by diffusion or migration. Yet culture change may also involve interacting social, economic, demographic, and ideological shifts that are unrelated to external influences but represent the outcome of adaptive choices between alternative strategies in a preexisting repertoire of information.[7] It is critical therefore to bear in mind that change involves complex permutations of new and old information and that available new information may long be rejected because existing adaptive solutions are perceived as satisfactory or as culturally or ecologically incompatible with such new information. Such lag phenomena consequently become potentially informative in their own right. At the same time, emphasis on the diffusion of visible traits can obscure the more fundamental, cumulative process of oscillating and "searching" trajectories that favor multiple stochastic development, and which may chance upon a new arrangement with emergent and latent possibilities.[8]

The relative importance of external diffusion versus internal adaptation will inevitably vary from one in-depth study to another, and it is precisely the case study that remains indispensable in understanding those complex interactive processes central to culture change. This chapter will outline one such example, dealing with changing subsistence strategies in Spain.

The focus is on *agrosystems*, here defined as successfully "tested" packages of technology and domesticates, integrated with basic patterns of behavior and perception and adapted to environmental variability at several scales. This conception of the agrosystem can serve as a useful inductive tool that mediates experience and tradition in the particular conditions of a place and season with a specific strategy. The more general concept of *lifeways* (analogous to the French *genre de vie*) can be used to describe basic economic behavior representative of a particular agrosystem. Finally, *life-style* is here employed to describe less fundamental social norms and institutions that provide alternative variety within a single mode of economic bahavior.

The Establishment of Early Agricultural Economies in Spain

The origins of agricultural lifeways in the Iberian peninsula date to the sixth millennium B.C. (calibrated C[14] years), as inferred from a range of Neolithic sites[9] and a period of intensely disturbed vegetation recorded in a long pollen core.[10] Such sites are found only along the Mediterranean perimeter of Spain and in coastal Portugal. The earliest ones pertain to the "Cardial" pottery sphere, shared with Italy and southernmost France, and are primarily located in caves. A later group ("El Garcel") is represented by small village and cave sites in southeastern Spain. The Neolithic economy was based on a mix of grain farming and livestock herding, a double strategy that presumably was intended to minimize risk. The cereals included einkorn, emmer, and bread wheats, as well as six-rowed and naked barley; the fauna was dominated by sheep, goats, and, to a somewhat lesser extent, pigs and cattle, with some wild game taken. Agricultural artifacts included sickles and primitive hoes. This rudimentary farming life-style appears to have been related to diffusion of pottery and agricultural traits (from Italy?) and acculturation of local hunter-gatherers, judging by the complete continuity of lithic assemblages between the prepottery and Neolithic levels in several key sites.

After about 5000 B.C. the number of Neolithic sites in eastern Spain declined, their inventories took on a decidedly regional character, and the pollen evidence indicates that forests expanded once more. However, the later Garcel Neolithic expanded to the central Portuguese coastal area, and a new culture group, associated with large, collective, stone burial structures (megaliths), made its first appearance in southeastern Spain at the end of the fifth millennium. Such architectural features extend from the Near East and North Africa up the coasts of Atlantic Europe and appear to have been linked with a specific type of social organization, the origin of which remains obscure. Their spread to Portugal and northern—ultimately, northeastern—Spain continued over almost fifteen hundred years and was later associated with copper spearheads. The megalithic economy is poorly understood but is believed to have included preeminent pastoral and hunting components. This lifeway, in conjunction with walled villages, penetrated farther into the interior than had earlier Neolithic cultures.

A second population expansion is indicated around 3000–2400 B.C. by more and larger shoreward village sites, as well as by another wave of deforestation.[11] Associated with copper implements and better, woodhafted hoes, this Iberian Chalcolithic includes the "Los Millares" archeological culture of southeastern Spain, with its metallurgy derived from trade and culture contacts with the Aegean world, and the more universal, later "Bell Beaker" complex, which probably evolved among the megalithic pastoralists of southwestern Spain. Bell Beaker sites are found scattered in the interior of the peninsula. The complex later spread rapidly to Britain and the Rhône and Rhine valleys. The animal economy included sheep, goats, cattle, and pigs, but with a greater emphasis on game than in the Neolithic period. The dominant wild animals in Spanish prehistoric sites are red deer and rabbit, both providing meat and skins but hunted by different and complementary strategies.

True bronze metallurgy was introduced during the subsequent period of population decline and woodland regeneration and was firmly entrenched, as shown by more numerous archeological sites, after 1900 B.C.[12] The Bronze Age settlement, represented by several regional variants, was characterized by fortified villages and towns, and the differential status of burials, including warriors in full military gear, is interpreted as evidence of a hierarchical society. The economy was based on cultivation of barley, wheats, and broad beans, with gathered acorns used as animal feed, and a heavy dependence on livestock, with cattle and pigs gaining importance. Bronze Age population growth in the peninsula was paralleled among related archeological cultures in western Europe and widely accompanied by deforestation and local soil erosion. The introduction of the light plow is probable, but not locally verified. The basic pattern of settlement, focused on defensible sites, continued until the era of Punic-Carthaginian, Greek, and Roman contacts, despite demic infiltration from France after 1100 B.C.

and unrest among the interior pastoral peoples when they were absorbed by Iron Age, in part Celtic, immigrants after about 900 B.C.

The picture of agriculture in the Iberian peninsula at the beginning of the last millennium B.C. is one of dry-farming, with supplementary livestock raising, around the coastal periphery and of cattle and sheep pastoralism, supplemented by small-scale grain cultivation, in the interior. Irrigation appears to have been used in the southeast since early Bronze Age times,[13] and probably expanded to the Guadalquívir lowlands of Andalusia, but was otherwise uncommon.

The development of this generally extensive, "primitive" agrosystem extended over some five thousand years, and was marked by several cycles of population growth and decline, in which each peak was progressively higher, judging by the distribution and density of sites. There is some evidence of immigration, but most of the shifts in social organization and technology appear to have been the result of maritime trade and culture contacts.

Equally fundamental was autochthonous adaptation to the constraints imposed by a modest biophysical environment. These processes of adaptation included a changing selection of cultivars and domesticated stock, experimentation with different cultivation and herding strategies in response to the moister coastal or drier interior ecologies, and a progression of settlement strategies that shifted from caves to open foothill sites and, later, to defensible hilltops, concomitant with a gradual expansion into the peninsular interior. Development of the "primitive" agrosystem can therefore be interpreted as a series of flexible adaptations to regional, ecological variability in the historical trajectory of cultural contacts.

Origin and Development of the Mediterranean Agrosystem

A vivid picture of the differential agricultural development of the regions of Iberia is drawn in the descriptions of Strabo[14] (ca. 20 B.C.) and Pliny[15] (ca. A.D. 75). Mineral resources were particularly important, with export of copper, silver, tin, lead, and iron from Andalusia. That area also produced a large surplus of wheat, olive oil, and salted fish, together with raw wool, artichokes, and wine. Beyond the irrigated breadbasket of the Guadalquivir basin, olive oil and wine were exported from the more developed Mediterranean environments of eastern Spain. The interior was characterized by predominantly pastoral economies, and the humid northwestern periphery by grain farming, fruit orchards, and ancillary cattle and goat herding for regional consumption. Forest products retained importance in the mountainous areas of the south and north, with pine timber and pig-herding characterizing the Pyrenean fringe, and pine resin and timber exported from the Isle of Ibiza. At this time, southern and eastern Hispania boasted large expanses of intensified Mediterranean-style agriculture, sharply demarcated from the backward, extensive agriculture or pastoralism of the interior and the northwest.

The intervening transformation was a result of the growing commercial integration of the Mediterranean basin, with the emergence of distant markets for regional produce and minerals. The fleets of Hiram of Tyre (969–936 B.C.) sought metals from the Andalusian entrepôt of Tarshish, near modern Seville or perhaps Huelva. During the seventh and sixth centuries the Carthaginians founded a string of commercial colonies along the southern coast from Cadíz to Murcia, before their destruction of Tarshish ca. 530 B.C. By then, Greek agrarian colonies were established and merchants active along the eastern coast. Rome succeeded to the Carthaginian and Greek commercial sphere during the last decades of the third century, transforming Baetica (Lower Andalusia) into a highly productive imperial province, with 175 towns and 19 Roman colonies by the time of Augustus. In the east, the native Iberians responded to the new market demand of the Roman emporia at Sagunto and Tarragona by intensifying their agriculture and by developing an urban commercial network that expanded far up the Ebro drainage. After all the peninsula had come under Roman domination, eastern and southern Spain continued to ship out Mediterranean produce on such a scale that it formed a major part of the revenue base sustaining Rome.

The full Mediterranean agrosystem differed from the earlier, double-strategy of grain cultivation and livestock herding by a range of important additions: olives and grapes, grafting as a technique to improve orchard crops, manuring to enhance cereal and other crop yields, fodder crops to feed selectively bred livestock, artificial terraces to allow hillside cultivation, and supplementary irrigation to facilitate late spring and summer plant growth.[16] The tree crops thus added another strand to what was now a three-pronged strategy: grain farming, livestock herding, and arboriculture. Each agricultural component was implemented in both extensive and intensive variants, depending on water, soil quality, and market access.

Finally, productivity was substantially increased and cultivation expanded at the expense of herding.

Substantial surpluses of grain, olive oil, wine, and purebred stock or animal products went beyond the needs of local market exchange or regional self-sufficiency; they paid off only in the context of sustained market demand by populous cities or distant emporia. The Mediterranean agrosystem was, then, both intensive and commercial; it required major labor or capital investment or both, and it atrophied rapidly as market demand slackened. Full implementation of this balanced agrosystem was therefore conditional on high population densities and strong urban institutions.

The origin and dispersal of the Mediterranean agrosystem must be viewed both as the sum of the individual cultivators and technologies as well as a composite socio-economic strategy. Although the key items and the triple strategy itself tended to appear simultaneously in the archeological or historical record, a lack of evidence for the diagnostic plants and techniques did not necessarily imply a lack of related information.

Evolution of this agrosystem is documented in Lebanon and Palestine from Chalcolithic times, ca. 3700–3100 B.C.[17]—contemporary with the growth of cities, early plow cultivation, and extensive canal irrigation on the floodplains of desert Mesopotamia. It was a matter of parallel intensification specific to the Mediterranean environment and its mild, rainy winters and dry summers. The Levantine hallmarks were commercialization of wheat cultivation, planting of vineyards on unproductive slopes, and intercropping of grains and olives—to provide edible oil without competing for space as in the case of flax/linseed oil.

A similar process is historically documented in and around the Nile delta during the Old Kingdom (2760–2225 B.C.),[18] significantly followed by widespread forest regeneration and an abrupt decline of olive cultivation during the urban demise and demographic decline of the Greek Iron Age (ca. 1200–700 B.C.).[19] The Punic, Canaanite, Egyptian, and Greek contexts document that the new economic strategy was tightly integrated with the ritual sphere and ideology, with olive oil used to anoint kings and fuel sanctuary lamps, and wine serving as a link between gods and humans, its prestige documented by storage and inscriptions according to vintage and origin.

Following the disruptions of the Iron Age, Punic and Cretan Bronze Age contacts with the western Mediterranean were resumed during the tenth century B.C. They encompassed the apparent founding of Carthage in 814 B.C., the poorly dated (eighth-century?) lore and legends incorporated in the Odyssey, the intensification of Etruscan and Roman agriculture during the ninth and eighth centuries, and the Carthaginian and Greek colonial settlements along the Spanish, French, and Italian littorals during the course of the seventh and sixth centuries. The question of whether olives, grapes, and other specific Mediterranean cultigens were known or used in the western Mediterranean basin prior to this developmental process is secondary to their economic and ritual integration within a nascent, commercialized agrosystem. For Spain, our earliest record of thriving olive groves and vineyards is the *Ora Maritima*, a Greek navigation guide of 530 B.C.,[20] about two hundred years younger than related archeological evidence in the Roman-Etruscan sphere. The intensification of agriculture in Spain can be understood only in this broader, Mediterranean setting as a response to Carthaginian and Greek demand and, ultimately, urban growth within the peninsula. But its continuity was ensured only by the integration of specific agricultural practices and products in a system of belief as well as in a set of diversified, polycultural mixes.

The Hispano-Roman Agrosystem

The full complexity of the classic Mediterranean agrosystem can best be appreciated from the instructive writings of the Greek and Roman agronomic authors, especially Theophrastus[21] (ob. ca. 285 B.C.), Columella[22] (writing about A.D. 60–65, born and raised in Baetic Spain), and Pliny[23] (ob. A.D. 79). The essential elements of this triple strategy in regard to cultivars and cropping practices, tree grafting, fertility management, and irrigation technology have already been outlined.[24] The agricultural calendar spanned the entire year, including a succession of irrigated, summer crops. Two-field cropping was the norm, but the three-field system was practiced in at least some areas; the qualities of mineral and organic fertilizers, as applied to different crops and soils, were basically understood, as was the use of nitrogen-binding plants. The disproportional attention paid to vineyards and olive cultivation testifies to the extraordinary interest in and economic significance of wine and olive oil. Last but not least, the Roman agronomists make abundantly clear that agriculture, in their view, was a commercial rather than subsistence enterprise. They dealt explicitly with the economics of management, labor supplies, slaveholding, and market access.

This orientation is corroborated by the archeological evidence for mass production and processing of commercial crops in large, rural villas.

Beyond the original, Near Eastern staples, all the indigeneous Mediterranean cultivars or condiments found in Greek, Italian, or Spanish cuisine were well known, as were most varieties of the standard tree crops. Noteworthy is the familiarity of Theophrastus and Pliny with exotic, "eastern" cultigens, some of which, like alfalfa, the carob, date palm, and sorghum, had either been tested or successfully incorporated within the Mediterranean agrosystem. Others, such as sugar, rice, and indigo, were known to grow in India, whence they were at least occasionally imported, in classical times. They were later adopted in Islamic Egypt and Spain. Spring wheat had been introduced to the Roman Mediterranean from temperate Europe and was popular because of its rapid growth.

"Eastern" irrigation devices were also studied and modified or adopted, in part by classical engineers and architects such as Vitruvius[25] (ca. 25 B.C.): the Archimedean screw (adapted as a water pump), the animal-driven waterwheel (or *noria*, modified as an impractical, human treadmill), the pole-and-bucket *shaduf* to lift water (already recorded in Visigothic Spain), and water-mining of aquifers by *qanats* (verified in Roman Tunisia and adapted elsewhere as a siege device). Theophrastus, Pliny, and Vitruvius effectively show that the Mediterranean agrosystem was "open" to the testing and acceptance or rejection of new information, and that evolutionary change was the result of rational decisions.

The centers of agricultural productivity in Hispania can be identified from the archeological and documentary record: the irrigated lowlands of the Guadalquívir[26] and Ebro rivers,[27] and the several key irrigation networks on the eastern, coastal plain.[28] The surviving physical evidence shows that Roman irrigation generally was as extensive as that of the nineteenth century. Systematic agricultural colonization is indicated by extensive traces of centuriations, both within and outside the irrigated areas,[29] complementing the inference for a high rural population density. As a functional counterpart, urbanization was strong in these same areas,[30] at least until the economic and demographic crisis of the mid–third century A.D. Cities were supplied by elaborate waterworks and aqueducts,[31] and linked by road systems.[32] All the evidence points to a high degree of economic integration between intensive production in the agricultural sector and urban market demand—and, ultimately, that of the city of Rome.

The apogee of Hispanian prosperity was probably attained under the

emperors Trajan and Hadrian (A.D. 98–138), both natives of Baetica. During the anarchic decades of the mid–third century the decline of Roman
administration in Hispania, together with its social inequities, became
painfully obvious in the wake of a relatively minor barbarian incursion
around A.D. 260. Peasant revolts destroyed many of the increasingly prominent latifundia, and cities were sacked and depopulated. The shrunken,
walled shells of late third-century urban centers provide archeological testimony for catastrophic demographic decline, a trend that was decisively
reversed only after A.D. 800. Excessive Roman taxation pressure continued
to accelerate rural depopulation during the fifth century, and repeated
waves of bubonic plague, A.D. 542–88, reduced the population from at least
6 million in the second century to perhaps 3.6 million around A.D. 590.[33] By
this time the Visigothic kingdom (emplaced after A.D. 507) was severely
underpopulated and characterized by a rural society, with a poorly integrated and rudimentary market economy.[34]

Yet even the much-maligned Visigothic era saw a modest revival during
the century prior to A.D. 680, with expanding agriculture, forest clearance,
reclamation of wasteland, and planting of new olive groves documented in
the Visigothic law code.[35] Isidore of Seville,[36] writing in about A.D. 630,
gives the only known Latin list of water-lifting devices and devotes a chapter to house gardens (*horti*), arguing that good plowing, fertilization, and
fallow were essential to achieving the productivity of former times. The
persistence of some measure of intensive, commercial agriculture can be
inferred from Spanish exports of wheat, olive oil, and possibly, horses.[37]
Consequently, even in the twilight of the Roman world, Visigothic Spain
retained most of the information critical to an intensive Mediterranean-
style agrosystem, and the basics of that system remained in operation, although in atrophied and skeletal form, in several parts of the country. The
complementary interactions of the various components of the system
were essential, thus preserving its variability and assuring equilibrium
maintenance.

The Islamic Agrosystem of Spain

The first fifty years following the Arab-Berber conquest of Spain in A.D.
711–16 were chaotic in the extreme, so that it can be questioned whether
the first documentary evidence for a *qanat* near Córdoba in A.D. 754 does

indeed refer to an Islamic introduction. Abd al-Rahman I (A.D. 756–88) is known to have created gardens with exotic, "eastern" plants and ornamental trees, and ninth- and tenth-century rulers laid out irrigation works.[38] A hybrid, Christian-Islamic agricultural almanac, known as the *Calendar of Córdoba* (ca. A.D. 961),[39] provides detailed insights on renewed intensification of Andalusian agriculture on the Roman model. It also verifies introduction of the silk industry and a range of new, Egyptian, Mesopotamian, Indian, or even Chinese cultivars such as lemon, apricot, rice, cotton, banana, cauliflower, watermelon, eggplant, henna, safflower, and jasmine. During the next two centuries various Spanish-Arabic writers attest to the further addition of sugar, grapefruit, taro, indigo, sorghum, and spinach.

Irrigation development and effective incorporation of the new cultigens in Spain appear to date from around A.D. 800–1100, simultaneous with the archeologically and historically verified demographic expansion and economic revival that characterized Islamic Spain. This revival began in the south, in Andalusia and Murcia, with a two-century time lag prior to similar developments in the lower and middle Tajo basin, the Ebro drainage, and the Valencian coastal plain.[40]

Since Arab and Berber immigration was small, and substantially less than the Visigothic influx of the 490s and early 500s, the Islamic intensification of Spanish agriculture must be seen as a matter of autochthonous growth, coupled with introduction of new cultivars and technology. The population had expanded to at least 7 million by A.D. 1000 and continued to grow until the mass emigration of Muslims after the fall of Córdoba (1236) and Seville (1248).[41]

It is significant that only 10 out of 134 economic plants and trees listed by the Islamic agronomists of Spain were "new" to the region.[42] Many of the Islamic introductions were important as commercial crops, but they only supplemented a market economy based on much more common and productive traditional staples. The Roman agrosystem had been based on winter wheat and barley, as well as a range of summer crops generally grown with supplementary irrigation—namely, spring wheat, two millets, a dozen or so orchard trees, and a wide range of fodder plants and vegetables. To this broad array the Arabs added sorghum, four fruit trees, and commercial crops such as rice, sugar, and cotton, that generally remained beyond the means of the bulk of the peasantry.[43] Crop rotation had been a standard Roman practice, and the Islamic technology of soil fertilization, tree grafting, and improved fruit varieties was explicitly based on Roman models.[44]

The Valencian evidence indicates that the Islamic agrosystem revived but did not substantially expand the large-scale irrigation networks, although the new animal-driven waterwheel made shallow piedmont aquifers accessible and irrigation was notably extended to the hill country. Irrigation organization was made more efficient by introduction of a proportional water measure (the *fila*) and a water clock. But these changes were a matter of detail for the sophisticated and well-established Roman irrigation technology.[45]

The renewed, Islamic intensification of the Hispano-Roman agrosystem was momentous in that it revived agricultural productivity and amplified it with methods and cultivars already tested and perfected in India, Persia, Mesopotamia, Syria, and Egypt. But Islamic intensification was evolutionary, rather than revolutionary. It contributed significantly to renewed expansion and further development of the Spanish agrosystem. But the Hispano-Roman counterpart had not been fundamentally different, and it survived intact throughout the late Roman and Visigothic economic depression. Islamic reintensification represented a revival of the Hispano-Roman system, fundamentally rooted in the triple strategy described above, during a new cycle of demographic and economic growth. Change and elaboration are indeed important, and the Islamic era was critical in terms of renewed information flow and increased productivity. But equally impressive is the long-term stability of technology, domesticates, and organizational strategies of the Hispano-Roman agrosystem.

Conclusions

The processes of diffusion become intelligible in an economic and cultural context: the development of demand, the facilitation of supply, and social acceptance. Watson, in illuminating diffusion and implementation of the key elements of the Islamic agrosystem, underscores the economic factors but also discusses the role of familiarization with and popularization of new foods among the middle classes.[46] But in his preoccupation with the Islamic phenomenon, he overlooks the long-term familiarity of the classical authors with exotic plants, grown at or beyond the perimeter of the Mediterranean coastlands. Through travel and trade, Greek and Roman agronomists had already developed a sustained interest in several of the cultivars that were later successfully introduced by the Arabs. Irrigation technology, including the *qanat* and *shaduf*, was already diffusing in the western Mediterranean basin during Roman times. The dramatic westward dispersal of information and material culture that followed the Islamic expansion was in many ways analogous to the Carthaginian and Greek impact on this same region following a similar, extended period of demographic and economic decline during the early Iron Age. Less distinct but at least suggestive are the earlier, prehistoric transformations following the introduction of agriculture and during the successive elaborations of rural lifeways in the Iberian peninsula.

Some basic regularities appear to emerge from the bigger picture. Demographic expansion, especially when accompanied by urbanization, required greater productivity, while tending to create new markets. Such population growth in Spain also appears to have been favored by the increased profitability of foreign exports, as seen in the Tartessian trade, in the Carthaginian and Greek mercantile links, and in the indirect advantages of the *Pax Romana* in return for the tribute funneled to Rome. In the case of Islamic Spain, exports to the Christian North, Africa, and the East were also important, but a more critical stimulus seems to have been provided by the autochthonous emergence of a strong, urban society within the peninsula itself.

Given the free flow of information so characteristic of the Mediterranean basin, trade and new settlers assured either the importation of new foods or products, or better, a broad and sustained information base as to their use and manipulation. Thus a clear perception of potential incorporation or potential substitutability of new components within the existing repertoire was likely. Eventually an economic and decision-making threshold would be passed in regard to the profitability of substituting or incorporating a particular item. In the case of Tartessian or Iberian agriculture, this involved extensive application of irrigation to summer cultivation and the large-scale development of olive groves and vineyards. In the case of Islamic Andalusia, it involved silkworm cultures in expanded mulberry plantings, and the addition of rice paddies, sugar or cotton fields, and citrus orchards to the agricultural landscape.

But neither the essential information repertoire nor the principles of economic demand and facilitation of demand explain how the process of adaptation worked. To allow the import of new cultivars and technology, in a format that allows local experimentation and adjustment, requires more than a suitable ecology and favorable economic circumstances. Equally critical are cultural values, social organization, and political institutions.

Migration and military dominance were integral to at least some of the

prehistoric economic shifts, and certainly to Roman and Islamic development of the peninsula. But the original process of intensification during the
last millennium B.C. was accomplished largely though indigenous social
adaptation, beyond the fringe of foreign-controlled coastal towns. Unfortunately the archeological record is inadequate to illustrate the details of this
change. But numerous symbolic details do record the impact of extraneous
culture traits and ideas on the iconography of the Tartessians and Iberians.
These include plows, olive branches, and date palms shown on coins, as well
as the practice of minting coins itself. The decorative arts incorporated
foreign styles, such as human representation, into pottery decorations or
sculptures, which, however, expressed indigenous values through elaborate symbolic associations. Pottery forms were expanded, for example, to
include the amphoras essential to long-distance trade, but otherwise remained conservative in rendition or finish. Alphabets were adopted, but
then rapidly modified to conform to regional styles and phonetic requirements. The identity of political communities was subsequently proclaimed
by coin inscriptions. These material objects indirectly show how indigenous values and institutions were modified to incorporate new goals and
ideas, and to accommodate new social and political needs.

The Roman subjugation of Spain, involving two centuries of bitter warfare, had profound social and political impact on Iberia, but did not fundamentally change the sustaining agrosystem. Productivity was indeed expanded, but
the dietary and technological repertoire remained much as it was. As in the
case of Egypt, where Christianity changed social institutions and ethnicity,
the romanizatin of Iberia transformed life-styles and identity more than it did
basic lifeways.

To some degree, the same applies to the arabization of Romano-Visigothic
Hispania and its conversion to Islam. The *Calendar of Córdoba* develops a
harmonious seasonal evolution that was deeply rooted in more ancient
lifeways.[47] Silk was produced for urban markets rather than for local use.
Rice and cotton were known, but the information on planting and harvesting
is incomplete, suggesting that these new commercial crops were less familiar. All of the detail is in fact devoted to the standard grains, the relay of seasonal
vegetables, the range of fruit crops, and the harvesting and application of
wild condiments or medicinal plants. This innate conservatism restricted
the cultivation of cotton and bananas in Islamic Spain to a few locations,
relegated rice and sugar cane to a secondary or tertiary role in even the most
productive irrigated lands, and limited citrus trees to ornamental status in
elite gardens.[48]

The human actors in the intensified agrosystem that had emerged shortly before Roman domination of Hispania could afford to be conservative, because their three-pronged strategy minimized risk and was reasonably successful in long-term maintenance. They did respond positively to the protracted flow of new information, but limited their receptivity to palatable garden plants or to tree crops requiring little labor investment. The only new grain—assuming that spring wheat was seen as a variety—was sorghum, and it always lacked prestige and was possibly favored by Berber immigrants. Despite its suitability to a semiarid environment, sorghum remained a minor component and was later completely displaced by maize (a fodder crop) so completely that even its name was appropriated. The staple human foods, as demanded by taste and diet, and as embedded in values and ritual, had become sacrosanct. Once the dietary package had been fully assembled and integrated into the cultural sphere, the Spanish farmer, much like his Italian and Greek counterparts, became highly circumspect about new foods. He did respond to market demand by cultivating more and by improving his technology. But he resisted any further, fundamental change in his cuisine. Thus, subsequent economic factors controlled the level of energy flows, but left dietary preferences and related values essentially unaffected.

In sum, diffusion appears to operate differently for isolated or weakly linked culture traits and for ecological "packages" with strongly interlinked traits. Isolated traits are, by virtue of such a dichotomy, not integral to such packages, and their adaptation is more likely to be a simple embellishment on a complex repertoire. The packages, on the other hand, include elements that participate in strong feedback chains that involve broad and positive social and ideological responses. They are thus inherently much more stable, and the mechanics of diffusion are infinitely more complex. Packages involve information, material culture, peoples and values that span a wide range of potential applications, economic roles, and social classes. The development of demand and the facilitation of supply will proceed at variable rates for each element, as well as for the networked components to each element. A package therefore seldom diffuses intact.

Another distinction must also be drawn, between "peripheral" and "central" traits. In the Spanish historical example developed here, labor investment and technology appear to have been less "central" than dietary preferences. Specific foods, in other words, are far more deeply embedded in culture (as ends, rather than means) than are specific work habits, which are merely a matter of life-style.

Finally, in regard to external diffusion vis-à-vis internal, systemic evolution, it can be argued that positive response to new information is an ongoing process insofar as it does not require a reevaluation of deeper-seated cultural values. More difficult, because of the problem of rigorous definition of such deeper-rooted values, is the question, whether systemic evolution also is a continuing process. If the distinction between life-style and lifeway has some merit, at least in the present context, then the former is likely to be less stable. This suggests that the most interesting issues in regard to diffusion are an evaluation of the feedback mechanisms triggered by new information and the degree to which these processes adjust to maintain a similar equilibrium mode or, instead, permit fundamental, systemic evolution.

Notes

1. David L. Clarke, *Analytical Archaeology* (London: Methuen, 1978), p. 86.
2. See Alexander Alland, "Adaptation," *Annual Review of Anthropology* 4 (1975): 49–73.
3. See William Buckley, "Society as a Complex Adaptive System," in W. Buckley, ed., *Modern Systems Research for the Behavioral Sciences* (Chicago: Aldine, 1968), pp. 490–513.
4. See Karl W. Butzer, *Archaeology as Human Ecology* (New York: Cambridge University Press, 1982), pp. 290–94.
5. Torsten Hägerstrand, "Migration and Area," *Lund Studies in Geography*, series B, vol. 13 (1957): 27–158.
6. Peter R. Gould, *Spatial Diffusion*, Resource Paper 4 (Washington, D.C.: Association of American Geographers, 1969). See also Lawrence A. Brown, *Innovation Diffusion: A New Perspective* (New York: Methuen, 1981).
7. See William M. Denevan, "Adaptation, Variation, and Cultural Geography," *Professional Geographer* 35 (1983): 399–406.
8. See Clarke, *Analytical Archaeology*.
9. See Bernat Martí Oliver, *El nacimiento de la agricultura en el País Valenciana* (Valencia: Universidad de Valencia, 1983); Martí Oliver, "Los estudios sobre el Neolítico en el País Valenciano y áreas próximas," in *Arqueología del País Valenciano: panorama y perspectivas* (Alicante: Universidad de Alicante, 1985), pp. 53–84; Jean Guilaine et al., "Prehistoric Human Adaptations in Catalonia (Spain)," *Journal of Field Archaeology* 9 (1982): 407–46; Jean Guilaine, ed., *Premières communautées paysannes en Méditerranée occidentale*, Actes du Colloque International de Préhistoire, Montpellier, 1983 (Paris: Colloques Internationaux du Centre National de la Recherche Scientifique, forthcoming); David S. Geddes, "Mesolithic Domestic Sheep in West Mediterranean Europe," *Journal of Archaeological Science* 12 (1985): 25–48; J. G. Lewthwaite, "From Menton to Mondego in Three Steps: Application of the Availability Model to the Transition to Food Production in Occitania, Me-

diterranean Spain and Southern Portugal," *Arqueologia* (Porto) **3** (1986): 95–119.

10. Dating interpolated for the core from Torreblanca (Castellón); see Josefa Menéndez Amor and Franz Florschütz, "Contribución al conocimiento de la historia de la vegetación en España durante el Cuaternario," *Estudios Geológicos* 17 (1961): 83–99.

11. See H. N. Savoury, *Spain and Portugal: The Prehistory of the Iberian Peninsula* (London: Thames and Hudson, 1968); Enrique Pla Ballester, ed., *Nuestra Historia*, vol. 1 (Valencia: Mas-Ivar, 1980); Martí Oliver, *El nacimiento*; Martí Oliver, "Los estudios." In regard to the dating framework, see Antonio Gilman and John B. Thomes, *Land-Use and Prehistory in South-East Spain*, London Research Series in Geography no. 8 (London, 1985), pp. 20–23.

12. Ibid.

13. See R. W. Chapman, "The Evidence for Prehistoric Water Control in South-east Spain," *Journal of Arid Environments* 1 (1978): 261–74.

14. *The Geography of Strabo* (London: Heinemann, 1942–49), vol. 8, book 3; *Livy* (London: Heinemann, 1943), vol. 7, 30.26.5.

15. *Natural History* (London: Heinemann, 1940–55), vol. 10, 3.3 and 4.20–22.

16. See Karl W. Butzer, Juan F. Mateu, Elisabeth K. Butzer, and Pavel Kraus, "Irrigation Agrosystems in Eastern Spain: Roman or Islamic Origins?" *Annals*, Association of American Geographers, vol. 75 (1985): 470–509.

17. See Lawrence E. Stager, "The First Fruits of Civilization," in Jonathan N. Tubb, ed., *Palestine in the Bronze and Iron Age* (London: Institute of Archaeology Monograph, University of London, 1985), pp. 172–88, and "The Finest Oil in Samaria," *Journal of Semitic Studies* 28 (1983): 241–45. The co-diffusion of wine and religious practices is treated by Dan Stanislawski, "Dionysis Westward: Early Religion and the Economic Geography of Wine," *Geographical Review* 65 (1975): 427–44, but the narrative must be read with considerable reservation.

18. See Karl W. Butzer, *Early Hydraulic Civilization in Egypt* (Chicago: University of Chicago Press, 1976), pp. 24, 93–95.

19. See Butzer, "Irrigation Agrosystems."

20. See Adolf Schulten, *Iberische Landeskunde: Geografie des antiken Spaniens* (Strasbourg: Heitz, 1957), vol. 1, pp. 549, 553.

21. *Enquiry into Plants* (London: Heinemann, 1941), vol. 2.

22. *On Agriculture* (London: Heinemann, 1941–55), vol. 3.

23. Pliny, *Natural History*.

24. See Kenneth D. White, *Roman Farming* (Ithaca, N.Y.: Cornell University Press, 1970); Lucie Bolens, "L'eau et l'irrigation d'après les traités d'agronomie andalous au Moyen-Age (XIe–XIIe siècles)," *Options méditerranéennes* 16 (1972): 64–77; Bolens, "Agronomie andalous du Moyen Age" (Geneva: Institut d'Historie, Université de Genève, *Etudes et Documents* 13 (1981): 1–305; Butzer, "Irrigation Agrosystems."

25. See Aage G. Drachmann, *The Mechanical Technology of Greek and Roman Antiquity* (Madison: University of Wisconsin Press, 1963), pp. 11, 151–55.

26. See José María Alvárez Blázquez, *Estructura económica y social de Hispania durante la Anarquía Militar y el Bajo Imperio*, Cuadernos de la Cátedra de Historia Antigua de España, vol. 1 (Madrid: Universidad de Madrid, 1964), esp. pp. 10–51; L. Casal Abad, *El Guadalquivir: via fluvial romana* (Seville: Diputación Provincial de Sevilla, 1975); M. Ponsich, *Implantation rural antique sur le Bas-Guadalquivir* (Paris: Publications de la Casa de Velásquez, 1973–79), vols. 2 and 3.

27. See Antonio Beltrán Martínez, "El Ebro en la Antiguedad," *Boletín*, Real

Sociedad Geográfica 97 (1971): 7–35; G. Fatás Cabeza, "Nota sobre el dique romano de Muel," *Caesaraugusta* 21–22 (1963): 174–77.

28. See Antonio López Gómez, "El origen de los riegos valencianos: los canales romanos," *Cuadernos de Geografía*, Universidad de Valencia, 15 (1974): 1–24.

29. See Antonio López Gómez, ed., *Estudios sobre centuraciones romanas en España* (Cantoblanco: Universidad Autónoma de Madrid, 1974).

30. See R. Thouvenot, *Essai sur la province romaine de Bétique* (Paris: Bibliothèque des Ecoles françaises d'Athènes et de Rome, 1940), pp. 379–544; Julio Mangas, "Hispania romana," in Manuel Tunon de Lara, ed., *Historia de España*, vol. 1, *Primeras culturas e Hispania romana* (Barcelona: Labor, 1982), pp. 197–446; Enrique Llobregat Conesa, "La historia antigua Valenciana," *Nuestra Historia*, vol. 2 (Valencia: Mas-Ivar, 1980), pp. 9–200.

31. See Klaus Grewe, "Römische Wasserleitungen in Spanien," *Schriftenreihe*, Frontinus-Gesellschaft (Bonn), 7 (1985): 7–48.

32. See J. M. Roldán, *Itineraria Hispana* (Valladolid: Anejos de Hispania Antigua, Universidad de Valladolid, 1975).

33. See Josiah M. Russell, "Late Ancient and Medieval Population," *Transactions*, American Philosophical Society, 48/3 (1958): 1–152, esp. 73–75; the second-century estimate is widely considered too low, by as much as 40%, because of the unrealistically low urban densities postulated by Russell. A figure of about 2.5 million is more probable for the late sixth century, in view of the minimal archeological record of the period, evaluated on a province-by-province basis. In regard to the evidence for economic and urban decline, see Javier Arce, *El ultimo siglo de la España romana: 284–409* (Madrid: Alianza Universidad, 1982), pp. 85–136.

34. See P. D. King, *Law and Society in the Visigothic Kingdom* (Cambridge: Cambridge University Press, 1972), pp. 190–200.

35. Based on statements in the Visigothic legal code; see K. Zeumer, ed., *Leges Visigothorum*, Monumenta Germaniae Historica, Legum, section 1, vol. 1 (Hannover: Hahn, 1902), 2.1.12; 8.2.2–3; 8.3.1, 7; 8.4.23, 28, 31; 8.12.2.D; 8.13.15; 10.1.3, 6–7, 9, 13. See summary in Butzer, "Irrigation Agrosystems."

36. In W. M. Lindsay, ed., *Isidori Hispalensis Episcopi: Etymologiarum sive originum* (Oxford: Clarendon Press, 1962), see 17.2, 17.10, and 20.15.

37. See King, *Law and Society*, pp. 195, 215.

38. See Miquel Barceló, "Qanat(s) a al-Andalus," *Documents d'Anàlisi Geogràfica* (Universidad Autónoma de Barcelona, 1983), vol. 2, pp. 3–22.

39. See Charles Pellat, *Le calendrier du Cordoue* (Leiden: Brill, 1961).

40. Butzer, "Irrigation Agrosystems."

41. See Russell "Late Ancient," esp. pp. 91–92, 102–105, and *Medieval Regions and Their Cities* (Bloomington: Indiana University Press, 1972), pp. 178–86. Again the estimate is low, and 8.5 million is more realistic in view of the settlement density verified from Arabic sources, in comparison with a lesser degree of urbanization in the interior during Roman times or with respect to provincial population densities documented by the first censuses of the late sixteenth century.

42. See Butzer, "Irrigation Agrosystems."

43. Ibid.

44. See Bolens, "L'eau" and "Agronomie."

45. See Butzer, "Irrigation Agrosystems."

46. Andrew M. Watson, *Agricultural Innovation in the Early Islamic World: The*

Diffusion of Crops and Farming Techniques, 700–1100 (Cambridge: Cambridge University Press, 1983), pp. 87–122.

47. See Pellat, *Calendrier*.

48. Watson's specific regional crop entries (*Agricultural Innovation*) give an essentially complete list of the Arabic sources, a more detailed analysis of which goes beyond the scope of this chapter.

CHAPTER SIX

Technology Diffusion in the World Automobile Industry, 1885–1985

Peter J. Hugill

The history of the world automobile industry appears complex. The pattern of production shifts, industrial giants rise and fall, the variety of product bewilders. Yet the fundamentals are simple. Innovation has been highly concentrated in Europe and America. New technologies have been freely and rapidly diffused in a highly competitive environment.[1]

Although diffusion has been massive, it is clear that both innovation and adoption have frequently depended upon the adoption environment. Early European innovations often did better in the more favorable American adoption environment. After an early period of experimentation, automobile design stabilized by 1902 and did not change radically until after 1959. In Kuhnian terms, a period of "normal technology"[2] was then followed by a technological revolution, the precursors of which had been developing in the 1920s. A new period of normal technology was entered in the 1960s. After 1900 only two basic types of automobiles have been mass produced, although the first type was progressively refined as producers attempted to miniaturize it. Normal technology is here defined as that technology adopted by almost all producers in a given period, thus excluding as radical technologies those used successfully by only one or a limited number of companies.

The development of automobile technology encompasses three major periods:

1. The Experimental Period, 1885–1902.

2. The First Normal Technology, 1902–59.
   a. The development of a technically competent, large, front-engined, rear-drive automobile in Europe and its diffusion to America, 1902–09.
   b. The mass production of cheap automobiles in America, 1909 onward.
   c. The miniaturization of first-period automobiles by European companies and American companies investing in Europe and Japan. This stage included within it the seeds of the second period of normal technology in the development of several radical technologies.
3. The Second Normal Technology, 1959 onward.

Thus far this third period has had only one phase. The technically competent, small, transverse-engined, front-wheel drive automobile was born in mass-produced form in England in 1959. It superceded the earlier technology, first in Europe, then in America, and finally in Japan. By 1985 the only remaining large-scale producer of front-engined, rear-drive vehicles was Ford Europe, and then not for its biggest-selling car, the Escort.

The Emergence of the First Normal Technology in the Experimental Period, 1885–1902

Early automobile designers had to cope with very poor roads, unskilled drivers, and unreliable engines. They therefore preferred a very strong chassis and very flexible, accessible, engines that required little use of the transmission. The first cars often mounted the engine within the wheelbase, ahead of the driven rear axle (Fig. 6.1). Such a mounting was inaccessible for repairs, it limited engine size to one or two cylinders, kept speed and performance low, and required drivers and passengers to clamber up to seats above the motor.

In 1891 the Frenchmen Panhard and Levassor developed the *système Panhard* (Fig. 6.2), mounting the engine vertically at the front, just behind the steered wheels, and driving the rear wheels. This improved engine accessibility and the grip of the steered wheels,[3] and also made it easier for driver and passenger to board.[4] The *système Panhard* diffused rapidly throughout Europe, but it was not until a decade later that its real advantage was fully exploited by mounting a large, flexible, four-cylinder engine that was both

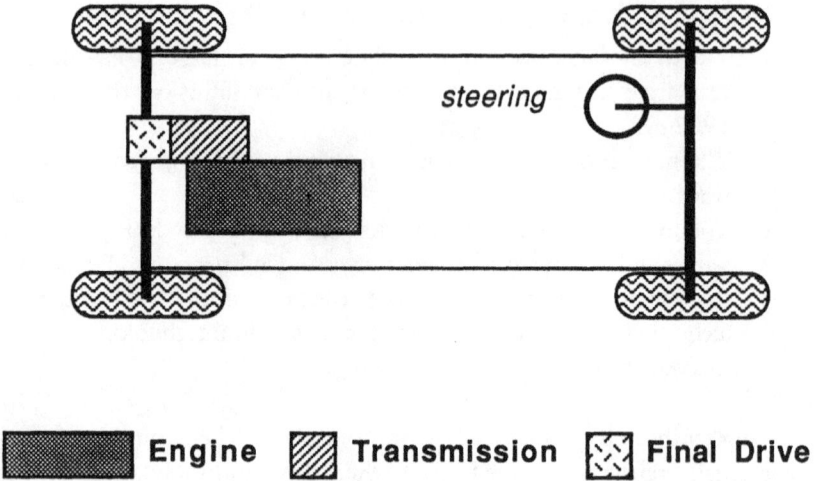

Engine   Transmission   Final Drive

Figure 6.1.   The Gas-Buggy

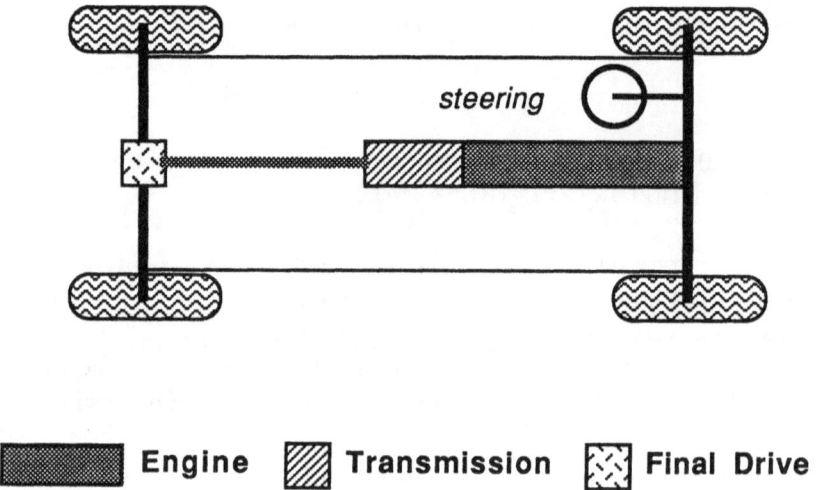

Engine   Transmission   Final Drive

Figure 6.2.   The *système Panhard*

easier to drive and endowed the automobile with exhilarating performance—the 1901 Mercedes.[5] It has been described as "more completely
definitive [in design] than anything in the next fifty years," and it was immediately copied by all automobile designers in Europe and America.[6] Built by
Daimler in Germany, it was designed by Daimler's finest engineer, May-

bach, at the urging of Daimler's sales agent in Nice, Emil Jellinek.[7] Jellinek was obsessed with speed and hill-climbing ability: "If I cannot get from an automobile more than from a horse carriage, I might as well drive with horses."[8] Maybach's design gave him both and more. The Mercedes allowed its owners to travel point-to-point in privacy at speeds hitherto impossible except by railroad.[9] The privacy of the automobile appealed to the wealthy and they could afford the price: a Mercedes 35 hp tourer sold for $12,450 in New York in 1904 at a time when a working man made under ten dollars a week.[10]

Radicals in the Experimental Period

Many other technologies might have become normal during the experimental period that led up to the emergence of the first normal technology. Steam and electric motors were tried, but steam cars took too long to start and consumed too much water, and electric batteries were heavy, slow to recharge, and gave too short a range. Despite its other flaws, the combination of easy starting, easy refuelling, and abundant power gave the gasoline engine a huge advantage.

Different layouts of the gasoline engine and transmission were tried in this period. Two of them deserve brief commentary because they have a great deal to say about the importance of adoption environments. Lanchester, in England, approached the problem from first principles and produced an automobile as a complete system, not a collection of components.[11] He commented that three things reduced the likelihood of success for a British automobile: draconian legislation to keep automobiles off the roads; the economic depression that followed the Boer war; and an obsession on the part of the aristocracy with things French.[12] Although Lanchester was well acquainted with the work that was being done on the Continent, he found none that could be taken as a guide.[13] He devised a sophisticated, rigid, unit-construction hull,[14] springing that "matched the natural frequency of rise and fall of the human body when walking," and seating that allowed him "to set the driver's eye level at the same height above the road as if he were standing."[15]

Unfortunately, central engine mounting made it impossible to add more cylinders as demands for speed and horsepower rose (Fig. 6.1). All designers until Maybach and Jellinek seem to have been convinced that 10 hp was sufficient and that, in Lanchester's own words, "to declare too high a horsepower would have terrified many possible purchasers."[16] By the time

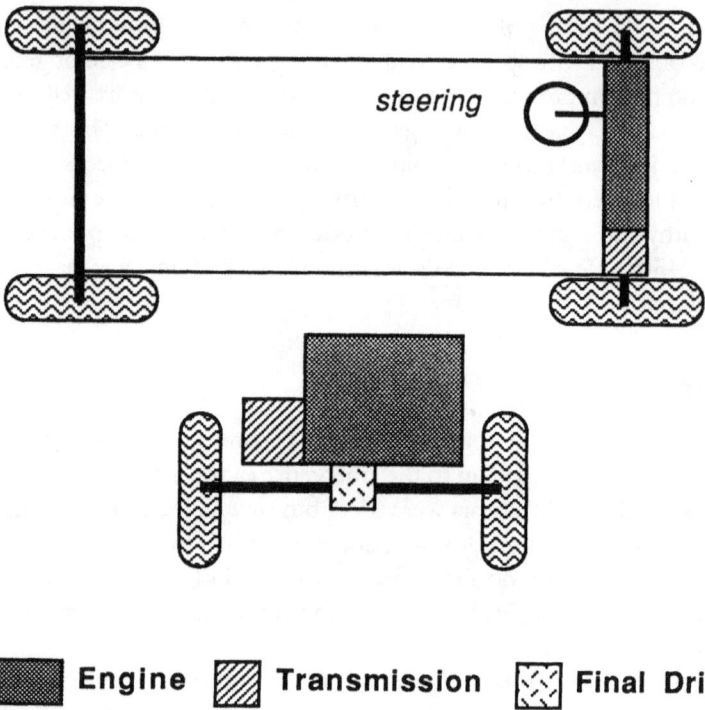

Engine **Transmission** **Final Drive**

Figure 6.3. Christie's Front-Wheel Drive

Lanchester's first production models reached the public in 1901, all eyes were on the 35 hp Mercedes. Lanchester's firm was undercapitalized[17] and Lanchester's backers nagged him to put vehicles into the hands of the public before he was ready,[18] then to adopt the long hood of the Mercedes so that his cars would look "conventional."[19]

The second great radical was Walter Christie in America.[20] In 1908 he patented a design that was the clear ancestor of the second normal automobile technology: a transversely-mounted front engine and transmission driving the front wheels (Fig. 6.3).[21] For all its brilliance the 1908 design suffered from lack of constant-velocity joints to transmit power smoothly from the final drive to the wheels at high steering angles. Having "solved" the problem of the automobile to his own satisfaction, Christie's interests shifted: to front-drive fire engines, four-wheel drive trucks and, finally, tanks.[22] At no time did Christie seem to have taken production seriously. Many of his unending financial failures were really failures of his backers.[23]

By 1908, in any case, the focus of the American automobile industry had moved to Detroit and Christie remained in New York.

The Transfer of the First Normal Technology to America, 1902–1906

The Mercedes took Europe by storm and when it was shown at the New York Motor Show in 1902 it had an equally galvanic effect in America. American manufacturers quickly abandoned the centrally mounted engine for cars "built on the accepted French lines with a good-looking body, motor in front, and the other up-to-date features of 1906 design."[24] America's 45 percent tariff on imported manufactures discouraged much direct importation,[25] although the first *Handbook of Gasoline Automobiles* listed eleven imports out of thirty-five marques, albeit at an average price of just over $8,000.[26] Between 1904 and 1909 the Mercedes itself and seven European copies were assembled or license-built in America.[27] New American companies sprang up by hiring European engineers or blatantly copying Mercedes. Packard, for example, hired a French designer, Charles Schmidt, who had worked for Mors in Paris, a company that produced excellent copies of the Mercedes.[28] The founder of Continental Motors made a complete set of drawings of a 1901 Mercedes while repairing it for its owner in that year. He even had casts made of some parts.[29]

American-made copies of the Mercedes were relatively cheap. In 1904 thirteen of the twenty-four American members of the Association of Licensed Automobile Manufacturers cataloged Mercedes copies, with an average price of $3,700.[30] Only two years later all of the association's twenty-seven American members cataloged designs clearly derived from the 1901 Mercedes.[31]

From the outset, however, the trend in America was toward automobiles for everyone.[32] This was achieved through high quality and low cost, using mass-production and the innovations of Henry Ford's Model T.[33] Between 1909 and 1929 the automobile matured in America into an all-weather, easily handled, reliable device with closed all-steel bodywork, self-starter, electric lighting, balloon tires, four-wheel brakes, and hydraulic shock absorbers.[34] Of these six major innovations, only four-wheel brakes were perfected in Europe.[35] Four more major innovations that refined and gave final form to first-period automobile technology were developed in production form in the 1930s: the mass-market V8 engine, automatic transmission, independent front suspension, and unit-construction. The mass-market V8 and automatic transmission made even large automobiles extremely smooth and easy to drive. Independent front suspension and unit-construction allowed miniaturization on a hitherto unprecedented scale. All but the mass-market V8, cast in a single block and perfected by Henry Ford,[36] were European ideas brought into production in America or by American companies. The ease of diffusion was remarkable, not least because of well-distributed technical literature.

It was based on these technical improvements that Detroit came to dominate the world automobile industry after 1909. Although the automobile was basically European in origin, its natural adoption environment, given the technology of the first two decades of this century, was America. Between 1911 and 1913, America produced over one million automobiles, 78 percent of the world total.[37]

Detroit also dominated world exports well into the 1920s, supplying almost 80 percent of all motor vehicles exported. France and Italy supplied most of their own automotive needs, but as late as 1923 nearly a quarter of the new cars registered in Britain were American. Australia, Brazil, and Argentina were utterly dominated by American automobiles in the early 1920s, with American penetration over 90 percent.[38] Many of the reasons for this were commented on by America's chief competitors. One British engineer commented:

Small, high speed engines are quite unsuited to colonial conditions; that alone is probably one reason why the American manufacturer has ousted us. . . . Engines should be of 12/14 hp with 4 cylinders, and *must* be water cooled. . . . Engine bearings should be generously proportioned. . . . Many overseas users are frequently two or three days at a stretch on the road.[39]

Added problems were poor roads and much more severe climatic variations than in Europe.[40] The main problem, however, was distance, and the best solution, well adapted to both the severe climate and poor roads of America in the early 1920s, was the generously proportioned, large-engined automobile.[41] The infrastructure could grow up around large automobiles in countries of recent settlement and population growth. In Europe the automobile had to fit into an existing commercial and industrial infrastructure that had produced tightly packed, pedestrian-oriented cities. Between cities the fragmentation of landholdings over a long period of settlement made it difficult to develop a rational system of relatively straight roads. Streets and highways meandered along the gaps between holdings, or were oriented merely for the convenience of landowners.[42]

Although tires were a major problem and expense for early automobile owners, the problems they posed were uninfluenced by infrastructure. European roads were better than American ones, and the rate of punctures was probably lower. The principal technical problems lay in producing engines that did not burn out their bearings, produced enough power to handle rough terrain, and cruised at a reasonable speed for very long trips. The large engine resolved all these problems, particularly before leaded fuels became available in the early 1920s.

Upper-class and, later, middle-class automobiles had large engines. Buick had 6 cylinders, high power outputs, and generous bearing-surfaces in the early 1920s, could carry heavy coachwork, and still enjoy a high weight-to-power ratio and a low wear factor (Table 6.1). Ford's Model T produced only 20 brake horsepower (bhp) from a 2.9 liter engine on the poor fuels of the early 1920s, but this was enough for a reasonable weight-to-power ratio in an open touring car of only 1,600 pounds. More to the point, cylinders of almost four-inch bore allowed generous big-end bearings that could stand up to considerable abuse, and low speeds on poor roads meant that a relatively high wear factor was not so serious.

Leaded fuels almost doubled power output in the mid-1920s. Ford's Model A of 1928 achieved 40 bhp from a 3.3 liter engine, and had a slightly larger bore size than Model T. Part of the improved weight-to-power ratio allowed cheap cars to carry heavy sedan bodies. Part went to improved acceleration and higher top speed. The makers of cheap cars, Ford and Chevrolet, competed to continually increase power output and bearing surface in vehicles with only moderately heavier bodies. The last design for which Henry Ford was personally responsible, his great V8 of 1932, achieved 85 bhp from a 3.6 liter engine. Its bearing surface was nearly three times that of the Model T and more than twice that of the Model A, yet the car weighed only 200 pounds more than the Model A (Table 6.1). Not surprisingly the longevity of Ford's first V8 became legendary.

In sum, the natural adoption environment for the first normal technology was America. A new infrastructure could grow around the automobile, and gasoline was plentiful. Europeans could afford neither to replace infrastructure to suit large automobiles, nor the political and economic costs of large-scale gasoline importation. Ford's V8 reflects the plateau of the first normal technology. From the early 1930s such technology was progressively refined. More powerful engines were developed in the 1950s, but vehicles became much heavier.

Table 6.1 Automobile Construction, Type, Dimensions, and Engine Wear Characteristics: Selected Vehicles

Year	Vehicle (sedans unless indicated as tourers)	Engine capacity (cc.)	Vehicle length (inches)	Weight (lbs.)	bhp	Weight-to-power ratio (lbs./bhp)	Chassis	Construction system	Engine wear index[a]
1904[b]	Mercedes 40 tourer	6785		2300	45	51.1	F	SP	—
1923[c]	Austin 7 tourer	747	106.0	784	10.5	74.7	F	SP	3176
1925[c]	Buick Standard	3392		3155	65	48.5	F	SP	1061
1925[c]	Ford Model T tourer	2896		1607	20	80.4	F	SP	2538
1928[c]	Chevrolet 6	3163		2500	46	54.4	F	SP	1003
1928[c]	Buick 116	3918		3215	74	43.4	F	SP	851
1928[c]	Ford Model A	3286		2336	40	58.4	F	SP	1445
1933[d]	Ford Model Y8 2dr	939	141.0	1540	22	70.0	F	SP	—
1935[c]	Opel Olympia 2dr	1288	155.5	1918	26	73.8	U	MSP	—
1935[d]	Morris 8 Pre-Series 2dr	918	141.0	1652	23.5	70.3	F	SP	—
1936[d]	Vauxhall 12 4dr	1530	160.5	2632	36	73.1	F	MSP	—
1937[c]	Opel Kadett 2dr	1074	150.0	1676	23	72.9	U	MSP	—
1938[c]	American Austin/Bantam	747	129.5	1200	20	60.0	F	SP	3911
1938[c]	Chevrolet Master	3548	190.0	2840	85	33.4	F	SP	546
1938[d]	Ford V8 85	3621	189.0	2800	85	32.9	F	SP	397
1938[d]	Vauxhall 12 4dr	1442	163.0	2072	35	59.2	U	MSP	—
1939[f]	Morris 8 Series E 4dr	918	144.0	1736	29.6	58.7	U	MSP	—
1939[f]	Fiat 700 2dr	700	144.1	1433	22	65.1	U	MSP	—
1957[d]	Vauxhall Victor I	1507	167.0	2296	55	41.8	U	MSP	—
1959[d]	BMC Mini	848	120.0	1267	34	37.3	U	ICS	—
1959[d]	Ford Anglia 105 E	997	153.5	1624	39	41.6	U	MSP	—
1959[c]	Auto Union 1000S 2dr	980	166.3	2050	50	41.0	P	DFD	—
1960[c]	Volkswagen Beetle 1200 Export	1192	160.2	1676	34	49.3	P	RLR	—
1962[d]	BMC 1100 4dr	1098	146.8	1820	48	37.9	U	ICS	—

1962[d]	Ford Cortina 4dr	1198	168.5	1736	48.5	35.8	U	MSP	—
1964[d]	Vauxhall Victor 4dr	1594	174.8	2268	76	29.8	U	MSP	—
1966[g]	Fiat 124	1197	158.7	2007	65	30.9	U	MSP	—
1969[g]	Fiat 128	1116	151.2	1742	55	31.7	U	ICS	—
1976[g]	Chevrolet Impala 4dr	5736	222.7	4222	145	29.1	F	SP	—
1979[g]	Chevrolet Impala V8 4dr	4097	212.0	3500	115	30.4	F	SP	—
1979[g]	Toyota Corolla 4dr (U.S.A. series)	1588	165.2	2270	75	30.3	U	MSP	—
1979[g]	Volkswagen (U.S.A.) Rabbit 4dr	1457	155.3	1779	71	25.0	U	ICS	—
1982[g]	Chevrolet Citation V6 4dr	2837	176.7	2490	135	18.4	U	ICS	—

CHASSIS TYPES
F = perimeter frame; U = unit-construction; P = backbone/punt frame

CONSTRUCTION SYSTEM
SP = Système Panhard (normal technology); MSP = Modified Système Panhard (modified by unit-construction and independent front suspension; normal technology); DFD = DKW front-wheel drive (radical technology); RLR = Rumpler/Ledwinka rear-drive (radical technology)

NOTES
a. (piston travel ÷ bearing area) × (weight ÷ bhp), where bearing area = the sum of main and big-end bearing surface in square inches; piston travel = the number of feet traveled by each piston per mile, and equal to engine revolutions × engine stroke; and engine revolutions per mile = (63360 ÷ tire diameter in inches) × final drive ratio.
b. ALAM, *Handbook of Gasoline Automobiles*, 1904–1906.
c. *Automotive Industries*, year of vehicle, March statistical issue.
d. David Culshaw and Peter Horrobin, *The Complete Catalogue of British Cars* (New York: William Morrow, 1974).
e. Werner Oswald, *Deutsche Autos 1920–1945* (Stuttgart: Motorbuch Verlag, 1983); *Deutsche Autos 1945–1975* (Stuttgart: Motorbuch Verlag, 1984).
f. Dante Giacosa, *Forty Years of Design with Fiat* (Milan: Automobilia SRL, 1979).
g. Automobile Club of Italy, *World Cars* (New York: Herald Books, year of vehicle).

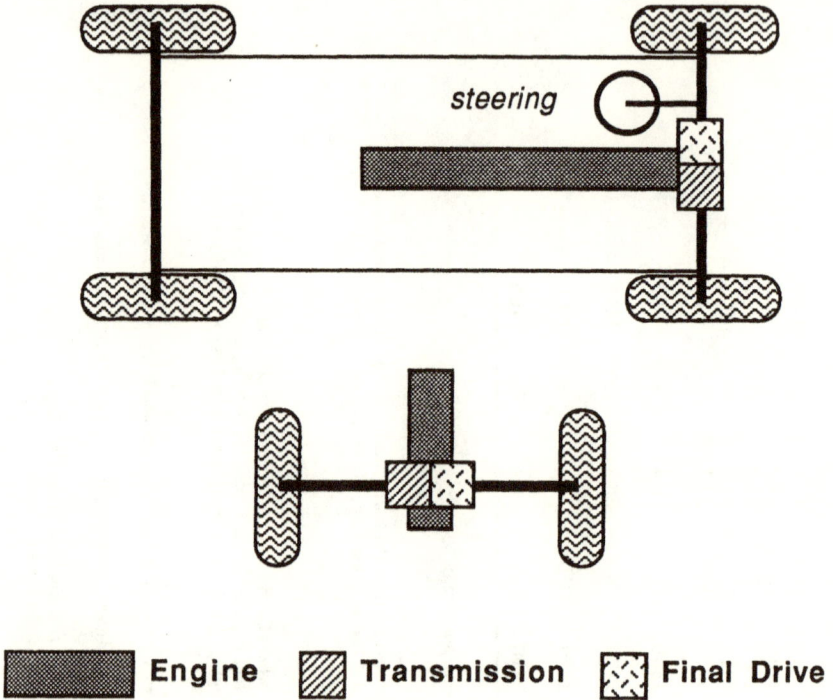

Engine **Transmission** **Final Drive**

Figure 6.4.   Miller's Front-Wheel Drive

Radicals in the First Normal Period of Automobile Technology

The *système Panhard* was challenged twice in the 1920s and 1930s: four different systems of front-wheel drive were developed in America and Europe; rear-engine, rear-drive vehicles were developed in Europe alone. Despite Christie's pioneering use of transverse engines and front-wheel drive nearly twenty years earlier, the impetus for the development of front-drive in the 1920s was clearly from Miller's victory at Indianapolis in 1925.[43] Miller mounted the engine behind the front wheels to enable him to use a long, straight-eight engine. The gearbox and final drive remained transverse (Fig. 6.4). Cord bought Miller's patents and even produced the prototype of the Cord L-29 of 1930 in Miller's workshop.[44]

Patent activity for the constant-velocity joints needed to transmit power to the steered wheels was intense in the late 1920s.[45] Workable constant-velocity joints were patented by, among others, Fenaille in France in 1926, Weiss in America in 1925, and Rzeppa in America in 1935.[46] French information clearly did not diffuse well to the United States, perhaps because language was a barrier, perhaps also because American companies were concentrating on the British market. In a major survey article of 1926 only the Weiss joint was mentioned.[47] Two universal joints with identical joint operating angles could be used, but the turning circle was very restricted as a result.[48] Miller could avoid the use of constant-velocity joints on the shallow turns of the racetrack, but Cord had to adopt the Weiss joint for street use. Only the much later Rzeppa joint allowed a good turning circle, and by then alternatives to front-wheel drive were clear.

The attention given front-wheel drive in the 1920s was an attempt to resolve three problems with the *système Panhard* as then produced. First, the new, closed steel bodies of the early 1920s had to be mounted high to clear the driveshaft to the rear wheels, which made for poor roadholding. Front-drive cars could be much lower. Secondly, the use of beam front-axles made for poor ride qualities, which the independently suspended wheels of front-drive would improve. Thirdly, front-drive would allow braking of the front-wheels by engine compression rather than with a complex mechanical linkage to brakes on the steered wheels.[49]

All three problems were solved by refining existent technologies. In 1929 Packard introduced the hypoid rear axle, which allowed the drive shaft, and thus bodies, to be lowered.[50] Simple independent front suspension had been introduced by Morgan in England as early as 1910, and adopted by several other European manufacturers.[51] General Motors pioneered its adoption on mass-market American cars in the mid-1930s, entirely for reasons of ride improvement.[52] Also as early as 1910 Henri Perrot had produced workable, mechanically-operated front-wheel brakes for the Scottish Argyll.[53] Lockheed's much simpler hydraulically-operated system was adopted with great success by Chrysler in 1924.[54] With these improvements front-drive offered no marked advantages to American companies.

A second, more efficient front-drive layout than that of the Miller was used by the British company Alvis (Fig. 6.5) two months before the Miller debut.[55] The American company Budd, whose main business was steel body panels, produced an all-steel, unit-construction, Alvis-style, front-drive prototype in 1926, but could not sell it in Detroit. It was taken up in the early 1930s by Budd's French license-holder Citroen, in an attempt to rescue his company from bankruptcy.[56]

A third layout for front-wheel drive emerged in 1931 when Deutsches Kraftfahrzeug Werke (DKW) licensed Fenaille's constant-velocity joints and mounted a two-cylinder engine transversely just behind the front

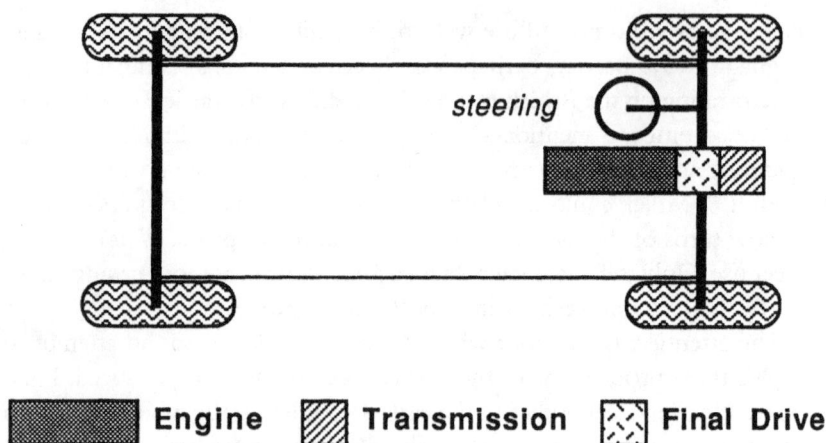

Engine ▨ **Transmission** ▩ **Final Drive**

Figure 6.5. Alvis's Front-Wheel Drive

wheels (Fig. 6.6). The DKW was not shown outside Germany until 1935, and only then did a good account of its innovative layout appear in English.[57] Language barriers and the rise of Nazism were probably responsible. DKW also pioneered the production of the fourth front-drive layout in 1940, with a three-cylinder engine mounted in front of the drive wheels (Fig. 6.7).[58] These two DKW designs have proven very long-lived. They were the basis for the Saab 92 and 93, when the Swedish airplane company entered automobile manufacture after World War II. After the war the DKW tooling remained in the Soviet bloc. As late as 1984 the two-cylinder design was still in production as the East German Trabant 601; the three-cylinder DKW design was the basis for the East German Wartburg and the Polish Syrena 105.[59] Both were also produced in Japan by Suzuki as the Fronte 360 and 800.[60] However, only Audi, one of DKW's sister companies in Auto Union, took the development of the second DKW design beyond its starting point.

The 1920s and 1930s also saw a second radical approach to lightening and cheapening the automobile. This was to drive the rear wheels with a rear-mounted engine. In 1921 Rumpler, in Germany, mounted an engine just ahead of the rear axle to allow him to streamline his automobile (Fig. 6.8). The engine thus intruded into the passenger space.[61] Rumpler's design was very influential, although Ledwinka, who had served under Rumpler at Tatra, later remounted the engine behind the rear axle to improve passenger space (Fig. 6.9). Ledwinka's design was copied by Porsche for his

122

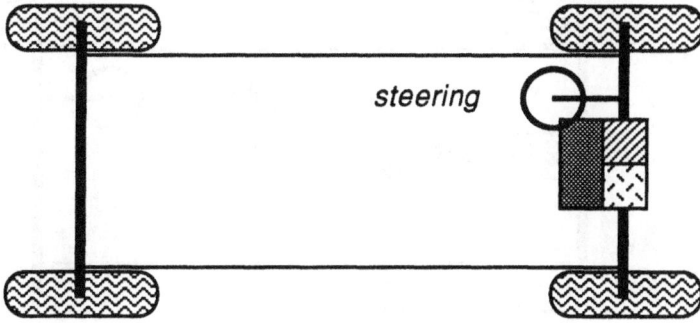

Figure 6.6.   DKW 2-cyl. Front-Wheel Drive

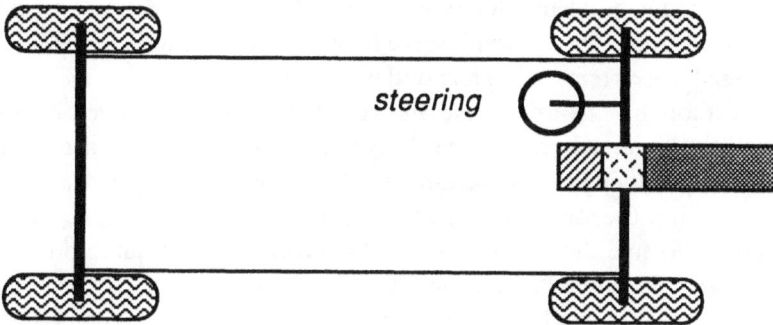

Figure 6.7.   DKW 3-cyl. Front-Wheel Drive

Volkswagen. The copy was so blatant that Volkswagen settled out-of-court for $2,130,000 when sued by Tatra in 1967.[62]

By the early 1930s the advantages of rear-engined cars were well understood. They were seen as easier to streamline and the engine position eliminated the long propeller shaft, and reduced the problems of engine noise, heat, and odors.[63] However, suspension design in the 1930s was not up to

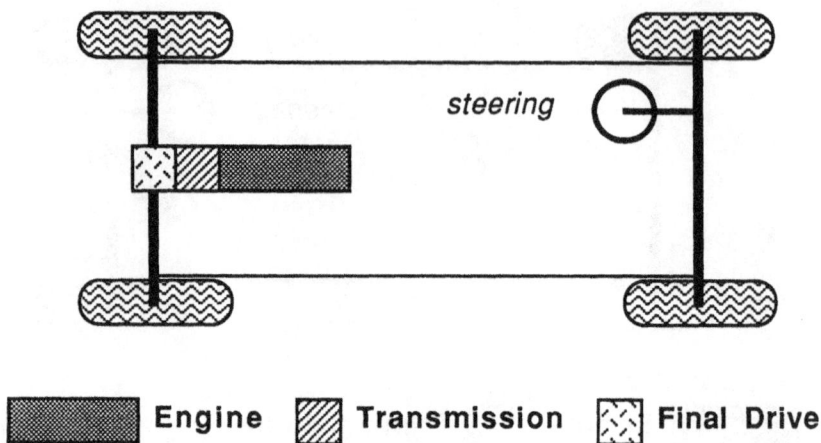

Engine **Transmission** **Final Drive**

Figure 6.8.   Rumpler Rear-Engine/Drive

the handling problems caused by a rear-weight bias. Rear-engined cars also suffered from a lack of trunk space between the front wheels, because the steered wheels required a great deal of turning room.

Although both front-drive and rear-engine vehicles offered considerable theoretical advantage over the *système Panhard*, both required considerable development and investment. Only the Volkswagen was able to successfully use one of these technologies in the interwar period. This was largely because the company was able to command the full resource base of Nazi Germany: a "car for the masses" was one of Hitler's pet projects.

After World War II it seemed at first that Ledwinka's rear-engined layout would become a normal technology for the small, light cars needed in the cramped infrastructure of Europe and Japan. In 1947 the French company Renault, assisted by Porsche, designed a successful rear-engined car: the cramped and underpowered 4cv. Renault licensed this design to Hino in Japan in 1953.[64] The Italian company Fiat produced its rear-engined 600 in 1955, but Giacosa, the chief designer, spent a great deal of development time on suspension because "when cornering at speed it looked as if it were going to overturn."[65] When Renault enlarged the 4cv to make the more powerful Dauphine, it ran into serious handling difficulties. Fiat's large rear-engined car, the Simca 1000, designed for its French associate company, developed an equally unenviable reputation.[66] Chevrolet's very Volkswagenlike Corvair ended as the subject of numerous lawsuits because of its handling peculiarities.[67]

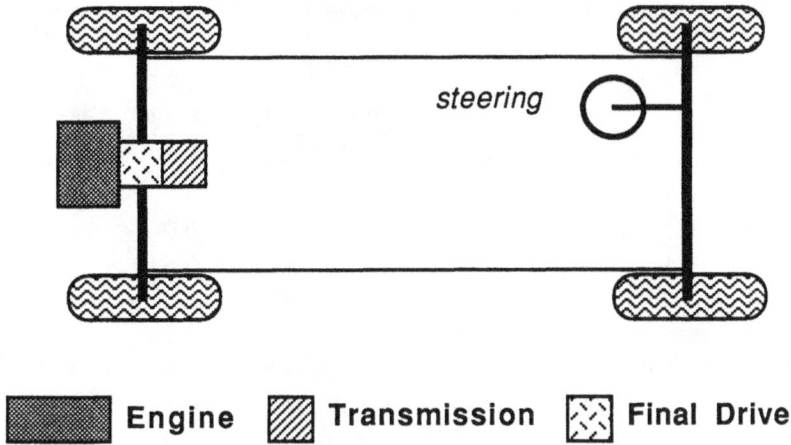

Engine   **Transmission**   **Final Drive**

Figure 6.9.   Ledwinka/VW Rear-Engine/Drive

Only Porsche's Volkswagen could thus be counted a success. Its engine power was low, and rear-overhang and weight were reduced by a short, flat-four engine, which was expensive to build in labor terms and used expensive, light alloys to keep weight down. Renault and Fiat used cheap, in-line, cast-iron, four-cylinder engines. Chevrolet used a light-alloy, flat-six engine and the Corvair should have handled well, but the company tried to save money on suspension and omitted a very necessary stabilizing bar.[68]

In Kuhnian terms, both front-drive and rear-engine designs were challenges to the prevailing paradigm, the established normal technology of the *système Panhard*. Such challenges failed in America, but were moderately successful in Europe. There were two reasons for this. By the 1920s American corporations had invested a huge amount of money in the *système Panhard*, and were unwilling or unable to change direction. The European motor industry was very much smaller (Table 6.2) and thus able to invest in radical new technologies. The Volkswagen plant, for example, was built completely from scratch in the late 1930s.[69]

Miniaturizing the Système Panhard

Although European attempts at miniaturizing the automobile began with the 1898 Renault,[70] the first really successful miniature was the two-seat Baby Peugeot of 1912.[71] World War I made American cars and production techniques familiar in a Europe whose industry had been devoted to

Table 6.2   World Automobile Production 1922–82, Selected Years

Year	Total	Percentage of Total Production				
		U.S.A. Canada	W. Europe	Japan	U.S.S.R. E. Europe	Rest of World
1922	2,602,727	92.1	7.9	—	—	—
1927	3,570,608	86.4	13.6	—	—	—
1932	1,596,790	74.3	24.8	*	0.9	—
1937	5,010,042	81.2	18.1	0.1	0.6	—
1938	3,045,193	69.8	28.6	0.3	1.3	—
1947	4,125,844	90.3	9.5	*	0.2	—
1952	5,924,626	77.7	21.0	0.1	0.5	0.7
1953	8,068,658	80.3	18.8	0.1	0.4	0.4
1954	7,964,360	73.4	24.9	0.1	1.0	0.6
1956	9,076,342	68.2	28.9	0.4	1.5	1.0
1957	9,793,306	65.9	31.1	0.5	1.5	1.0
1958	8,685,724	52.3	41.8	0.6	2.4	2.9
1962	14,011,817	52.6	39.8	1.9	2.4	3.3
1967	18,750,787	43.4	41.5	7.3	3.1	4.7
1969	23,752,251	39.0	42.6	11.0	2.9	4.6
1972	28,728,672	34.7	42.1	14.0	4.4	4.8
1977	30,975,303	33.5	38.9	17.5	3.7	6.4
1982	27,497,289	21.3	40.1	25.1	7.5	6.0

*less than 0.1% of world production
SOURCES
1922–38, *Automobile Industries*
1947–69, *Automobile Facts and Figures*
1972–82, *Ward's Automotive Yearbook*

war for four years. It also made it clear that large American cars fitted the European infrastructure poorly. After 1918 three major companies began mass production of miniature automobiles: Citroen in France with the 5cv in 1921, Austin in Britain with the 7 in 1922, and Opel in Germany with the Laubfrosch of 1923. Their designs were, like the Peugeot, simple miniatures of American cars, although Opel was (unsuccessfully) sued by Citroen for copying the 5 cv. The Austin 7 was also produced under license in France, Germany, and America, and was illegally copied by DAT in Japan as the Datson (later Datsun).[72] Citroen, Austin, and Opel all bought machine tools and components from America.[73]

The ease with which the Citroen, Austin, and Opel corporations were able to grow in the early 1920s despite American dominance of the world automobile market requires explanation. Part of their success was infrastructural: an eight-foot, ten-inch long Austin 7 simply fit more easily into the crowded environment of pedestrian cities than did Ford's Model T, eleven feet long. Part of it hinged on the European adoption of tax systems designed to restrict petroleum imports by favoring small engines, as well as tariffs against American imports. Part of it was also Ford's insistence that European dealers accept the unpopular American franchise system in 1919. Ford's English dealer strength dropped abruptly from twelve hundred to four hundred and companies like Austin stepped into the breach.[74]

Citroen, Austin, and Opel achieved acceptable performance only with light, open bodies designed for two or three persons. Their engine bearings were small and their wear index was high (Table 6.1). In the late 1920s demand for closed steel sedans that could accommodate four persons increased. In the American market closed sedans accounted for 43 percent of sales in 1924 and 85 percent in 1927. Such sedans offered far better all-weather utility for the automobile,[75] but the penalty was a sharp rise in weight. The American Austin sedan therefore suffered heavily compared to the open tourer version of the Austin 7 (Table 6.1).

In America the increased weight of the closed body was compensated for in two ways. Engines were enlarged, often by adding more cylinders, and leaded fuels that extracted more power from engines of the same size were introduced. Because of high taxes European makers rarely increased engine size. They did, however, gain about 30 percent more engine power from leaded fuels. Leaded fuels entered the American market in 1924[76] and the European market in 1926.[77]

American companies operating in Europe were slow to respond to European tax changes. Ford continued to assemble the Model T, shifting European assembly plants to Model A at the same time as in America. General Motors, without European assembly plants, sought to buy existing companies as it grew to challenge Ford's world dominance in the early 1920s. To gain entry to the European market General Motors made an offer to buy Citroen in 1919[78] and Austin in 1925. Both deals fell through.[79] General Motors was able to buy the British company Vauxhall in 1925. Although its annual production was less than 1,500 high-priced, sporting cars, Vauxhall's staff was attractive to General Motors because the burgeoning American market in automobiles made seasoned automobile engineers and managers very scarce.[80] In 1929 General Motors purchased Europe's third mass-producer, Opel, and completed construction of a large assembly plant at Antwerp.[81]

Neither Ford nor General Motors made any effort to compete with the European miniatures until the Depression made its effects thoroughly felt. Hardest hit was Ford, which in 1929 had begun construction of the largest European integrated plant at Dagenham, England. This plant was designed to serve the whole of Europe and the British empire with the manufacture of two hundred thousand units a year.[82] Ford sold one hundred thousand units in Britain in 1929—meaning that it would have to double sales to absorb Dagenham's production.[83] In 1928, when Henry Ford was drawing up plans for Dagenham with Sir Percival Perry, he had shown Perry plans of a proposed light car to compete with Austin's well-established 7.[84] Perry preferred the Model A, but Ford had fifteen European miniatures shipped to Detroit for evaluation. When Dagenham opened at the height of the Depression in 1931, sales of Model A hardly reached ten thousand. Perry now begged Henry Ford for a miniaturized car to save Dagenham. Ford himself began design of the latter in October, 1931, and prototypes were shown in London in February, 1932.[85]

Model Y was an instant success in Britain, but Depression-era France, Germany, and Italy closed their doors to imports. Ford opened assembly plants for Model Y at Köln and at Poissy, outside Paris, but was kept out of Italy.[86] Model Y was a brilliant synthesis of the European designs examined by Ford, and was well made with high-quality materials.[87] Morris, then a distant third behind Ford and Austin, quickly produced a fine copy of Model Y, the pre-series 8. This model soon superceded the Y as the most popular British car.[88] Toyota's first postwar cars were patterned after the prewar British Ford Model C, itself an updated Y.[89]

The most powerful response to Ford's Y was by General Motors. GM pioneered the mass-production of two important technologies: independent front suspension and unit-construction. In the American market independent front suspension was adopted because it gave a superior ride. It also allowed the engine to be placed forward between the front wheels (Fig. 6.10). In the European market this translated into more space for passengers within the same size automobile.[90]

Unit-construction removed the need for a separate, heavy, space-consuming frame, although it produced noise, vibration, and harshness problems that required much attention to suspension and tire design. General Motors introduced this refinement through its German subsidiary,

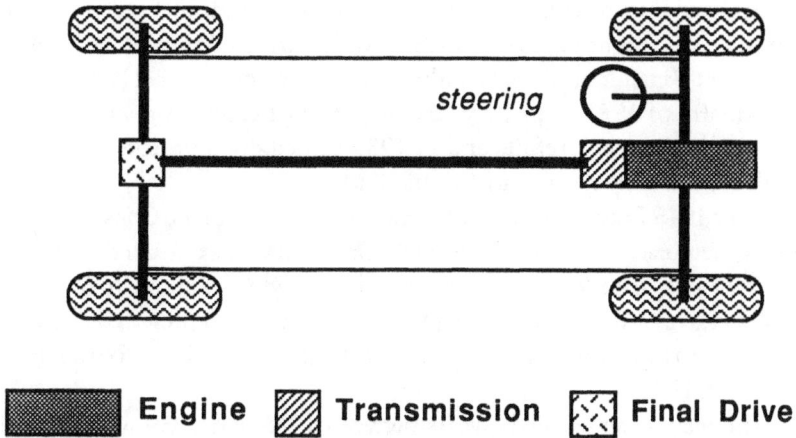

Engine **Transmission** **Final Drive**

Figure 6.10. *Système Panhard* with Independent Front Suspension

Opel, on the Olympia of 1935, and continued it in the smaller Kadett of 1937.[91] Vauxhall, the General Motors British subsidiary, introduced its more powerful version of the Olympia in 1938 as the Vauxhall 12. Compared to the separate chassis Vauxhall 12 of 1936, the 1938 unit-construction car was very slightly larger and 21.3 percent lighter (Table 6.1). The design work and body-tooling for these new European models was all done in Detroit.[92] The revolution this brought about in Europe has been very much underrated, not least because General Motors remains a rather secretive company with no coherent archives. Unit-construction and independent front suspension allowed weight-to-power ratios to jump in Europe in the late 1930s in much the same way they had in America in the late 1920s with the introduction of leaded gas and larger engines.

Unit-construction requires large-scale production to be profitable. Lancia and Rumpler had developed the innovation in Europe in the early 1920s but were low-volume producers. General Motors did not adopt it for American vehicles until 1980, because it believed they could not hold noise, vibration, and harshness to acceptable levels without a separate frame. In the European market they were the first to adopt it for small, cheap vehicles, to try to gain an advantage over Ford. Only a company of General Motors size could risk such a gamble. Once begun, however, all other companies had to follow if they were to hold their weight-to-power ratios to acceptable levels. The nature of the adoption environment clearly affected this diffusion of technology across the Atlantic and back again.

All over Europe companies followed the GM lead. In England Morris produced the Eight Series E of 1939, and Hillman the Minx Mk I of 1940.[93] In France Renault produced a rather blatant copy of the Opel Kadett as the Juvaquatre of 1937.[94] In Italy Giacosa, the Fiat chief designer, examined the Opel Olympia carefully and in 1939 turned out a prototype Fiat 700 with considerable resemblance to the Kadett.[95]

After 1945 European companies, including Ford with the Consul of 1950, quickly embraced unit-construction.[96] Only a few mass-market companies retained a separate frame, and that mostly the light, backbone frame of the Volkswagen, or its derivative, the punt frame that Austin preferred.[97] Austin switched to unit-construction for its smallest cars in 1951 and for the rest of its line in 1954.[98]

The main changes in the years between 1945 and 1959 were in fuels, oils, and bearings rather than in body construction or the layout of the engine and transmission. The genesis of these improvements was prewar, but the exigencies of the war-in-the-air forced frantic improvements in both technology and production. The 65-octane leaded fuels of the late 1920s matured into 87-octane fuels in the late 1930s, enough for steady improvements in weight-to-power ratios. In turn these gave way to 100-octane fuels after the war.[99] The postwar successor to the Vauxhall 12, the 1957 Victor, was 11 percent heavier than the 1938 model yet had a 30 percent better weight-to-power ratio (Table 6.1).

Improvements in oils, bearings, and fuels continued in the late 1950s, allowing engine speeds to rise. Vauxhall's Victor 101 of 1964 represented the last big jump in power output, most of which came from 100-octane fuel: a 38 percent horsepower gain over the 1957 model with an increase in engine capacity of less than 6 percent (Table 6.1). Compared with the 1936 Vauxhall 12 the difference is even more noticeable: a much roomier interior, a nearly 14 percent reduction in weight, and a 145 percent improvement in weight-to-power ratio.

Although the refinement of unit-construction made much lighter *système Panhard* automobiles possible, the longitudinal engine mounting of the first normal technology still imposed minimum-length limits. By the late 1950s a relatively cramped European vehicle for four adults and luggage, such as the British Ford Anglia 105E, still required nearly thirteen feet of road space. Rear-engine mounting suffered handling problems and loss of luggage space. The DKW second front-drive system gave satisfactory handling and luggage space, but the turning circle was very poor. The Ford Anglia 105E, the Volkswagen Beetle, and the Auto Union 1000S all accommodated four adults in relative discomfort, and were all around thirteen feet long, with the Ford clearly shortest. Turning circles were 32'5'' for the Ford, 36'7'' for the Volkswagen, and 38'4'' for the Auto Union, which made the latter very hard to parallel park on a crowded city street. The Volkswagen's poor turning radius was because room for the wheels to turn was sacrificed for luggage space in the front trunk; that of the Auto Union was caused by the use of constant-velocity joints derived from the Fenaille design.

The Emergence of the Second Normal Technology, 1959 Onward

By the late 1950s Europe was entering the phase of mass-automobile adoption that America experienced in the 1920s. The European share of world automobile production accelerated from over 20 percent (1952–55) to consistently around 40 percent after 1958 (Table 6.2). This was despite the Suez Canal crisis of 1956, which temporarily disrupted the flow of petroleum to Britain and France.

In the four major European nations the automobile-oriented infrastructure varied substantially. France and England recovered relatively quickly from World War II, Germany and Italy only slowly. France's legendary *Routes Nationales* were a legacy of a long history of centralized government under Louis XIV, Bonaparte, and Napoleon III. Germany and at least northern Italy had the legacy of excellent freeway networks begun by their fascist governments as make-work projects in the Depression. Hitler had even propounded a policy of *Motorisierungpolitik* to link his ideas for a people's car, the Volkswagen, and the autobahns into a prescription for economic recovery before rearmament.[100] Centralized governments have a major advantage over more democratic ones when it comes to road construction. Local interests can be ignored and it is difficult for a small group of landowners to block a major highway. Such blocking tactics had been common in Britain since the days of the railways.[101]

The problems of economic recovery did not help. Postwar British governments spent their limited capital on more critical problems when railways and buses seemed able to cope with transportation.[102] When spending did begin, it was on a national freeway system rather than on city streets. This emphasis, coupled with the rapid rise in car ownership, particularly in the London region, caused a near crisis in the London traffic situation in 1958.[103] Lack of off-street parking meant that the on-street parking situation worsened considerably.[104] On-street parking was then reduced to ease traffic flow. The number of parking spaces in central London was still declining in the late 1960s: 1966 to 1971 saw a reduction from 125,000 to 116,000.[105] By 1964 the British minister of transport, Ernest Marples, commented:

Just as towns of the future must be rebuilt to come to terms with the motor vehicle, so the motor vehicles must be designed to come to terms with those towns. For example, can't we design vehicles whose size, power and manoeuvrability make them more suitable for town use?[106]

Marples had a particular vehicle in mind. The British Motor Corporation (BMC), responding in part to the 1956 Suez Crisis and petroleum rationing, had begun work on a car to carry four persons and luggage at 50 miles per hour at 50 miles per imperial gallon.[107] This car, the Mini, came onto the market in 1959. The BMC chief designer was Alec—later Sir Alec—Issigonis. Issigonis rejected rear-engines as inherently unstable but recognized that to achieve a compact front-drive system required a radical rethinking of front-drive technology. Mounting the engine transversely was his solution. Transversely-mounted engines had been developed by Christie early this century, but were impractical before the development of the constant-velocity joint. Issigonis recognized the importance of a good turning circle for a small car. He chose the Rzeppa joint as improved by an English company, Birfield. These joints offered a turning-circle of thirty one feet. Just under ten feet in length, the Mini could be parked in a space just eighteen inches longer. Transverse engine mounting allowed 80 percent of the interior of the car to be devoted to passengers: "the leg-room front and back was identical to the average space offered in the American cars of the day,"[108] and was much greater than that of such contemporaries as the Ford Anglia 105E.

The great achievement of the Mini was packaging excellent interior room in minimal exterior space, while maintaining the performance standards of larger cars. Its excellent weight-to-power ratio was made possible by the radical weight reduction of a car some 25 percent shorter than its peers. It was the first inexpensive European car to approach the weight-to-power ratios of such inexpensive, prewar American cars as the Chevrolet Master and Ford V8.

The Issigonis/Christie System was next applied by Issigonis to an even more important car, the 1962 BMC 1100. In a package just over 12 feet long Issigonis offered more interior space than cars that were nearly 30 inches longer. The 1100 was much more beguiling to the majority of car owners than was the Mini. It offered performance and ride comfort comparable with such standard European family cars as the Ford Cortina or the Vauxhall Victor FC 101, at least as much interior room, better gas mileage, and was much easier to park.[109]

The Mini and the 1100 shook European designers. Fiat, for example, diverted all its efforts into front-wheel drive. Giacosa commented:

The appearance of Alec Issigonis' Morris Mini in 1959 had been a discouraging blow for us all. I knew that the Morris company had been testing the vehicle for some time, but I never imagined it was so small and so amazingly successful in design. I was shaken and felt regretful that I had not persisted with my studies for a front-drive transverse engined auto after the design for the little "100" in 1947.[110]

Fiat rushed a transverse-engined, front-drive vehicle into production through its subsidiary, Autobianchi, but it did not reach the market until 1964. Its introduction coincided with that of the last Fiat rear-engined car, the 850. Giacosa still found time to innovate in his design for Autobianchi. Once he had incorporated Issigonis's design into his thinking:

The restless spirit of rivalry sprang up and we let ourselves be led by it. . . . I wanted an extremely simple machine which could be manufactured without having to set up costly or ambitious plant so that it would be easier to get the works to approve of it.[111]

Giacosa had never been keen on one part of Issigonis's solution to front-drive, the placement of the engine and gearbox on top of each other (Fig. 6.11). Such a layout resulted in high noise levels, loss of power from a long gear train, higher weight, and greater costs. Giacosa reduced the space taken by the clutch and laid the engine, clutch, and gearbox out in-line (Fig. 6.12).[112] This arrangement has since been adopted by all the big auto makers and has become the standard pattern for front-drive.

Despite Giacosa's refinement of Issigonis's design, Fiat hedged its bets by producing the *système Panhard*, unit-construction 124 design in the mid-1960s. The first Issigonis/Christie car sold as a Fiat, the 128 of 1969, was introduced a decade after the Mini. Since then, however, the world's automakers have shifted almost entirely to the Issigonis/Christie system. The last major native European producer to convert to this system was Volkswagen with the Golf in 1974, and then only after near bankruptcy.[113]

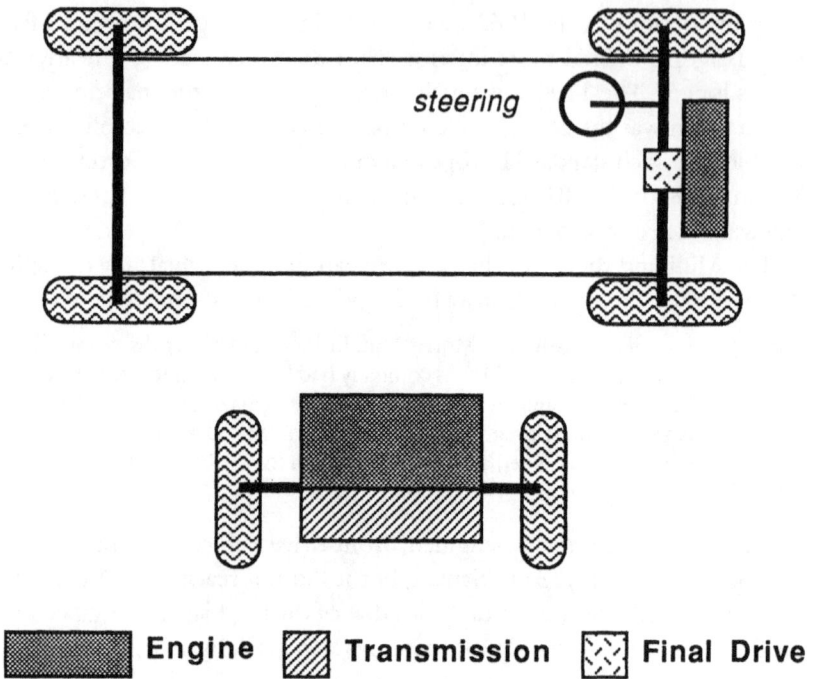

Engine **Transmission** **Final Drive**

Figure 6.11. Issigonis/Christie Front-Drive System

The diffusion of the Issigonis/Christie design to America and its adoption by the major automakers there was chiefly attributable to political rather than infrastructural considerations. A change in consumer demand after the oil shortages of 1973–74, coupled with the imposition of the Corporate Average Fuel Efficiency (CAFE) standards by Congress, forced Detroit to downsize its automobiles. Initially this was achieved by simple scaling down of separate-chassis, *système Panhard* vehicles (compare the 1979 and 1976 Chevrolet Impala in Table 6.1). However, dramatic improvements were achieved with the Issigonis/Christie system Chevrolet Citation of 1980. It was two feet shorter yet had more interior room and a far better weight-to-power ratio than the seventeen-foot 1979 Impala. Ford followed suit with the much smaller Escort, designed by Ford Germany. Chrysler declined to near bankruptcy and recovered only because it was able to buy three hundred thousand engine and transmission units per year from Volkswagen,[114] install them in body shells derived from the design of the Simca Horizon of its French subsidiary, and sell them as the Dodge Omni/Plymouth Horizon.

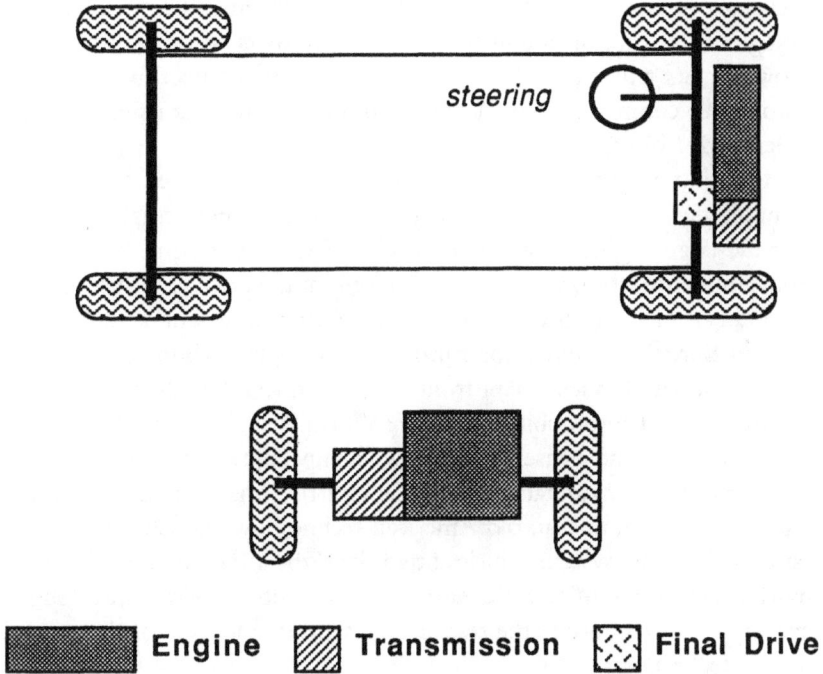

Engine **Transmission** **Final Drive**

Figure 6.12.   Issigonis/Christie System as Modified by Giacosa

Japan moved more slowly. The Japanese motor industry depended heavily on European technology and designs until the mid 1970s. Some American technology was imported, but the Japanese infrastructure was even tighter than that of Europe, and most American designs were unsuitable. Innovative Honda produced the first successful Japanese Issigonis/ Christie system car in its 1973 Civic. Conservative Toyota switched to the Issigonis/Christie system for its biggest seller, the Corolla, in 1984, thus completing the revolution of the second normal technology begun by BMC in 1959.

Conclusion

The diffusion of technology has occurred on a grand scale in the automobile industry. It has been facilitated by a widespread technical literature,

exchange of personnel, judicious purchase of licenses for specific technologies, and careful examination of the products of other companies.
However, its true extent has been hidden by the competitive nature of
automobile companies. No company wishes to admit that its basic design
differs little from that of others.

Adoption environments are critical to the diffusion even of advanced
technologies. Europe and Japan could not rebuild their infrastructure to
suit the large-engined, long automobiles of the first normal technology.
Some miniaturization was possible, but only at the price of vehicle longevity and carrying capacity. American manufacturers seeking a competitive
edge in Europe combined the European developed technologies of unit-
construction and independent front suspension to refine the miniaturized
système Panhard automobile just before World War II. After 1945 Europe
began to enter the phase of mass-ownership enjoyed by America after
1918. European manufacturers accelerated the phase of mass-adoption
after 1959 by refining an old American technology: the Christie system.
Issigonis/Christie system vehicles fitted the tight infrastructure of Europe
much better than miniaturized *système Panhard* automobiles. The oil shortages of 1973–74 pushed the rest of the world to adoption of this second
normal technology.

High technology paradigms thus diffuse and are adopted along lines similar to those described by Kuhn for scientific paradigms. At any one time a
single paradigm dominates. In time, refinement of that paradigm occurs to
make it suit newer observations or conditions. Some persons never accept
the paradigm and continually attack it, usually proposing revolutionary alternatives: theories in the case of science, new technologies in the case of
engineering. When one of these displaces the existing paradigm, a new
paradigm has been established. The reason for displacement, however, is
that the adoption environment has changed to the point where it is willing
to concede the advantages of the new technology or theory.

Notes

1. The literature on automobile design is voluminous, but two types of data
source stand out. Trade and professional journals were heavily depended upon for
contemporary information. The American weekly, *Automotive Industries*, proved an
excellent guide to events between 1918 and 1941, when the world industry was
heavily dominated by American capital and technique. It is a poor guide to events

after World War II. The *Journal of the Society of Automotive Engineers* is an excellent guide to American technology. *The Automobile Engineer* provides a similar overview of technological developments in the English industry. Considerable interchange was obvious between the two journals. A second major source was autobiographies by, and biographies of, the chief mechanical engineers of major automobile companies. Two stand out: Dante Giacosa, *Forty Years of Design with Fiat* (Milan: Automobilia SRL, 1979) and Maurice Platt, *An Addiction to Automobiles: The Occupational Biography of an Engineer and Journalist* (London: Frederick Warne, 1980). Vauxhall is the General Motors English subsidiary. Japan was covered from a combination of Japanese-language company sources: Toyota Motor Company, *Thirty-Year History of Toyota Motor Company* (Toyota City: Toyota Motor Company, 1967); and enthusiast literature in Japanese: Jun Aoyama, ed., *Post-War Japanese Cars*, I and II (Tokyo: Nigensha/Car Graphic Library, 1971, 1977), and German; Halwart Schrader and Peter J. Viererbl, *Datsun: Automobiles from Japan* (Munich: Schrader & Partner, 1976); the English translation from the German is not always accurate. For the German industry I leaned heavily on Oswald's excellent work: Werner Oswald, *Deutsche Autos 1920–1945* (Stuttgart: Motorbuch Verlag, 1983) and *Deutsche Autos 1945–1975* (Stuttgart: Motorbuch Verlag, 1984). The poorest coverage is that of the French industry.

2. Thomas S. Kuhn, *The Structure of Scientific Revolutions* (Chicago: University of Chicago Press, 1962). The notion that changes in technology follow Kuhn's model for changes in science is well developed in Edward W. Constant's study of changes in aviation powerplants, *The Origins of the Turbojet Revolution* (Baltimore: Johns Hopkins University Press, 1980).

3. See T. R. Nicholson, *The Birth of the British Motor Car 1769–1897* (London: Macmillan, 1982), p. 319.

4. See Peter J. Hugill, "Good Roads and the Automobile in the United States, 1880–1929," *Geographical Review* 72 (1982): 334.

5. Jellinek is considered to have used his daughter's name, Mercedes, to encourage better sales in anti-German France. David Burgess-Wise, *The Illustrated Encyclopedia of Automobiles* (London: Hamlyn, 1979), p. 235.

6. L. J. K. Setright, "Cars of Ten Decades: 1896–1905," *Car Magazine* (July 1984): 100–103.

7. Guy Jellinek-Mercedes, *My Father Mr. Mercedes* (Philadelphia: Chilton, 1961), pp. 89–98.

8. Ibid., p. 79.

9. See Peter J. Hugill, "The Elite, the Automobile, and the Good Roads Movement in New York," Department of Geography, Syracuse University, Discussion Paper #70, 1981.

10. Association of Licensed Automobile Manufacturers, *Handbook of Gasoline Automobiles* (1904–1906), (Reprint, New York: Dover, n.d.), p. 70. The average weekly wage in manufacturing was $9.74 in 1909: see Thelma Leisner, *Economic Statistics, 1900–1983* (New York: Facts on File, 1985), p. 56.

11. See L. J. K. Setright, *The Designers: Great Automobiles and the Men who Made Them* (Chicago: Follett, 1976).

12. Frederick W. Lanchester, "The Gas Engine and After" *Proceedings*, Institute of Mechanical Engineers, 136 (1937): 200.

13. Ibid., p. 211.

14. Ibid., p. 212.

15. Setright, *Designers*, p. 169.

16. Lanchester, "Gas Engine," p. 212.

17. Ibid., p. 20.

18. See Setright, *Designers*, p. 170.

19. See John Bolster, *The Upper Crust: The Aristocrats of Automobiles* (Chicago: Follett, 1976), p. 97.

20. See Stan Grayson, "The Front-Wheel-Drives of John Walter Christie, Inventor," *Automobile Quarterly* 14 (1976): 260.

21. See J. Edward Christie, *Steel Steeds Christie: a Memoir of J. Walter Christie* (Manhattan, Kans.: Sunflower University Press, 1985), p. 11.

22. Ibid., pp. 14–20.

23. Ibid., p. 12.

24. Note that the Mercedes was regarded as a French car even in America: Harry B. Haines, "The Recent Improvement in Automobiles," *Country Life in America* 9/6 (April, 1906): 784.

25. See James J. Flink, *America Adopts the Automobile, 1895–1910* (Cambridge: MIT Press, 1970), p. 61.

26. See ALAM, *Handbook*.

27. These were: (1) American Simplex—a Dutch copy of a Benz copy of the Mercedes (Burgess-Wise, *Encyclopedia*, pp. 77, 301); (2) Napier—a British copy with the first six-cylinder engine (Bolster, *Upper Crust*, pp. 97–98); (3) American Mors—a French copy (Andrew D. Young and Eugene F. Provenzo, Jr., *The History of the St. Louis Car Company* [Berkeley, Calif.: Howell-North, 1978], pp. 62–69); (4) American Mercedes—assembled by the Steinway company, which had previously assembled Daimler engines in America (W. Robert Nitske, *Mercedes-Benz: A History* [Osceola, Wis.: Motorbooks International, 1978], pp. 121, 150); (5) American CGV—the Charron, Girardot, and Voight was a French copy (Burgess-Wise, *Encyclopedia*, p. 118); (6) Berg—a license-built Panhard copy. (Burgess-Wise, *Encyclopedia*, p. 99); (7) American Berliet—a French copy, licensed by the American Locomotive Company and later called ALCO (Burgess-Wise, *Encyclopedia*, p. 70); (8) American Chocolate—imported parts assembled by a company better known for candy-bar machines (Burgess-Wise, *Encyclopedia*, p. 75).

28. See Jan P. Norbye, *The 100 Greatest American Cars* (Blue Ridge Summit, Penn.: TAB Books, 1981).

29. See William Wagner, *Continental! Its Motors and Its People* (Fallbrook, Calif.: Aero Publishers, 1983).

30. See ALAM, *Handbook*.

31. Ibid.

32. See Hugill, "Good Roads," p. 336.

33. See Allan Nevins, *Ford: The Times, The Man, The Company* (New York: Charles Scribner's Sons, 1953).

34. See Hugill, "Good Roads," pp. 345–47.

35. See Platt, *Addiction*, pp. 46–52.

36. Ibid., p. 81.

37. See George Maxcy, *The Multinational Motor Industry* (London: Croom Helm, 1981).

38. See K. W. Stillman, "U.S. and Canada Supply 60% of Cars in Use Abroad," *Automotive Industries* 55 (1926): 848–50.

39. F. A. Stepney Acres, "Design of Cars for Use in the Tropics Needs to Be Changed," *Automotive Industries* 51 (1924): 289.

40. Ibid., pp. 286–87.

41. See U.S. Department of Transportation, *America's Highways, 1776–1976: A History of the Federal Aid Program* (Washington, D.C.: U.S. Department of Transportation, 1979).

42. See David Ward, "The Pre-Urban Cadaster and the Urban Pattern of Leeds," *Annals*, Association of American Geographers, 52 (1962): 150–66.

43. There are three links between Miller and Christie. Jan Norbye (*The Complete Handbook of Front Wheel Drive Cars* [Blue Summit, Penn.: TAB Books, 1979], p. 269) claims that Miller influenced a man named Gregory, who took out several front-drive patents that he sold to Miller in 1923. Norbye also points out that the 1925 Indianapolis car was built for Jimmy Murphy, and that Murphy's riding mechanic, Riley Brett, was "an old Christie fan" (ibid.). Miller was also close friends with Barney Oldfield, who told Miller of "running the first 100 miles per hour lap at Indianapolis, April 1916, with the last and fastest of the Christies" (Mark Dees, *The Miller Dynasty* [Scarsdale, N.Y.: Barnes, 1981], p. 138).

44. See Dees, *Miller Dynasty*, p. 322.

45. See Norbye, *Complete Handbook*, p. 48.

46. Ibid., pp. 50–52, 276.

47. C. W. Spicer, "Action, Application and Construction of Universal Joints," *Journal of the Society of Automotive Engineers* 19 (1926): 625–34. Fenaille also had a reputation for being secretive.

48. See Norbye, *Complete Handbook*, p. 49.

49. See P. M. Heldt, "Impasse in Car Development May Be Circumvented by Front Wheel Drive," *Automotive Industries* 56 (1927): 831–37.

50. See John Day, *The Bosch Book of the Motor Car: Its Evolution and Engineering Development* (New York: St. Martin's, 1975), p. 122.

51. Ibid., p. 163.

52. See Alfred P. Sloan, Jr., *My Years with General Motors* (Garden City, N.Y.: Doubleday, 1964), pp. 230–34.

53. See Platt, *Addiction*, p. 46.

54. Ibid., p. 54.

55. See David Owen, "The Hare and the Eagle . . . A History of Alvis," *Automobile Quarterly* 16 (1978): 434.

56. Norbye, *Complete Handbook*, pp. 283–88. See also Stan Grayson, "The All-Steel World of Edward Budd," *Automobile Quarterly* 16 (1978): 352–67.

57. See *The Automobile Engineer* (1935): 124–26, 440.

58. The design was first used on a fire truck by Christie: Christie, *Steel Steeds*, p. 14.

59. See Automobile Club of Italy, *World Cars, 1984* (Pelham, N.Y.: Herald Books, 1984), pp. 104, 105, 224.

60. See Automobile Club of Italy, *World Car Catalogue* (Bronxville, N.Y.: Herald Books, 1967), pp. 465–66.

61. See *The Automobile Engineer* (1922): 194–203.

62. See *Car* (January, 1985): 136. An earlier suit was less successful, though Volkswagen was found guilty on one of three charges in a Düsseldorf court in 1961 (Griffith Borgeson, "In the Name of the People: Origins of the VW Beetle," *Automobile Quarterly* 18 [1980]: 361).

63. See P. M. Heldt, "Will Rear-Engine Design Come Back?" *Automotive Industries* 64 (1931): 646–50.

64. See Michael Sedgwick, *The Motor Car, 1946–1956* (London: Batsford, 1979), p. 80: Aoyama, *Post-War*, II, p. 126.

65. Giacosa, *Forty Years*, p. 147.

66. Ibid., p. 203.

67. See Ralph Nader, *Unsafe at Any Speed: The Designed-in Dangers of the American Automobile* (New York: Grossman, 2nd ed., 1972).

68. See Ed Cray, *Chrome Colossus: General Motors and Its Times* (New York: McGraw-Hill, 1980), p. 410.

69. See Jerry Sloniger, *The VW Story* (Cambridge: Patrick Stephens, 1980).

70. See C. F. Caunter, *The Light Car. A Technical History of Cars with Engines of Less than 1600 c.c. Capacity* (London: Her Majesty's Stationery Office/Science Museum, 1970), p. 19.

71. Ibid., p. 50.

72. See ibid., p. 72; Roy Church, *Herbert Austin: The British Motor Car Industry to 1941* (London: Europa, 1979), pp. 76–78; Karl Ludvigsen and Paul Frere, *Opel: Wheels to the World* (Princeton, N.J.: Automobile Quarterly, 2nd ed., 1979). Opel's design was so like the Citroen 5 cv that Citroen sued for patent infringement, albeit unsuccessfully (p. 38). The Austin 7 was built under license in France as the Rosengart and in Germany as the Dixi, where it laid a profitable base for BMW. Sir Herbert Austin himself founded American Austin, later Bantam. DAT copied the Rosengart. Austin discovered this and negotiated a license with DAT (Church, *Herbert Austin*, pp. 94–96).

73. See *Automotive Industries* 49 (1923): 1124.

74. See Church, *Herbert Austin*, p. 70.

75. See Hugill, "Good Roads," p. 345.

76. See Sloan, *My Years*, p. 224.

77. See Platt, *Addiction*, pp. 70–74.

78. See Frederic G. Donner, *The World-Wide Industrial Enterprise: Its Challenge and Promise* (New York: McGraw-Hill, 1967), p. 18. Donner followed Sloan as chairman of General Motors.

79. See Church, *Herbert Austin*, pp. 103–105.

80. See Donner, *World-Wide*.

81. See Herbert Hosking, "General Motors Purchase of Opel Affects International Market," *Automotive Industries* 60 (1929): 510–11, 516; W. F. Bradley, "General Motors New Antwerp Plant to Be One of Best in Europe," *Automotive Industries* 61 (1929): 229–30.

82. See M. W. Bourdon, "Ford in Europe," *Automotive Industries* 60 (1929): 396–402.

83. See R. J. Politzer, "Double or Lose Seen as Ford's Answer in Europe," *Automotive Industries* 66 (1932): 145–48.

84. See Ian Ward, *Motoring for the Millions* (Poole, Dorset: Blandford), p. 81.

85. Ibid., p. 82.

86. See Maxcy, *Multinational*, pp. 79–81. Italy refused Ford permission to buy Isotta-Fraschini in 1930 as a way into the Italian market (Michael Sedgwick, *Fiat* [New York: Arco, 1974], p. 168).

87. See D. G. Rhys, "Concentration in the Inter-War Motor Industry," *Journal of Transport History* 3 (1976): 241–64. Ford could have undercut the price of local competitors considerably but elected to put its price advantage into better materials and assembly (p. 248).

88. Morris procurred a Model Y Ford and used "data" from the completely stripped-down engine to "expedite" its own design (Harry Edwards, *The Morris Motor Car, 1913–1983* [Ashbourne, Derbyshire: Moorland, 1983], p. 195). Less

polite commentators have called the Morris 8 a "blatant crib" of the Ford Y (Ward, *Motoring*, pp. 97–98). Other British and European manufacturers followed suit.

89. See Toyota Motor Company, *History*, pp. 249–52.

90. See Laurence E. Pomeroy, "The Automobile over 75 Years," *Chartered Mechanical Engineer* 10 (1963): 84.

91. See Ludvigsen and Frere, *Opel*, p. 52; Oswald, *Autos, 1920–1945,*, p. 326. By the mid-1920s Detroit was looking expectantly to Germany: Edwin P. A. Heinze, "Germany Best Potential Automobile Market in Europe," *Automobile Industries* 55 (1926): 1082–83.

92. See Platt, *Addiction*, p. 98.

93. See Michael Allen, *British Family Cars of the Fifties* (Newbury Park, Calif.: Haynes, 1985), p. 81.

94. See Patrick Fridenson, *Histoire des Usines Renault: Naissance de la Grande Enterprise, 1898–1939* (Paris: Editions du Seuil, 1972), p. 145.

95. Giacosa, *Forty Years*, pp. 57–59.

96. See Allen, *British*, p. 53.

97. See Day, *Bosch*, pp. 132–33; R. J. Wyatt, *The Austin, 1905–1952* (Newton Abbot, Devon: David and Charles, 1981), pp. 228–30.

98. See Allen, *British*, pp. 20, 30, 38.

99. Ronald W. Harker (*The Engines Were Rolls-Royce: An Informal History of That Famous Company* [New York: Macmillan, 1979], pp. 58–62) indicates how crucial 100 octane aviation fuel was to winning the Battle of Britain in 1940. Bearing technology was forced in prewar Germany, which encouraged much use of diesel engines to conserve fuel (P. M. Heldt, "Bearing Materials: The Past with Its Developments—the Present with Its Newest Materials," *Automotive Industries* 78 [1938]: 412–22; Edwin P. A. Heinze, "Economy of Materials and Use of Substitute Materials Marked at the Berlin Automobile Show," *Automotive Industries* 78 [1938]: 442–47, 457–58). Detergent oils further helped raise power output (H. R. Ricardo, "[Report on] Engine Lubrication [Internal Combustion Engines]," *Proceedings*, Institute of Mechanical Engineers, 136 [1937]: 132–38). It was only after the war, however, that German bearing technology and Anglo-American oil chemistry were "married" to resolve the problems of bearing wear in high-performance engines (J. J. Broeze, "Automobiles and Petroleum: Past, Present, and Future," *Proceedings*, Automobile Division, Institution of Mechanical Engineers, 7 [1953–54]: 135–45; A. Towle, "Some Problems in Lubrication and the Substances Called Additives," *Proceedings*, Automobile Division, Institution of Mechanical Engineers, 2 [1954–55]: 57–66). This "marriage" caused corrosion problems, but these were considered resolved by 1962 (J. Thiery, "Some Technical Aspects of the Motor Oils Market in France and Europe," ASTM Special Technical Publication #334 [1962]: 89–97).

100. See R. J. Overy, "Cars, Roads, and Economic Recovery in Germany 1932–8," *Economic History Review* 28 (1975): 472, 476.

101. See Frank Ferneyhough, *The History of Railways in Britain* (Reading: Osprey, 1975), pp. 70–72.

102. See David Starkie, *The Motorway Age: Road and Traffic Policies in Post-War Britain* (Oxford: Pergamon, 1982), pp. 1–9.

103. Ibid., pp. 17–18.

104. Ibid., pp. 20–21.

105. Ibid., p. 53.

106. The Times, June 11, 1964.

107. An imperial gallon is 5 U.S. quarts. This would translate as around 40 miles per U.S. gallon.

108. Rob Golding, *Mini* (London: Osprey, 1979), p. 44.

109. See Jeff Daniels, *British Leyland: The Truth about the Cars* (London: Osprey, 1980), pp. 337, 50–51.

110. Giacosa, *Forty Years*, p. 246.

111. Ibid., p. 249.

112. Ibid., p. 250.

113. See Sloniger, *VW Story*, p. 166.

114. Ibid., p. 187.

CHAPTER SEVEN

The Diffusion of Science into Engineering

HIGHWAY RESEARCH AT THE BUREAU
OF PUBLIC ROADS, 1900–40

Bruce E. Seely

In 1893 Congress created a new agency in the Department of Agriculture that would eventually receive the name Bureau of Public Roads (BPR) and become the single most important arbiter of this nation's developing road system. One reason for its stature was a research program undertaken by the bureau after 1900, research that made the BPR almost the only source of technical information for engineers confronting the demands of first bicyclists and then automobile owners for improved highways.

Initially, BPR researchers utilized traditional engineering methods in their work, relying upon experience and empirical observation in conducting systematic tests. After World War I, however, federal engineers embraced a different set of research methods that emphasized the development of theoretical understandings of nature and the expression of results in mathematical form. In other words, the BPR research program after 1918 borrowed methods and attitudes usually associated with science. This change provides an opportunity to examine one of the more interesting examples of the diffusion of ideas in the last hundred years—the diffusion of science into engineering.

In common usage the words "science" and "technology" have become interchangeable and this discussion might sound like hairsplitting. Most persons consider the development of the atomic bomb during the World

---

This chapter is based on work supported by the National Science Foundation under Grant SES 80–07899.

War II and the landing of men on the moon scientific achievements. In reality, however, both owed more to the organizational and problem-solving skills of engineering than they owed to science. Moreover, since the 1960s historians of technology have demonstrated that until quite recently science and technology had represented entirely separate realms of knowledge and activity.[1] Only in the second half of the nineteenth century was unity between the two established in the electrical and chemical industries, where new products and processes developed through a reliance on scientific knowledge and methods. This began the widespread diffusion of science into engineering in the twentieth century.[2]

The research efforts of engineers at the BPR fit this larger trend. Although some bridge builders, led by the French in the late eighteenth century, had begun to develop mathematical approaches to the analysis of stress, most civil engineers in 1900 worked in a "low-technology" field when compared with the "high-technology" realms of electricity and chemistry.[3] A number of factors prodded BPR engineers to bring their efforts into conformity with the broad changes sweeping all engineering after the First World War. Many who have considered this type of change have assumed that engineering automatically benefited from such an introduction of scientific methods and attitudes, but diffusion rarely works in such a smooth fashion, and the case of the BPR research program provides a cautionary reminder about the impact of new ideas. In the wake of changes in its research approach, the agency encountered serious difficulties producing information of direct utility to practitioners in the field. The most clear-cut, but not the only, instance, involved a twenty-year study of the effect of vehicle impact on pavements.

Federal Highway Research, 1893–1918

To understand the shift that took place in the BPR research program, we must first survey quickly its style of investigation before the First World War. That style reflected the purpose assigned the Office of Road Inquiry (ORI) in 1893 by Congress. American roads were truly abysmal—mud holes in spring, dust traps in summer, rutted always. Under pressure from bicycling groups, Congress directed the new ORI to collect and disseminate information on road materials and construction methods. Knowledge alone, the argument ran, would lead to better roads. The ORI compiled information for an impressive collection of bulletins on the location of materials. The office also emulated other agencies in the Agriculture Department, such as the Bureaus of Plant Industry, Animal Industry, and Entomology, and the agriculture experiment stations, that assigned university-trained scientists to solve practical problems through research.[4]

By 1897 the ORI had combined the information-gathering and practical research approaches, concerning itself with classifying and grading construction materials. This work culminated in the opening of a physical testing and chemical laboratory in 1900 that examined materials at no charge to the public. ORI engineers soon turned to determining the optimal use of materials, introducing new ones, studying the effect of the automobile on roads, and developing tests to measure the suitability of materials. They had, by 1905, become the foremost source of technical information relating to roads.[5]

Significantly, BPR investigators relied on a wide variety of full-scale tests and laboratory methods. In many cases, federal engineers designed tests to compare several types of construction and material on existing sections of highway. After 1910, the office conducted this type of study at its own experiment station in then-rural Arlington, Virginia. As always, the focus fell on field testing, but this work was supplemented by the free laboratory testing program, from which emerged procedures for measuring the strength of materials, especially sand and stone. By 1911, federal researchers had enough information from these two sources to issue typical construction specifications and standard methods of testing materials that state and local road building agencies rapidly adopted.[6] Moreover, they provided satisfactory answers to practical problems facing road builders.

BPR engineers operated systematically, but never saw themselves as scientists. They showed little concern for general theories of material behavior and made little use of mathematics. Instead, their work relied on cut-and-try investigations that identified the best material through actual use. In fact, the office did not even use the word "research" to describe its activities until 1916. Even so, federal engineers believed they understood how to build durable roads. Their main concern lay in improving the efficiency and skill of local road officials, not in developing new technical understandings. Their confidence, however, was destroyed in an unprecedented destruction of roads during the winter of 1917–18. East Coast ports were jammed with material for France that choked the railroad yards, so motor trucks were loaded with supplies near their midwestern factories and driven to Philadelphia and Baltimore. Before spring arrived, hundreds of miles of roads including some of the best in the country, were all but impassable.[7]

Federal engineers quickly launched a series of field tests to identify the causes of the massive road failures. Their findings pointed to two culprits— water frozen in the soil foundation and heavy trucks. They found that traditional designs failed to drain the soil under a road, especially in clay soils, and trucks could crush the cracked surfaces that the bad foundations created.[8] In short, the field investigations undermined the basic assumptions of highway design.

In some respects, this situation repeated the events of 1905, when it had been discovered that rapidly increasing numbers of automobiles were destroying common, macadam-type, earth and gravel roads. The BPR, under the direction of Logan Page, had relied on full-sized field investigations to identify methods that would halt this problem.[9] But in 1918 the BPR reacted to the new challenge in a markedly different manner, moving away from studies of individual materials and field tests. One researcher explained a year later that "with the rational design of road surfaces as a goal, the Bureau of Public Roads has begun experiments to find out something of the fundamentals affecting road design."[10]

This comment contained two signals of change. The first was the use of the word "rational," indicating a desire for a general theory to guide all road construction. The second was the reference to fundamentals. In scientific circles, fundamental research referred to pure rather than applied studies that aimed to solve a specific problem. The BPR researcher did not adopt this distinction totally, coming closer to the definition of engineering science developed by historian David Channel—concern for modifying the ideal laws of nature to explain real behavior. This outlook combined the traditional empirical approach of engineering with science, but kept attention on utilization.[11] At the BPR, this shift was reflected in changes in research method, as engineers attempted to adopt what they saw as the essence of science—a concern for the acquisition of precise quantitative data and the expression of results using mathematics. The BPR chief engineer expressed the agency's goal in 1922 when he explained that he hoped their work would "establish the art of road building as an exact science and to this end let us obtain and use the underlying fundamental facts."[12] Thus the highway failures of 1917–18 led BPR investigators to abandon not only the old rules of road construction but also their traditional methods of research.

Truck Impact Investigations, 1918–32

The changing research style emerged slowly. In late 1918, federal engineers set out to determine more precisely the effect on pavements of trucks, one of their targeted culprits. This first investigation operated in the traditional fashion of field studies, as BPR researchers placed pressure cells under full-sized concrete slabs at the Arlington station and drove trucks over the surface to measure the impact force. To their surprise, they found that the force of a truck's tires slamming into the slab was much larger than the static weight of the vehicle.[13]

They turned, therefore, to measuring impact with carefully designed apparatus to crush copper cylinders in a field situation in their main investigation in 1919, the first movement toward fundamental studies. The force of impact obtained in field experiments could be estimated by comparing similar pieces crushed in the laboratory by a hydraulic press. Impact was found to be five times greater than the weight of the vehicle, although follow-up studies indicated that pneumatic tires could substantially reduce that force.[14]

From this first round of tests federal engineers learned the major factors behind impact damage, and they released a series of practical recommendations. These included urging even distribution of weight between a truck's axles, constructing smooth pavements, using pneumatic tires, and building thicker slabs to bridge bad subgrade formations. All were commonsense suggestions, indicating that a rational theory for highway design had not appeared.[15]

The second set of investigations begun at the end of 1920 turned more noticeably toward scientific styles, focusing on developing quantitative data. The goal of this investigation was to determine how a slab reacted to impact, while measuring the force applied. Because the initial apparatus could not meet this purpose, engineers constructed a tower that could deliver a simulated truck impact to fifty-six slabs of different thickness and construction at the Arlington station. The same soil foundation was maintained for all slabs.[16]

By the end of 1921, the BPR had completed the tests, repeating the application of force until severe cracks showed in each slab. They considered releasing the information in tabular form to guide designers in their choice of slab thickness and materials, but chose not to for reasons that clearly demonstrated the growing desire to act in a scientific rather than an engineering fashion. First, the results really fitted only one soil type. Secondly, a table struck the researchers as "not very scientific and . . . only . . . a preliminary step."[17] Instead, the engineers wanted to release numerical data. But calculation of the impact force required more equipment—in this case a mechanism for recording the movement of the tower parts over time. Moreover, actually making the calculations took two years.

As a result of this decision, the test results were not ready until 1923. Nor was this delay the only effect of the new research style. Using machinery to simulate a truck eliminated the factor of speed from the calculations, and the tower was built to apply impact only at the center of a slab, even though researchers knew the greatest damage came on the edges and corners. The demand for numbers introduced artificiality into the whole system and de-layed results. Moreover, the most prominent "result" was a call for further research, a noticeable difference when compared with the suggestions issued after the first battery of tests.[18] The engineers' theory still eluded them.

The Bates Test Road, 1921–24

Even as federal engineers pushed forward with their new testing appara-tus, the Illinois State Highway Department was engaged in a test that high-lighted the shift underway in the BPR research style.[19] In 1920 the highway department constructed a two-mile oval of asphalt, concrete, and brick on which trucks of various sizes repeatedly circled. By the end of 1922, they had destroyed fifty sections of pavement. Federal engineers observed the Bates test, provided trucks and measuring equipment, but Clifford Older of Illinois ran the test.

In startling contrast with the BPR investigations, the Bates test showed that the proper design for a concrete slab was thicker at the edge than in the center, exactly the reverse of the prevailing pattern. Moreover, because the oval encompassed several soil types, the results suggested construction standards and materials to highway engineers encountering similar condi-tions. *Engineering News-Record* correctly observed that "test roads have sel-dom given results so positive that a radical change in pavement design followed," as most states quickly adopted the design indicated by the Bates test. But the Arlington station could not confirm these findings: its samples did not include a thickened-edge slab.

The crucial explanation for the differences in the tests lay in the goals set by the investigators. Illinois highway engineers intended to find the most durable slabs for various soil conditions, and to that end they built a full-size road and used real trucks in order to re-create real conditions as closely as possible. They were utilizing the methods used by federal engineers before the war. The BPR, however, was even then turning to smaller slabs, complicated equipment, and increased artificiality in order to meet their goal of developing numerical data on impact force. By acting as they believed scientists acted, they laboriously succeeded in isolating each variable and obtaining precise, unequivocal data. But the results were of limited utility, unlike those of the Illinois tests. Moreover, the Illinois engineers had not ignored BPR interests: they installed a variety of measuring instruments that in some instances produced better data than the Arlington experiments. Nonetheless, BPR engineers considered this test and a similar study by the California State Highway Department to be flawed: "Too much emphasis has been laid on the destruction of slabs and too little on obtaining scientific data during the destruction phase."[20] Yet precisely because they de-emphasized such goals, the empirical Bates and Pittsburg (California) test roads gave engineers clear choices of pavement under several soil conditions, whereas the federal engineers were still calculating the force of impact from their graphs.

Continued BPR Impact Tests, 1924 – 40

This difference in research approaches was further emphasized by the approach taken at the BPR as it continued its impact investigations after 1923. These new investigations not only continued to employ complicated mechanical apparatus to simulate real conditions, but also showed the greater emphasis being placed on the acquisition of quantitative data. As a result, the problems evident in the second round of experiments, especially the limited utility of the findings for practicing engineers, increased.

This pattern showed quite clearly in the third set of BPR impact investigations. The 1918 studies had focused on the reaction of pavement slabs to trucks, and the 1919–23 tests had considered the magnitude of impact, but attention in 1924 turned more deliberately to combining these goals. The chief barrier remained the difficulty in measuring impact without altering the pavement itself, for the engineers were dissatisfied with the cumbersome system of graphs used in the 1921 investigations. Their solution was to design an accelerometer that mounted on the wheels of a truck and graphed the movement of tires and springs. The investigators also developed a device called a profilometer to measure the irregularities in a pavement surface. They hoped to combine this equipment so that they could drive a truck over a real highway and record the impact forces caused by imperfections in the surface. They would then apply an impact of the type recorded by the truck to slabs prepared at the Arlington station with recording devices, using a modified version of the device built for the 1921 test.[21] In this way, they hoped to re-create real conditions in a controlled environment that would permit them to develop the desired numerical information.

Unfortunately, the engineers encountered serious difficulties in carrying out this ambitious plan. Difficulties with the accelerometers delayed actual recording efforts until 1927, and further problems arose in calibrating the new impact machine, despite the assistance of the National Bureau of Standards. In 1933 the BPR announced in its *Annual Report* that it had succeeded in measuring the force of impact. It continued, "Attention is now turning to the equally important question of the effect on road surfaces of the suddenly-applied forces of motor vehicle impact."[22] This was, of course, the goal initially announced for this experiment in 1924, indicating that the investigators' efforts had fallen short. They simply lacked the means of gaining the precise mathematical data they desired, while maintaining some sense of real highway conditions. Worse, it seems plain that in their quest to imitate science, federal highway engineers had lost sight of the initial problem that had justified the research in the first place—helping highway engineers build better roads. By the 1930s, they were engaged in an intriguing challenge to their ingenuity, and this, more than the initial engineering problem, explained the design of the test.

The fourth round of the investigation merely confirmed this point, as BPR engineers announced in 1933 that they were moving ahead in their effort to simultaneously measure impact and record the effect of the forces applied. For this effort, they completely abandoned the plan of copying reality in their experiment and turned instead to a laboratory setting that was the most artificial research environment yet witnessed. Rather than testing a real highway section, researchers designed a pendulum-type machine that applied impact to a much smaller slab than any previously used. A wheel mounted on the end of the pendulum was fitted with new accelerometers to record the force of impact; improved strain gauges on the back of the slab measured the reaction. Equipment bugs were not worked out until 1936, and not until 1937 did the bureau announce, "The work is necessarily slow and painstaking. With the special testing equipment designed and built for this research many thousands of observations have been made."[23]

That was the last word from the BPR about its impact investigations. Once again the investigators had failed to reach their initial goal of simultaneous measurement and observation, and the more general purpose of developing an overall theory of highway design. As before, basic problems appeared because of the artificiality of the experiment. The apparatus took no account of the cushioning of the soil and foundation under a slab, applying impact to a small piece of concrete cantilevered in the air. The shape was different from a pavement slab, and the actual application of force also differed from real conditions, ignoring the effect of the springs and suspension on a real truck. Finally, the apparatus made no provision for dual-tired trucks. Thus at the end of twenty years, the Bureau of Public Roads impact investigations had offered very little guidance for highway engineers attempting to build roads capable of supporting the increasingly heavy trucks on American highways.

One can almost detect a comedy of errors about this long-running investigation, but before we are too hasty in condemning the BPR engineers for mismanagement or stupidity, we should recognize that their research efforts were consistently acclaimed throughout this entire period as setting the standards for other highway research groups. T. D. Mylrea, head of the Department of Civil Engineering at the University of Delaware, visited the BPR in 1938 to witness a series of tests on the last impact machine. His evaluation represented most engineers' attitudes to the bureau's achievements: "The care with which these tests are being conducted has impressed me very much, and I have come to the conclusion that it would do our senior students a great deal of good to witness this test procedure."[24]

Even so, the most interesting footnote to these investigations came after the Second World War, as the BPR began to develop standards for the construction of the interstate highway system, which it knew would face heavy demands from large trucks. A crucial research tool for this effort was a series of road tests that resembled the Bates Road Test in plan and operation. Four major investigations were carried out. The Hybla Valley Test (1944–54) at Arlington studied asphalt pavements; Road Test One (1949) in Maryland, the WASHO Road Test (1952–54) in Idaho, and the AASHO Test (1958–60) in Illinois all tested multiple materials and construction techniques on a variety of soil conditions. Each relied on real trucks to provide the impact forces. All utilized sophisticated measuring devices to determine the effects of the trucks, but the basic purpose of the tests had returned to the question asked in the late 1910s: How are we to build a durable pavement? The answers were sought using the older empirical methods of observations and full-sized field investigations that had served the BPR so well earlier in the century.[25]

Why This Diffusion?

Not all BPR research endeavors followed this pattern, but the general trend in its investigations during the period between the wars was toward the development of theoretical statements and a greater reliance on mathematics as the language for results. Indeed, the BPR enjoyed a number of successes, especially in the area of bridge design and in a series of studies carried out by University of Illinois engineer H. H. Westergaard on the theoretical analysis of stresses in concrete slabs. But there were other projects that also encountered difficulties in producing findings of use to road builders, for many of the same reasons that plagued the impact studies. The impact studies, therefore, cannot be dismissed as an aberration.[26]

A variety of factors help explain the persistence of BPR efforts to emulate the activities and goals of scientists during this period. Heading the list was the movement of engineering as a whole toward scientific attitudes and a reliance on mathematics. As noted earlier, this shift accelerated after the electrical and chemical industries began to harness science during the last third of the nineteenth century. The real catalyst, however, was the enormous enthusiasm for scientific research that followed the highly successful contributions of scientists to such First World War projects as radio and submarine detection.[27] Abundant evidence attests to the responsiveness of the engineering profession to this new approach to solving problems.

Leading figures in the field, such as Alfred D. Flinn, director of the Engineering Foundation and one of the forces behind the creation of the Division of Engineering in the National Research Council in 1920, strongly encouraged such efforts. Numerous articles in professional journals after 1920 joined Flinn in promoting the introduction of scientific approaches.[28] Mathematics and physics began to receive much greater emphasis in the engineering classroom. A. Hunter Dupree and Daniel J. Kevles have discussed the explosion of scientific research in American business during the

1920s, as the number of corporate research laboratories increased from 300 in 1920 to 1,625 only a decade later. By 1935 the dean of engineering at Virginia Tech could summarize the situation by noting that "The scientist is pretty much of an engineer and the engineer must be a fair sort of scientist."[29]

This persistent pressure to shift the direction of engineering toward the attitudes and methods of science certainly carried the BPR along its path. In 1935, the director of the Highway Research Board, a branch of the National Research Council, argued that the highway industry needed to conduct more studies along the lines of the BPR impact investigations. Road builders needed to start more research that involved "scientific study rather than experimentation. Much of our present-day practice is based upon the experimental method applied in the field, but from now on, we must go much deeper into fundamentals."[30] The BPR efforts to inaugurate that pattern of study after 1918 would seem, given the general consensus of opinion, to have been the proper course. The highway failures of 1917–18 seemed to indicate the bankruptcy of both existing construction approaches and of empirical research methods, whereas the new scientific methodology promised to rectify the situation as it had in many other fields of engineering. But a closer examination of the events of the period suggests that the research methods initially adopted by the BPR at the turn of the century retained their merit, largely because of the complexity of the problems under investigation. They were not susceptible to a reductionist approach of finding the one best answer or general formula. Both the Bates Road Test of the 1920s and the battery of road tests in the 1940s and 1950s indicated the continued viability of the older research style.

In spite of the difficulties encountered by the BPR investigators, which hindsight reveals so clearly, they chose to move in the new directions, encouraged by additional considerations beyond the shifting attitudes of their peers. Of equal influence was the public perception of science and scientists as the heroes of the First World War. Engineers saw the suddenly increased prestige of scientists and hoped that copying scientific techniques could connect engineering to the new enthusiasm. The activities of Thomas H. MacDonald, chief of the BPR from 1919 to 1953, plainly exhibited such motives. He had long been a proponent of highway research, both as highway engineer in Iowa and as head of the BPR. His mentor at Iowa State College had been Anson Marston, a pioneer in soil investigations, who passed on to MacDonald the emphasis on scientific approaches to engineering he had gained from his mentor at Cornell, Robert Thurston. Thus the postwar excitement about research struck a responsive chord in the BPR chief.[31]

MacDonald's concern for raising the status of engineers through research became apparent in a paper he read in 1923 entitled "The Objectives of Research":

> Why has not the engineer been accorded more readily and more consistently the leadership and the rewards, not necessarily material, which generally accrue to recognized authority?
>
> And the answer, which is reasonably sufficient to me . . . is . . . the lack of engineering research . . . If the engineer is making progress, and if he is succeeding, if he finally proves beyond all doubt the ability of the engineer to master and thus lead in a new transition in our national life, it will be through research.[32]

Not surprisingly, MacDonald played a leading role in the establishment and early operation of the Highway Research Board in the Division of Engineering of the National Research Council.[33] Based within the National Academy of Science, MacDonald believed that highway engineers could share the prestige with which that body emerged from the war. Indeed, this viewpoint enjoyed wide currency among engineers, including Marston, who had pushed for the creation of the Division of Engineering after 1919.

A third factor in the BPR embrace of scientific research involved MacDonald's concern for the prestige of the BPR itself. By 1900 the BPR had been recognized as the pacesetter in highway engineering practice and the leading source of all types of technical information. This position had permitted Logan Page, BPR director from 1905 through 1918, to guide the general development of highway policy at the state and federal levels in matters related to many topics outside technology because of the agency's established expertise; this included the introduction of systems of administration at the local and state level, and state and federal legislation as well. MacDonald strengthened the BPR position as the final arbiter of American highway policy in legislative, educational, research, and technical matters by enhancing the agency's reputation as the consummate expert. But because the BPR entry into all these policy arenas rested on its genuine technical expertise, MacDonald believed it essential that the BPR remain on the cutting edge of road building technology and research.

It was this sentiment that no doubt motivated a federal engineer to suggest in 1927 that the "energies of the Bureau, except in rather exceptional cases, should be expended on basic research."[34] This proposal, however, would have reversed the entire justification for BPR research developed over thirty years—that it solve practical problems. As a result, the idea never became official policy. But the fact that state highway engineers, in the words of the director of the Highway Research Board, "do not have time for long-range scientific inquiry," encouraged the BPR to emphasize fundamental research projects.[35]

Another component of this awareness of the prestige of expertise appeared in the BPR response to criticism directed at it after the road failures of 1917–18. At that time, the agency was struggling to develop the administrative procedures for overseeing the first federal-aid highway funds, which Congress had authorized in 1916. The outbreak of the war in Europe vastly complicated the BPR task: its efforts to install guidelines and begin construction of roads to meet wartime demand were frustrated by shortages of personnel and materials, as well as by chaos on the nation's railroads. The BPR seemed to many to be inept and inefficient, with the failures adding fuel to the fire. A broad-based movement appeared to create a national highway commission to replace the BPR. But the BPR research efforts provided a means of demonstrating its ability and expertise, for by wrapping their efforts in the cloak of fundamental research, BPR engineers undercut their critics' arguments.[36] Interestingly, it was after MacDonald had defused this potentially dangerous threat to the existence of the BPR, and after the urgency to explain the road failures of 1918 had abated, that the swing to scientific research began in earnest.

The final factor in the BPR's steady adherence to the new style of research was the internal motivation of the engineers themselves. Federal highway engineers found themselves confronting challenging obstacles in their pursuit of precise quantitative data, and the solutions required sophisticated equipment that pressed, and in some cases exceeded, their technical abilities. Caught up in their enthusiasm for such efforts, they pursued the possibilities to their logical conclusion. They were having fun, of course, but in the process, they redefined the problems they had set out to solve. The acquisition of data, rather than the solution of engineering problems, became their primary goal and, not surprisingly, their work had little if any value to practicing engineers. But this pattern of activity reflected a broad current within all engineering that has only rarely been give recognition. Problems of greater sophistication and systems of greater complexity are inherently more fun than easy problems and simple technologies. The challenge of cutting-edge technologies is powerful, and the BPR impact investigations nicely demonstrated this fascination with a difficult problem and complex systems.[37]

These five factors—changing professional goals, public enthusiasm for science, concerns for institutional prestige, responses to outside critics, and the internal fascination with challenging problems—explain the BPR's initial adoption and persistent retention of the new scientific research methodologies. Through all their actions loomed a desire to be and act like scientists. The easiest way to prove that they were scientific was the emphasis on mathematical expression, for there was, and still is, a basic belief that the quantification of data was the essence of science.

The BPR investigations were carried on in accordance with the more recent sentiment of the mission chief scientist of the 1980 Voyager fly-by of Saturn, who observed "until you have numbers, you don't have science."[38] This definition of science is rather limited, yet however we judge its validity, it defines the attitude of engineers who desired to emulate science. For them, the precision of mathematical expression was the hallmark of scientific research. The current hierarchy of the sciences retains the same assumption. Theoretical physics stands at the top of the ladder because it, more than other scientific disciplines, is based on mathematics. It should not be surprising that engineering has continued its emulation of science by adopting a similar hierarchy, placing the fields that lean most heavily on mathematics at the pinnacle of the profession.[39]

Not all engineers have embraced this shift, as evidenced by a small but steady stream of letters to professional journals and a few articles complaining that university education represents the "'other world' of civil engineering which is considerably removed from reality." The writer went on to say he had dropped his subscription to one journal because "the papers contained therein were nothing more nor less than Ph.D.s talking to each other. They were of little value to a practicing engineer."[40] Another note of concern was raised by a British mechanical engineering professor at the Imperial College of Science and Technology in London, who explained, "Until a graduate has the attitude that analysis is a tool for him to use, and the laws of science are the rules of the game, but not the game itself, we have failed to produce an engineer."[41]

Notwithstanding these views, the great consensus of opinion is that the change that engineering has undergone as a result of the diffusion of science and its methods has proven beneficial; indeed, few engineers point to the types of problems mentioned just above. Certainly few observers saw any difficulty in the ponderous and ultimately fruitless BPR impact studies.

Thus the general tendencies of the past century, which have produced a greater unity of science and engineering, have continued to the present day.

Conclusion

This case study points to a lesson learned by historians who have studied the transfer of technology—that the exchange of ideas happens in a less than straightforward fashion. Factors having little to do with the virtues of new approaches can prove crucial to the adoption of new hardware and new ideas. In the case of the diffusion of science into engineering, one cannot deny that scientific methods and attitudes have provided powerful problem-solving tools for engineering and that many of the advances in contemporary technology rest on a scientific foundation. It is much less common in contemporary society than ever before to know *how* to do something before understanding *why* a process or machine works as it does.

But there have been unexpected results of this diffusion as well. For example, it seems more than an interesting coincidence that as engineering has moved toward the model of science, it has increasingly encountered public criticism brought on by problems, failures, or expectations not met. Complaints about highway construction through urban neighborhoods, the safety of nuclear power plants, and environmental pollution form only part of a lurking fear that technology may be out of control.[42] Some of the specific instances arousing complaints, moreover, can be traced to difficulties stemming from the absence of experience among engineers as they struggle to fit reality into a theoretical conception. In one celebrated example, the Bay Area Rapid Transit system met public opposition not only because of its cost overruns, but also because it failed to perform as promised. Its operating problems grew in part from the attempt to use aircraft engineers and systems analysts as designers instead of transit and street railway engineers with experience in subway operation.

This picture of difficulties growing from the diffusion of new ideas is repeated in studies of the transfer of a number of technical innovations within or between cultures. Historians of technology and social scientists have examined the spread of the clock and the printing press, the transfer of textile technology from England to America after 1780, the development of mass-production procedures in nineteenth-century America, the installation of electric power systems, the introduction of the snowmobile to the Arctic, and many others. Many of these studies emphasized the staggering changes that followed in the wake of new machines or technical ideas.[43] Yet running through the thought of historians is the question of why certain technologies were adopted slowly rather than quickly. The introduction of coke as fuel in the manufacture of iron is a case in point. Scholars have assumed that a lag in the adoption of coke by American iron makers in the early nineteenth century was evidence of backwardness. The slowness of diffusion then becomes the issue to be examined, even if the lag occurred for perfectly logical reasons.[44] Hesitation, in an age that celebrates progress, represents the anomalous. But the diffusion of science into engineering reverses the question, raising as a representative issue, why the BPR began a headlong rush to alter its research efforts.

The diffusion of science into engineering may prove to be as important a diffusion as any in the history of technology. But in common with other groups attempting to borrow ideas from outside their borders, the BPR experience in highway research after 1918 emphasizes the two-headed nature of the introduction of new ways of looking at and solving problems. The lesson that change always involves trade-offs, bringing undesirable as well as useful characteristics, is not new. It may, however, have special relevance for our heavily technological society, not to mention for the social sciences themselves, which seem every bit as eager to adopt the scientific method as the federal highway engineers at the BPR.

Notes

1. See the journal *Technology and Culture*; also A. R. Hall, "Of Knowing—and Knowing How to . . . ," in A. R. Hall and Norman Smith, eds., *History of Technology*, third annual volume (London: Mansell, 1978), pp. 91–103.

2. On the changing interrelationship of science and technology in the nineteenth century, see Edwin T. Layton, Jr., "Mirror-Image Twins: The Communities of Science and Technology in 19th-Century America," *Technology and Culture* 12 (1971): 562–80; David F. Channel, "The Harmony of Theory and Practice: The Engineering Science of W. J. M. Rankine," *Technology and Culture* 23 (1982): 39–52.

3. S. B. Hamilton, "Bridges," in Charles Singer et al., eds., *A History of Technology* (Oxford: Oxford University Press, 1958), vol. 3, pp. 417–37.

4. On the ORI, see Bruce E. Seely, *Building the American Highway System: Engineers as Policy Makers* (Philadelphia: Temple University Press, 1987), pp. 1–15. On science in the Agriculture Department, see A. Hunter Dupree, *Science in the Federal Government: History of Policies and Activities to 1940* (Cambridge, Mass.: Belk-

nap, 1958), pp. 323–57; Charles E. Rosenberg, "Science, Technology, and Economic Growth: The Case of the Agricultural Experiment Station Scientist, 1875–1914," *Agricultural History* 45 (1971): 1–20.

5. This work can be followed in the annual reports of the agency (which underwent several name changes before becoming the Bureau of Public Roads): U.S. Department of Agriculture (USDA), *Annual Report of the Secretary of Agriculture*, from 1893 to 1916. The following information is drawn from these reports, unless otherwise noted. One can also find information in the bulletins and circulars released by the office during this same period.

6. See correspondence in Files 10, 59, 335, and 470, General Correspondence, 1893–1916, Records of the Bureau of Public Roads, Record Group 30, National Archives, Washington National Records Center, Suitland, Maryland (hereafter Records, BPR); USDA, Office of Public Roads, *Methods for the Examination of Bituminous Road Materials*, Agriculture Department Bulletin no. 704, 1918; "Object Lessons in Road Building," *Scientific American* 106 (March 16, 1912): 232.

7. See U.S. Department of Transportation (USDT), *America's Highways, 1776–1976: A History of the Federal Aid System Program* (Washington, D.C.: USDT, 1977), pp. 90–100, 103–104, 117–19; "Our Highways and the Burden They Must Carry," *Public Roads* 1/2 (June, 1918): 4–29; Prevost Hubbard, "Efficiency of Bituminous Surfaces and Pavements Under Motor-Truck Traffic," *Public Roads* 1/10 (February, 1919): 25.

8. See J. L. Harrison, "Water and the Subgrade," *Public Roads* 1/12 (April, 1919): 11–17; W. W. McLaughlin, "Capillary Moisture and Its Effects on Highway Subgrades," *Public Roads* 4/1 (May, 1921): 6–8.

9. On Page's investigations of the effect of cars on macadam roads, see the OPR *Annual Report*, from 1905 to 1913; and Logan W. Page, "The Motor Car and the Road," *Scientific American* 102 (January 15, 1910): 46–47; "Automobiles and Improved Roads," *Scientific American* 109 (September 6, 1913): 178, 200–201; "The Selection of Materials for Macadam Roads," *Proceedings of the American Road Congress*, Detroit, Michigan, 1913 (Baltimore: Waverly Press, 1914), p. 170.

10. C. A. Hogentogler, "Tests of Impact on Pavements by the Bureau of Public Roads," *Public Roads* 4/6 (October, 1921): 3–18; "Bureau of Public Roads Subgrade Study," *Engineering News-Record* 84 (May 27, 1920): 1072–73.

11. Channel, "Harmony."

12. A. T. Goldbeck, "Highway Research and What the Results Indicate," *Good Roads* 62 (April, 1922): 238.

13. See A. T. Goldbeck and E. B. Smith, "An Apparatus for Determining Soil Pressures," *Proceedings of the American Society for Testing Materials*, 16/2 (1916): 306–19; A. T. Goldbeck, "Thickness of Concrete Slabs," *Public Roads* 1/2 (April, 1919): 34–38.

14. See Earl B. Smith and J. T. Pauls, "Preliminary Report of the Impact Tests of Auto Trucks on Roads," *Public Roads* 2/15 (July, 1919): 8–10; A. T. Goldbeck, "The Present Status of Impact Tests on Roadway Surfaces," *Public Roads* 2/18–19 (Oct.–Nov., 1919): 19–25; "Good Progress in Impact Tests," *Public Roads* 3/27 (July, 1920): 18; Earl B. Smith, "The How and Why of Motor Truck Impact," *Public Roads* 3/31 (November, 1920): 16–18; and correspondence for 1919–22 in File 890, Tests, Motor Trucks, Classified Central File, 1912–50, Records, BPR.

15. See Smith, "How and Why"; Thomas MacDonald to District Engineers, April 20, 1920, File 470, General Classified Central File, 1912–50, Records, BPR.

16. See Hogentogler, "Tests of Impact"; Prevost Hubbard, "Test and Re-

search Investigations of the Bureau of Public Roads," *Public Roads* 2/15 (July, 1919): 28–32; Earl B. Smith, "Motor Truck Impact Tests of the Bureau of Public Roads," *Public Roads* 3/35 (March, 1921): 3–36.

17. Hogentogler, "Tests of Impact," and "Tests of Impact . . . , Part 2," *Public Roads* 4/7 (1921): 1–18, 27.

18. See A. T. Goldbeck, "What the Arlington Tests are Showing," *Engineering and Contracting* 59 (February 7, 1923): 308; BPR, *Annual Report*, 1924, p. 10.

19. See Clifford Older, "Illinois Begins Traffic Endurance Test," *Engineering News-Record* 87 (August 18, 1921): 274–76; Illinois Department of Public Works and Buildings, Division of Highways, *Bates Experimental Road; or Highway Research in Illinois*, Bulletin no. 21, January, 1924; and correspondence for 1920–22, File 407, General, and 407, Illinois, Classified Central File, 1912–50, Records, BPR. Quotation from "Progress Made in Highway Engineering," *Engineering News-Record* 90 (January 18, 1923): 55.

20. "Results of Heavy Traffic on Pittsburg Test Road," *Engineering News Record* 88 (June 29, 1922): 732; see also A. T. Goldbeck to Thomas H. MacDonald, June 10, 1922, File 407, California, Classified Central File, 1912–50, Records, BPR.

21. See Leslie W. Teller, "Impact Tests on Concrete Pavement Slabs," *Public Roads* 5/2 (April, 1924): 1–14; "Accurate Accelerometers Developed by the Bureau of Public Roads," *Public Roads* 5/10 (December, 1924): 1–9; C. A. Hogentogler, "Status of Motor Truck Impact Tests of the Bureau of Public Roads," *Public Roads* 5/9 (November, 1924): 11–14; BPR, *Annual Report*, 1924, p. 42.

22. Quotation from BPR, *Annual Report*, 1933, p. 42; see also "Motor Truck Impact Tests Now in Progress," *Public Roads*, 7/11 (January, 1927): 231; "New Research Projects Initiated by Bureau of Public Roads," *Public Roads* 8/6 (August, 1927): 124; J. A. Buchanan and G. P. St. Clair, "Calibration of Accelerometers for the Use in Motor Truck Impact Tests," *Public Roads* 11/5 (July, 1930): 81–109; BPR, *Annual Report*, 1932, p. 40.

23. Quotation from BPR, *Annual Report*, 1973, p. 68; see also L. W. Teller, "A Machine for Impact and Sustained Load Tests of Concrete," *Public Roads* 18/10 (December, 1937): 185–94; BPR, *Annual Report*, 1934, pp. 58–59, 1935, p. 57, and 1936, pp. 65–66.

24. T. D. Mylrea to the BPR, December 8, 1938, File 890, Tests, Bridge Impact, Classified Central File, 1912–50, Records, BPR.

25. USDT, *America's Highways*, pp. 333–35. See also these reports by the National Academy of Science, National Research Council, and Highway Research Board: "Road Test One—MD," *Special Report* no. 4, 1952; "The WASHO Road Test," part 1, *Special Report* no. 18, 1954, and part 2, *Special Report* no. 22, 1955; "The AASHO Road Test: History and Description of Project," *Special Report* no. 61A, 1961.

26. See Bruce E. Seely, "The Scientific Mystique in Engineering: Highway Research at the Bureau of Public Roads, 1900–1940," *Technology and Culture* 25 (1984): 798–831.

27. See Dupree, *Science in the Federal Government*; Ronald Tobey, *The American Ideology of National Science, 1919–1930* (Pittsburgh: University of Pittsburgh Press, 1971), pp. xii–xiii, 35–37, 49–61; Daniel J. Kevles, *The Physicists: The History of a Scientific Community in Modern America* (New York: Vintage, 1979), pp. 72–73, 81, 95–96.

28. See Alfred D. Flinn, "Research Advances Civil Engineering," *Civil Engineering* 1 (October, 1930): 14–16; F. C. Lea, "Science and Engineering," *Engineering* 128 (August 28, 1929): 88; Mervyn O'Gorman, "Bringing Science into the

Road Traffic Problem," *The Engineer* 159 (January 11, 1935): 53; A. A. Potter, "Scientific Research and Future Roads and Street Building Programs," *Roads and Streets* 77 (March, 1934): 94; F. M. Dawson, "The Role of Fundamental Research," *Journal of Engineering Education* 39 (December, 1943): 195.

29. Earle B. Norris, "Research as Applied to Engineering," *Civil Engineering* 5 (May, 1935): 408; see also James Kip Finch, *The Story of Engineering* (New York: Doubleday, 1960), pp. 387–88; and Finch, *Trends in Engineering Education: The Columbia Experience* (New York: Columbia University Press, 1948), pp. 5–6. On research laboratories, see Dupree, *Science in the Federal Government*; Kevles, *Physicists*.

30. Roy W. Crum, "Highway Research," *Engineering News-Record* 114 (January 17, 1935): 75.

31. See Tobey, *American Ideology*, pp. 35–39, 49–61; Herbert J. Gilkey, *Anson Marston: Iowa State University's First Dean of Engineering* (Ames: Iowa State University, College of Engineering, 1968).

32. Thomas H. MacDonald, "Objectives of Highway Research," paper presented to the Advisory Board for Highway Research, November 9, 1923, pp. 2–3, copy in Thomas H. MacDonald Papers, Box 84–N, Bentley Library, University of Michigan, Ann Arbor, Michigan.

33. See Seely, *Building the American Highway System*, pp. 109–14; National Academy of Science, Highway Research Board, *Ideas and Actions: A History of the Highway Research Board, 1920–1970* (Washington, D.C.: Highway Research Board, 1971). On the motives of engineers for creating the Divison of Engineering, see correspondence between MacDonald, A. N. Talbot, and Marston, August to December, 1919, File 001.11, Classified Central File, 1912–50, Records, BPR.

34. E. F. Kelley to A. T. Goldbeck, September 29, 1927, File 001.11, Classified Central File, 1912–50, Records, BPR.

35. R. W. Crum, "Highway Research in the United States," *Chemistry and Industry* 57 (July 23, 1938): 697.

36. See Seely, *Building the American Highway System*, chap. 3.

37. See Eugene S. Ferguson, "Enthusiasm and Objectivity in Technological Development," paper read to the American Association for the Advancement of Science, "Symposium on Technology: Nuts and Bolts or Social Process," Houston, Texas, December 29, 1970; Tracy Kidder, *The Soul of a New Machine* (Boston: Little, Brown and Company, 1981).

38. Rick Gore, "Saturn: Riddle of the Rings," *National Geographic* 160 (July, 1981): 24.

39. Evidence of growing mathematization of engineering can be found in books promoting engineering as a career: Phillip Polluck, *Careers and Opportunities in Engineering* (New York: Dutton, 1967), pp. 54–56; Finch, *Story of Engineering*, pp. 387–88. See also Sally Hacker, "Mathematization of Engineering: Limits on Women and the Field," in Joan Rothschild, ed., *Machina ex Dea: Feminist Perspectives on Technology* (New York: Pergammon, 1983), pp. 38–58.

40. Henry D. Claybrook, "Readers Write," *Civil Engineering* 52 (May, 1982): 26. See also Eugene S. Ferguson, "The Mind's Eye: Nonverbal Thought in Technology," *Science* 197 (August 26, 1977): 827–36; John Huston, "Stop the World—I Want to Get Off," *Civil Engineering* 51 (December, 1981): 66–67; Douglas Lewin, "The Relevance of Science to Engineering—A Reappraisal," *Radio and Electronic Engineer* 49 (March, 1979): 119–24.

41. L. C. Laming, "Engineering Science Versus Technology," *Engineering* 216 (May, 1976): 352–54.

42. Leading critics of technology include René Dubos and Lewis Mumford.

For a good overview, see Langdon Winner, *Autonomous Technology* (Cambridge: MIT Press, 1978). See also E. F. Schumacher, *Small Is Beautiful, Economics as if People Mattered* (New York: Harper and Row, 1973). For a rejoinder, see Samuel Florman, *The Existential Pleasures of Engineering* (New York: St. Martin's, 1976).

43. See Carlo Cipolla, *Clocks and Culture, 1300–1700* (New York: Walker, 1967); David S. Landes, *Revolution in Time: Clocks and the Making of the Modern World* (Cambridge: Belknap, 1984); Elizabeth Eisenstein, *The Printing Press as an Agent of Change: Communications and Cultural Transformations in Early Modern Europe,* 2 vols. (New York: Cambridge University Press, 1979); David Jeremy, *Transatlantic Industrial Revolution: The Diffusion of Textile Technology between Britain and America, 1790–1830* (Cambridge: MIT Press, 1981); David A. Hounshell, *From the American System to Mass Production: The Development of Manufacturing Technology in the United States, 1800–1930* (Baltimore: Johns Hopkins University Press, 1984); Thomas Parke Hughes, *Networks of Power; Electrification in Western Society, 1880–1930* (Baltimore: Johns Hopkins University Press, 1983); Pertti J. Pelto, *The Snowmobile Revolution: Technology and Social Change in the Arctic* (Menlo Park, Calif.: Benjamin-Cummings, 1973).

44. See Bruce E. Seely, "Blast Furnace Technology in the Mid-19th Century: A Case Study of the Adirondack Iron and Steel Company," *Industrial Archaeology* 7 (1981): 27–54.

PART THREE

The History and Theory of Diffusion

Diffusion Research in the Context of the Naturalism Debate in Twentieth-Century Geographic Thought

J. Nicholas Entrikin

Diffusion studies have been a part of geographical research throughout the twentieth century, but the wide variety of such studies prohibits reference to a single diffusionist tradition within the discipline. The most useful framework for the discovery of order among this variety is to view diffusion studies as reflections of the major conceptual shifts in geography that have taken place during this century.[1] These shifts have not been related to empirical anomalies or to theoretical debate, but rather are related to changing perspectives concerning the basic goals of a geographical science. Central to this debate is the issue of naturalism: the view that the social sciences can be modeled on the natural sciences.[2] A consideration of the variety of interpretations given to the naturalist perspective by geographers provides an important component in a contextual understanding of twentieth-century geographic thought.

A Historical Schema

That geographic diffusion studies reflect these larger concerns of the discipline is illustrated by the fact that differing views of diffusion can be

I should like to thank that John Simon Guggenheim Memorial Foundation for its support of my research.

described in terms of the relatively standard schema of twentieth-century Anglo-American geographic thought. Within this schema, the discipline is seen as having passed through a sequence of stages from environmentalism to regional synthesis to spatial analysis and finally into the present, pluralistic stage best described as post-spatial analysis. As the name indicates, this last stage is the most difficult to characterize in that the only unifying theme appears to be the negative one of a reaction against the view of geography as a positivistc spatial science. Within discussions of diffusion, the manifestation of this discontent has been a criticism of the decontextualization of the diffusion process that is seen as resulting from an exclusive concern with modeling the spatial aspects of this process and from an overriding interest in the development of empirical generalizations concerning spatial form.[3]

Most attempts to characterize these shifts of focus, at both the disciplinary level of geography and at the subdisciplinary level of geographical diffusion studies, have relied in varying degrees upon the concepts used by the historian of science Thomas Kuhn in his research on paradigms and scientific revolutions.[4] The application of his model of scientific revolutions appears to be problematical, however. Among the difficulties are the ambiguous nature of the term "paradigm" and the question of the appropriateness of applying this term to the social sciences in disregard of Kuhn's claims concerning the "preparadigmatic" or "immature" nature of most social sciences.[5]

Despite these difficulties, Kuhn's research has served the positive function of stimulating study of the history and the sociology of science, which has been instrumental in highlighting the gap between the practice of science and normative versions of the nature of science. These studies have recognized the role of such things as epistemology, metaphysics, social norms, and cultural beliefs as important in understanding scientific change. Kuhn has restated his position in arguing that their interrelatedness should be noted but that they can "no longer be discussed as though they are one of a piece."[6] For example, naturalism has been described as the "primal" philosophical problem of the social sciences, but the impact of attempts at its resolution extend beyond philosophical discourse to influence group norms in the practice of science.[7] Social scientists have often responded to periods of disciplinary insecurity by redefining or clarifying the relationship of their disciplines with the more prestigious natural sciences.[8] The major themes in geographic thought, and more specifically in geographic diffusion studies, have both reflected and been supported by such redefinitions.

Environmentalism: Semple's Interpretation of Ratzel

The diffusionist ideas of the nineteenth-century German anthropo-geographer Friedrich Ratzel were introduced to American social science through several different sources, the most prominent of whom were the geographer Ellen Churchill Semple and the anthropologist Franz Boas and his students. The interpretation of Ratzel's work associated with the environmentalism of Semple appears quite different, however, from the interpretation found in the work of Boasian ethnographers. Carl Sauer, an intellectual descendent of both traditions, has explained this discrepancy in suggesting that Semple's work is essentially based upon the first volume of Ratzel's *Anthropogeographie*, a volume concerned with the environmental basis of civilization, whereas the Boasians, especially Sauer's Berkeley colleague Robert Lowie, had recognized a less deterministic Ratzel in volume two, a volume concerned with the topics of migration and diffusion.[9]

Semple's interpretation is most clearly presented in her 1911 work, *Influences of the Geographic Environment*, subtitled *On the Basis of Ratzel's System of Anthropo-Geography*.[10] In this volume, Semple addressed the spread and development of civilization through the movement of peoples driven largely by the forces of nature. The diffusion of ideas and innovations was thus seen in terms of these migrations. The scientific worldview associated with this conceptualization is evident in Semple's claim that the essential point of the Copernican revolution was the view of "a world in motion instead of a world at rest." Anthropogeography concerned itself with the "whole complex relation of unresting man to the earth."[11]

The specific model for such a science was for both Semple and Ratzel the life sciences, especially ideas of evolutionary biology and zoology: "Just as an understanding of animal and plant geography requires a previous knowledge of the various means of dispersal, active and passive, possessed by these lower forms of life, so anthropo-geography must start with a study of the movements of mankind."[12]

Following the lead of Ratzel, Semple identified the goal of anthropogeography as the discovery of natural laws. She credited Ratzel with "placing anthropogeography on a secure scientific basis," when he "first investigated the subject from the modern scientific point of view, constructed his system according to principles of evolution, and based his conclusions on world-wide inductions."[13] She recognized the immaturity of the scientific study of humankind as compared to other sciences, but argued that the laws of anthropogeography were nonetheless "well founded."[14]

Similar to other social scientists who played important roles in the early stages of academic specialization, Semple's discussions of the scientific nature of geography had among its goals the establishment of the scientific credentials of anthropogeography and the delimitation of its conceptual independence through the "carving out" of a distinctive subject matter. Both these functions were served by the identification of a single causal relationship between nature and man. According to Semple such a relationship was infinitely more complex than plant-environment relationships and thus was deserving of independent status from the biological sciences. Also, an anthropogeography based upon this relationship would be a unifying force among the human sciences, which she believed offered only "piecemeal and partial" explanations:

All these sciences, together with history so far as history undertakes to explain causes of events, fail to reach a satisfactory solution of their problems largely because the geographic factor which enters into them all has not been thoroughly analyzed.[15]

The "evolutionary environmentalism" associated with Ratzel and Semple was an extrapolation of evolutionary biology applied to the understanding of cultural differentiation.[16] Anthropogeographers sought mechanisms in the form of natural laws in which causes of cultural variations were found in the surrounding environmental conditions. Model mixed with metaphor in Semple's application of the science of anthropogeography to the Mediterranean as she described an evolutionary scheme in which diffusion played a vital role:

Whatever flower of culture each small region developed in its own garden plot was disseminated over the whole basin by the multitudinous paths of the sea. So varied were the local conditions of temperature, rainfall, soil, relief, area, coastline and vicinal grouping, that each district commanded some peculiar combination of natural advantages in the production of its distinctive contribution to the civilization as the whole. These cultural achievements in turn, transplanted to distant shores, took on new aspects in response to a changed environment or were remodeled by the genius or needs of new masters.[17]

Causal regularities associated with the laws of migration and geographical isolation proposed by Ratzel's teacher Moritz Wagner, as well as the neo-Lamarckian doctrines of the inheritance of acquired traits, were employed to provide the appearance of a scientific foundation for the study of cultural and regional differentiation.

Regional Geography: Sauer and Kniffen

Carl Sauer's cultural geography represented an attempt to carry on the traditions of Ratzel's anthropogeography and its concerns with cultural origins, migration, and diffusion, but at the same time to eliminate what he saw to be the a priori assumptions of his teacher Semple. He condemned the monocausal theories of the previous generations of human geographers, and presented instead the argument that human geography was a science that did not seek natural laws.[18] Sauer was antipositivist in that he condemned the idea of a human science based upon the model of physics, which sought explanations in terms of universal laws, but he was not antinaturalist. He stated that "If the social scientists are naively positivistic, that means only that they have learned badly from natural science."[19]

Sauer's scientific philosophy was an interesting combination of ideas derived from his training in the natural sciences, especially with geologist Rollin Salisbury, and his intellectual contacts with the Boasian ethnographers Robert Lowie and Alfred Kroeber. From the natural scientists, Sauer gained an appreciation for, and training in, natural history, and from the ethnographers he gained an appreciation for the culture history of Ratzel and Eduard Hahn, and for the neo-Kantian interpretation of historical science. He referred to his approach to the social sciences as culture history, and it was this approach that characterized his diffusion research and that of his student Fred Kniffen.

Sauer avoided the use of the term "anthropogeography" to describe his research because of its association with environmentalism, and he used instead the name "cultural geography." His cultural diffusion was much like the approach found in Semple's writing in that his model was drawn from the life sciences and his concern was for understanding the origin and dispersion of cultural artifacts as a basis for understanding areal and cultural differentiation. Unlike Semple, however, he did not see the purpose of such studies as the discovery of the natural laws that explained such differentiation. Also, Sauer removed the study of diffusion and of areal variation of culture from evolutionary environmentalism by detaching cultural origins from the causal mechanisms of environmental adaptation.

The relationship between the life sciences and Sauer's culture history

can be better understood through brief reference to the scientific philosophy of Sauer's Berkeley colleague Alfred Kroeber. Kroeber initially dis-
tanced anthropology from biology in order to more firmly establish the
logical independence of the science of culture, but after having accomplished this goal he once again noted the logical similarities between the
two fields.[20] Many of these similarities were rooted in the neo-Kantianism
of the German philosophers Heinrich Rickert and Wilhelm Windelband,
and their elaboration of the distinction between ideographic and nomothetic concept formation. Kroeber's view on this distinction changed from
originally conceiving of it as a basis for dividing cultural science from natural
science to more appropriately recognizing it as a description of two types of
concept formation found in varying degrees in all sciences.[21]

Contrary to the lore that surrounds the terms "ideographic" and "nomothetic" in geography and other social sciences, these terms did not refer
to distinctions between nature and culture, unique objects and general
objects, or description and explanation. They instead corresponded to a
distinction made concerning the goals of concept formation. Each could be
applied to the same aspects of reality but with differing results. In one case
"value is ascribed to knowledge of the general properties of reality," and in
the second case "value is ascribed to knowledge of its concrete and unique
properties."[22] Causality was a component of each model of concept formation, in the form of causal laws in the nomothetic mode and in the form of
causal sequences of events in the ideographic mode.[23]

The sciences in which the ideographic mode was most evident, according to Kroeber, were the historical sciences; cultural anthropology, geology, and biology. He criticized other social scientists, including his mentor
Boas, for not recognizing that it was the ideographic mode of concept
formation rather than an essential concern for the temporal that characterized the historical sciences:

I am convinced that the essence of the process of historical thought will continue
to fail of being grasped as long as time is considered most important in that
essence. This essence is the characterizing delineation of groups of phenomena
in context, into which both time and space factors enter.[24]

The nomothetic mode of concept formation destroys context in seeking as
its goal universal generalizations.[25]

Kroeber utilized a conception of cause as "formal cause," with which
one studies relationships such as antecedence, similarity, and contrast among
cultural forms.[26] The primary epistemological concerns in discussing cul-

tural forms became those of appropriate description, classification, and the tracing of their origins.[27] This method was similar to what Sauer referred to as the geographic method of seeking clues as to origins and dispersions from the study of distributions.[28] Although Sauer did not concern himself with the specifics of neo-Kantian philosophy, many of the ideas of ideographic concept formation are evident in his work. The goal of cultural geography was the understanding of the origin and dispersion of cultural artifacts in their phenomenal context of period and place. Theory and generalization were viewed in purely instrumental terms as steps in the process of the accumulation of facts about specific cultural forms.

Sauer's student Fred Kniffen has been the most significant contributor to diffusion studies in this culture history tradition. Kniffen describes his work as systematic geography, which, similar to systematics in evolutionary biology, has as its immediate goals accurate description and classification. Systematic geography was seen as a necessary step for the more general goal of regional synthesis. For example, in establishing the significance of his studies of the diffusion of the covered bridge, Kniffen wrote:

> Besides its romantic and antiquarian appeal, to the student of man and his work the covered bridge is a conspicuous detail of the cultural scene. By its presence or absence in a complex of traits it aids the recognition of regions. Knowledge of the origin and diffusion of the covered bridge contributes to an understanding of cultural differentiation.[29]

The model of the relationship of systematic studies, such as diffusion studies, and regional geography was that of biological ecology:

> Initially he [the geographer] studies these two groups of phenomena [natural and human] after the manner of taxonomy. Eventually, as a regional geographer properly grounded in systematic knowledge, he scrutinizes the man-land relations of a specific segment of the world, a procedure analogic to biologic ecology.[30]

Unlike the biologist or the ecologist, however, the problems of description and taxonomy often stretch one's concept of objectivity. For, as Kniffen suggests, cultural mixing poses problems not found in the biological sciences in that biologists do not concern themselves with the possibility of encountering "a tail of a lion grafted to the body of a cow."[31]

This overriding concern with description and classification was part of the impetus behind the spatial analysts' reaction against the regional theme in geography, and they found in the work of the Swedish geographer Torsten Hägerstrand a concrete example of what they perceived to be diffusion studies in the mode appropriate for a modern social science of geography.

Spatial Analysis: Interpretations of Hägerstrand

The diffusion model of Hägerstrand, similar to that of Sauer, can be seen as both a continuation of and a significant break from past traditions. The heritage of his research traces back to Ratzel and his own interest in ethnographic research.[32] In his autobiographical statement Hägerstrand noted the support that he found in what he saw to be the parallel research of Fred Kniffen.[33] Also, Hägerstrand has had a lifelong interest in natural history, biology, and ecology, a fact that I think is important for understanding the trajectory of his research interests, especially his current concern with time-geography. Recognition of these interests allows one to see the shift of his research interests away from explicit diffusion studies as an increase in the depth and breadth of an ongoing research program rather than as a radical change.[34]

This human ecological aspect of Hägerstrand's research has not been well understood in Anglo-American geography. Instead, greatest attention has been paid to the physicalist, reductionist, and quantitative nature of his studies of the spatial structure of diffusion, an emphasis that was due in part to the introduction of his work into the polarized debate in Anglo-American geography during the 1950s and the 1960s between the quantitative spatial-analytic tradition and the qualitative regionalist tradition. The spatial analysts placed emphasis on the differences rather than on the similarities between Hägerstrand's work and that of the cultural tradition because of their view of Sauer as a mandarin of the prescientific traditionalism of regional geography. Also, Sauer's intransigent view of mathematical model builders, as the most recent example of academic evangelists who had plagued twentieth-century American geography with programs that imposed a rationalist orthodoxy on the field, did little to encourage a sense of unity of purpose between the two groups.[35]

The Anglo-American spatial analytic tradition, which provided both an intellectual influence and a receptive audience for Hägerstrand's research, was perceived by its proponents as the vanguard of a modern social science, geography. The explicit philosophical justification for this approach was couched in the language of logical empiricism, in which the goal of all scientific inquiry was explanation involving scientific laws in the form of true, empirical generalizations. Explanation was seen as logically equivalent to prediction, and thus the "pragmatic criterion of predictive success" became the sole criterion of evaluation for such explanations.[36] The predictive success of physics made it the model science against which all others were judged. The reductive, quantitative, and theoretical mode of the physicist was the model employed by the spatial analysts seeking empirical generalizations, explanations, and predictions. It is within this intellectual context that Hägerstrand's approach to diffusion flourished.

Hägerstrand, like other spatial analysts, attempted to construct mathematical models that would provide the means for predicting or retrodicting the spatial spread of innovations. To accomplish this task, he made simplifying assumptions. The rationality of the decision-maker was assumed; the heterogeneity of places was transformed to the homogeneity of space; and the community became a set of discrete individuals linked by a communication system. Access to information was the primary variable and thus space itself became of fundamental importance.[37]

In spite of and, perhaps, because of his ties to earlier diffusionist traditions, Hägerstrand sought to apply the reductionist and mathematical strategies that he found to be so attractive in the philosophy of physicist Arthur Eddington. Also of interest to him was the social physics of the sociologist George Lundberg. Of Lundberg's influence, Hägerstrand wrote:

> By looking at the sentences I underlined in his book, I can easily reconstruct what I picked up with approval from him. Here is one example: "The ends of science are the same in all fields namely, to arrive at verifiable generalizations as to the sequences of events". . . . Today Lundberg's physicalism, behaviorism, positivism, or what you care to call it, may seem naive. But given the cackling in geography this new song sounded lovely in my ear.[38]

This concern with verifiable generalizations of sequences of events underlines the solidly empiricist quality of his work, which often moved from large-scale data collection and analysis to the abstraction of general relationships. Its search for explanation involved the Humean conception of cause as the constant conjunction of events and the belief that the truth of a scientific explanation is dependent upon the existence of such constant conjunctions or laws.

Post-spatial Analysis: Responses to the Hägerstrand Model

It has been suggested that all recent research in geographical diffusion can be interpreted as responses to the Hägerstrand model.[39] The nature of these responses has varied significantly, however. Many critics have sought to increase the complexity of the original model by expanding the number of variables studied and by removing many of the simplifying assumptions, without contradicting the basic empiricist philosophy underlying the model. Others have attacked this philosophical basis. Both groups share a common discontent with the extreme versions of spatial analysis that characterized the Hägerstrand model, in which most social, economic, political, and environmental factors were assumed away for the purpose of considering the spatial patterns of information flows and of innovation adoption. They also share an interest in reemphasizing the contextual elements of the diffusion process.[40]

These concerns are expressed in the words of Peter Gould, one of the pioneers of quantitative diffusion studies in the spatial analytic tradition, who states that the "traditional geographical analogy between particle physics and innovation diffusion has to be discarded." He illustrates this point through an example:

When Portuguese farmers live in small villages, and exchange information over a glass of wine in the evening, we can see how the restricted and unreflective tradition of functional thinking that leads to a least squares estimation of a mean information field actually crushes down, and totally misrepresents, the multidimensional complexity. We also see that innovations, considered as transmitted traffic, must have some structure, some backcloth of face to face communication upon which they can move, and that this geometry of connections will severely shape the actual course of diffusion.[41]

The social structure that Gould refers to is somewhat ambiguous, however, in that the term has been given two quite distinct meanings in geographical research, one as a set of empirical constraints on action and the other as a causally efficacious object. This first view has been evident in the empiricist tradition that works to expand and apply the Hägerstrand model. The second view is part of a nascent realist critique of this empiricist tradition.[42]

Thus far the realist contribution to diffusion studies has been largely programatic, critical of the goals of previous, empiricist diffusion studies.[43] Realists have argued that empiricism presents an incorrect description of the nature of science. They argue that scientific explanation is causal explanation, yet cause is not to be viewed in the Humean sense of the constant conjunction of empirical events but rather as residing in the nature of the object itself, as the causal power of the object to produce change. Within this view of science a causal explanation does not require universal generalizations or laws, and need not allow one to predict the occurrence of future events. Thus, criticism of Hägerstrand's diffusion studies is directed at the overemphasis upon the search for universal generalizations concerning spatial form, and at the neglect of the more causally significant aspects of the interplay between human agency and social structure.[44] The call is for a greater contextualization of diffusion processes, but the framework used for the argument is once again the issue of naturalism.

Conclusion

This brief overview of twentieth-century geographical diffusion studies has illustrated the relationships among the philosophy of science, human geography, and diffusion theory. It has questioned the accuracy of viewing such diffusion studies as part of a progressive, twentieth-century march from a prescientific past to a scientific present. Also, it has contradicted those arguments that have characterized diffusion studies as moving between the two poles of a scientific and a humanistic geography. Rather, members of the various diffusionist traditions in human geography have sought to present their research in accordance with the prevailing norms concerning the nature of social science. Changes in the diffusionist tradition reflect changes in these norms. Such an epistemological history provides a coherence to a seemingly disorderly tradition, but it does not address questions concerning the mechanisms of change and persistence.

Why do the norms guiding research in the social sciences seem to change with greater rapidity than do similar norms in the natural sciences? Why do these norms take on the particular form that they do? Why have the questions concerning diffusion persisted throughout the century as important research questions? How closely can this continued significance be linked to issues of practical utility associated with concerns of colonialism, nationalism, and the expansion of markets?[45]

Answers to such questions would contribute further to a contextual interpretation of diffusionism. In order to make sense of the history of diffusionism in geography and of the plurality of diffusionist traditions that currently coexist, one must recognize the manner in which basic cultural beliefs such as those concerning the nature of science infuse questions of significance, theory, and method.

Notes

1. See Lawrence Brown, *Innovation Diffusion: A New Perspective* (New York: Methuen, 1981).

2. See Roy Bhaskar, *The Possibility of Naturalism: A Philosophical Critique of Contemporary Human Sciences* (Atlantic Highlands, N.J.: Humanities Press, 1979); David Thomas, *Naturalism and Social Science: A Post-Empiricist Philosophy of Social Science* (Cambridge: Cambridge University Press, 1979).

3. See John Agnew, "Instrumentalism, Realism, and Research on the Diffusion of Innovation," *Professional Geographer* 31 (1979): 364–70; Piers Blaikie, "The Theory of the Spatial Diffusion of Innovations: A Spacious Cul de Sac," *Progress in Human Geography* 2 (1978): 268–95; James Blaut, "Two Views of Diffusion," *Annals*, Association of American Geographers, 67 (1977): 343–49; Peter Gould, "Statistics and Human Geography: Historical, Philosophical, and Algebraic Reflections," in G. Gaile and C. Willmott, eds., *Spatial Statistics and Models* (Dordrecht: Reidel, 1984), pp. 17–32; Derek Gregory, "Suspended Animation: The Stasis of Diffusion Theory," in Derek Gregory and J. Urry, eds., *Social Relations and Spatial Structures* (London: MacMillan, 1984), pp. 296–336; Avinoam Meir, "Spatial-Humanistic Perspective of Innovation Diffusion Processes," *Geoforum* 13 (1982): 57–68.

4. See Thomas Kuhn, *The Structure of Scientific Revolutions*, 2nd ed. (Chicago: University of Chicago Press, 1970); Mark Billinge et al., "Reconstructions," in Mark Billinge et al., eds., *Recollections of a Revolution: Geography as Spatial Science* (London: MacMillan, 1984), pp. 3–24; R. J. Johnston, *Geography and Geographers: Anglo-American Human Geography since 1945* (New York: Wiley, 1979); Brown, *Innovation Diffusion*; David R. Stoddart, "Ideas and Interpretation in the History of Geography," in David R. Stoddart, ed., *Geography, Ideology, and Social Concern* (Oxford: Blackwell, 1981), pp. 1–7.

5. See Barry Barnes, *T. S. Kuhn and Social Science* (London: MacMillan, 1982); Margaret Masterman, "The Nature of Paradigm," in Imre Lakatos and Alan Musgrave, eds., *Criticism and the Growth of Knowledge* (Cambridge: Cambridge University Press, 1970); David Thomas, *Naturalism*.

6. Kuhn, *Structure of Scientific Revolutions*, p. 182.

7. See Bhaskar, *Possibility of Naturalism*.

8. See Henrika Kuklick, "Boundary Maintenance in American Sociology: Limitations to Academic 'Professionalization,'" *Journal of the History of the Behavioral Sciences* 16 (1980): 201–19.

9. Robert Lowie, *The History of Ethnological Theory* (New York: Farrar and Rinehart, 1937).

10. Ellen Churchill Semple, *Influences of Geographic Environment: On the Basis of Ratzel's System of Anthropo-Geography* (New York: Holt, 1911).

11. Ibid., pp. 79–80.

12. Ibid., p. 80.

13. Ibid., p. v.

14. Ibid., p. vii.

15. Ibid., p. 2.

16. See J. A. Campbell and D. N. Livingstone, "Neo-Lamarckism and the Development of Geography in the United States and Britain," *Transactions*, Institute of British Geographers, new series, vol. 8 (1983): 267–94.

17. Ellen Churchill Semple, *The Geography of the Mediterranean Region: Its Relation to Ancient History* (New York: Holt, 1931), pp. 9–10.

18. See four studies by Carl Sauer: "The Morphology of Landscape," *University of California Publications in Geography* 2 (1925): 19–54; "Recent Developments in Cultural Geography," in E. C. Hayes, ed., *Recent Developments in the Social Sciences* (Philadelphia: Lippincott, 1927), pp. 154–212; "Regional Reality in Economy" (1936), Sauer Papers, Bancroft Library, Berkeley, California; "Foreword to Historical Geography," *Annals*, Association of American Geographers, 31 (1941): 1–24.

19. Carl Sauer, Letter to Joseph Willits, Dec. 18, 1947, Sauer Papers, Bancroft Library, Berkeley, California.

20. See George W. Stocking, Jr., *Race, Culture, and Evolution* (New York: Free Press, 1968).

21. See David Bidney, *Theoretical Anthropology* (New York: Columbia University Press, 1953).

22. Guy Oakes, "Translator's Note," *History and Theory* 19 (1980): 165–68.

23. See Wilhelm Windelband, "History and Natural Science," *History and Theory* 19 (1980): 169–85; Thomas Burger, *Max Weber's Theory of Concept Formation* (Durham, N.C.: Duke University Press, 1976).

24. Alfred Kroeber, *The Nature of Culture* (Chicago: University of Chicago Press, 1952), p. 102.

25. Ibid., p. 101.

26. Ibid., p. 107.

27. See Eric Wolf, "Alfred Kroeber," in Sydel Silverman, ed., *Totems and Teachers* (New York: Columbia University Press, 1981), pp. 35–55.

28. Sauer, "Foreword to Historical Geography."

29. Fred Kniffen, "The American Covered Bridge," *Geographical Review* 41 (1951): 114.

30. Fred Kniffen, "The Physiognomy of Rural Louisiana," in H. J. Walker and M. B. Newton, eds., *Environment and Culture* (Baton Rouge: Department of Geography and Anthropology, Louisiana State University, 1978), p. 199.

31. Fred Kniffen, "Louisiana House Types," *Annals*, Association of American Geographers, 26 (1936): 180; W. G. Runciman, *A Treatise on Social Theory: The Methodology of Social Theory*, vol. 1 (Cambridge: Cambridge University Press, 1983).

32. See Torsten Hägerstrand, "In Search for the Sources of Concepts," in A. Buttimer, ed., *The Practice of Geography* (New York: Longman, 1983), pp. 238–56; Allan Pred, "Postscript," in Torsten Hägerstrand, *Innovation Diffusion as a Spatial Process* (Chicago: University of Chicago Press, 1967), pp. 299–324.

33. Hägerstrand, "In Search."

34. See Torsten Hägerstrand, "Ecology under One Perspective," in E. Bylund et al., eds., *Ecological Problems of the Circumpolar Area* (Lulea, Sweden: Norrbottens Museum, 1974), pp. 271–76.

35. See J. Nicholas Entrikin, "Carl O. Sauer: Philosopher in Spite of Himself," *Geographical Review* 74 (1984): 387–408.

36. See Mary Hesse, *Revolutions and Reconstructions in the Philosophy of Science* (Bloomington: University of Indiana Press, 1980).

37. Hägerstrand, *Innovation Diffusion*, p. 6.

38. Hägerstrand, "In Search," pp. 247–48.

39. Brown, *Innovation Diffusion*.

40. See Blaikie, "Theory of Spatial Diffusion"; Blaut, "Two Views"; Brown,

Innovation Diffusion; Tommy Carlstein, *Time Resources, Society and Ecology: On the Capacity for Human Interaction in Space and Time*, vol. 1, *Preindustrial Societies* (London: George Allen and Unwin, 1982); Gregory, "Suspended Animation"; Meir, "Spatial-Humanistic Vision."

41. Gould, "Statistics and Human Geography," p. 23.

42. See Bhaskar, *Possibility of Naturalism*; Andrew Sayer, *Method in Social Science: A Realist Approach* (London: Hutchinson, 1984).

43. See Agnew, "Instrumentalism, Realism, and Research"; Gregory, "Suspended Animation."

44. See Gregory, "Suspended Animation."

45. See James Blaut, "Diffusionism: A Uniformitarian Critique," paper presented at the 25th International Geographical Congress, Paris, France, 1984.

CHAPTER NINE

Why Diffusion?

Philip L. Wagner

When an innovation is diffused, it is *communicated*. Not all communication is diffusion, however: only the latter implies repeated retransmissions of the message by receivers. Hence both its necessary properties and limitations as a process of communication, and the special conditions governing the actions of transmission and retransmission, together must construct the explanation of diffusion.

Universals of Communication

Current terminology is, like most communication, redundant, for not only diffusion, but any and all communication induces innovation or novelty.[1] An increment of information is by definition presupposed. Necessarily, communicative acts can be recognized only when some behavior of one party, the sender or transmitter, induces a detectable change, a response, on the part of another party, the receiver. Communication always constitutes a *dyadic* performance, or an indefinitely large set of parallel and sometimes simultaneous dyadic performances. At least one specific receiver must respond in some complementary fashion to the signal or message of a given sender. Only thus may the fact of a completed communicative event be established; any single receiver or respondent is relevant. Individuals always necessarily acquire sensory input *alone* and idiosyncratically, through their own bodily receptors and under locational and biographical circumstances (a perceptual screen) peculiar to each.

Furthermore, in order for a given transmission reliably to elicit a particular response, and therefore to exert a determinate effect upon receivers, the sender must *encode* it in such a way that it elicits, programs, or frames a small, finite set of possible elective responses. But, although essential, encoding only sets the stage for systematic communication. The interactive performance, according to a principle of biological economy, must not only convey (new) information to the receiver but also reward the sender with informative feedback, otherwise the effort of transmission would amount to a perilous and pointless prodigality of energy, and in the long run be disadvantageous to survival. Thus, in the completed dyadic interchange definitive of communication, an element of novelty must in here as well in the response as in transmission, and pure "one-way" communication must be seen as a contradiction in terms. This allows the inference that any communicative system incorporates a guarantee and requirement of some *freedom* of action for both dyad partners.

Encoded messages constitute at most an infinitesimal part of the flow of stimuli impinging on the senses. Thus, to the idiosyncracies of the particular receiver must be added all the concurrent sensory input from environmental sources, which will tend to modify and particularize *interpretation* of a coded message. The original message passes through a whole series of filters, or constraint processes, minimally including reduction to code form, the mechanics of transmission activity, perceptual detection by a receiver, code decipherment, and contextual evaluation. Additionally, inescapable random distortion or noise inheres in any of the filtering systems.

The minimal condition for communication of any sort is appropriation of a *channel* over which some novel message content may pass relatively intact, despite the inevitable attrition imposed by all these constant processes. A channel conforms, of course, to the dyadic form: it must successfully connect a given sender with some receiver in whom the message induces a response, although the identity of the particular receiver may be relatively inconsequential beyond species and social relationship. The availability of suitable channels may not suffice, however, to insure that a single code specification of each constituent information element of the total message will invariably penetrate through all the constraining screens mentioned. Hence a property of *redundancy* or duplicative encoding may reiterate many of those elements within a single message. Even the simultaneous employment of multiple channels may serve this function, but it may also introduce incompatible content items because of the resulting disparate filtering processes affecting different modes of transmission and reception.

The Human Communicator

The fundamental universals of communication just briefly outlined are all directly germane to diffusion. Certainly peculiarities of codes potentially, and in part distinctively, available to human communicators further characterize the cultural diffusion process. Absolutely any source of *controllable contrast* in sensory stimulus may furnish a basis for an operating code. The code must enable a sender freely and repeatedly to generate specific patterns incorporating novelty, which can attain a receiver's awareness. The repertoire of acts and objects potentially suited to this vicarious use is only limited by the capacity of a species to isolate, systematize, and operate such a code. Almost any ordered set of stimuli will do. However, throughout the animal kingdom communication codes tend to depend closely on bodily functions and features, constituted into various but not very numerous signifying *displays*, and the message content they are called on to transmit remains restricted to a few themes.[2] In the human case, the possibilities of code construction and employment much increase.

Any behavior, enacted as display, may lend itself to encoding and serve a communicative function. In particular the activity carried out by means of the "forward" regions of the human body enters heavily into encoded communicative behavior. The versatility developed in the human face, vocal tract, and auditory system, hands and arms, serves greatly to enhance transmission and receipt of information in the visual, aural, tactile, and even kinesthetic channels. Not only does the density of discriminate sensory events increase the range of controllable stimulus generation and capture, but manipulative propensities make possible the skilful creation of objects—artifacts—that may themselves serve to present communication. Artifacts as code components play a singularly fateful role in human social intercourse.

The second potentiating feature consists of a unique combinatorial capacity enabling human beings, in what seems an utterly unique development, to encode simultaneously on two levels, using the same set of natural code elements. Not only can human beings present action or artifact displays in concurrent arrangements—what Leroi-Gourhan calls "graphemes"[3] —but through systematic lineal, sequential ordering of individual elements, such as words or graphic units, they can secure the opportunity for encoding message content into the actual sequence of constituent elements, the *syntax*. The former, "analog" communicative option is thus powerfully supplemented, but by no means replaced, by a "digital" one.[4] The digital, syntactical mode of communication makes it possible to go beyond ostentive (demonstrative and evocative) performance and to encode *propositional* or declarative statements including contingent, transtemporal, extralocal, and even negative ones.

To sum up: members of our species possess particularly efficient means of producing and perceiving encoded displays, as well as a distinctive ability to create codable artifactual displays. Furthermore, they may so combine some of the basic units as to constitute them into superordinated syntactical *statements of relation*.

Social Interaction

But although the digital mode may superficially seem the more spectacular, the outstanding communicative achievement of humans probably lies in the elaboration of analog display in partial fusion or conjunction with the digital. The proliferation of artifactual codes richly implementing determinate sequences of analog display that, as *rituals*, become themselves syntactical, institutes an integrative framework for intensive *social interaction*. Authorities have commonly attributed development of artifacts to an ecological or utilitarian imperative, considering the survival or adaptive value of objects invented and used by human beings to lie primarily in such livelihood roles as defense and especially "production." Marx made the most inspired, but by no means the only or the last statement of this position. Most technologists, economists, archeologists, ethnologists, and even philosophers continue to subscribe to it. However, several astute recent critiques have called it into question.[5]

No doubts need attach to the assertion that artifactual creations of all kinds enter into communication, and even do so in a regular, sequential, syntactical way.[6] The ubiquity of explicit manufactured signs and guiding structures provides the indispensable contexts for our action and interaction. How many more concrete objects and spatial arrangements we learn from, are guided by, and conform to than we actually use ourselves in any productive fashion! Everything human-made around us can be "meaningful" to us, but little of the totality is immediately useful to our work or our defense.

In ritual proceedings or "formalized interactions" both artifact display and vocal or gestural utterances, together in syntactical composites, program human (and some animal) behavior.[7] As communication, please recall, this programing permits and requires a degree of freedom for each participant. As Goffman has convincingly argued, a large portion of human encounter behavior falls into astonishingly orderly, rituallike formats.[8] Investigation of the use of language, too, has revealed an overwhelming regularity in procedure, exposed for example in conversational "turn-taking" analysis and speech-act analysis.[9] The role of artifacts in such interaction has not so far come in for much comment, although the function of nonverbal bodily behavior has.[10] It is only just to postulate that artifactual displays—sometimes in prescribed sequence, as in ritual—enter fully into human communicative interactions, too. In summary, the artifactual order necessarily takes part constantly in both our organized behavior in general and our informal and formalized interactions with other persons. From this hardly debatable notion, one may infer certain more surprising consequences.

Geltung

Given an immense range of behavioral and artifactual components for communicative codes that may function simultaneously on two levels, human individuals can interact as eminently social beings. The conduct of their interactions always itself appears conformal to some "code" or set of prescriptive or at least interpretable rules. The order of interaction thus confers a particular communicative role or function on each participant at any given moment. One individual initiates, another attends; one transmits, the other receives—in a regular progression of phased and complementary performances. In order for communication to proceed, this systematic *alternation* must occur, so that it effects a reciprocal exchange of information. But the process shows another crucial feature: the *initiative* in opening and concluding such dialog depends on factors other than those regulating the alternating performances themselves. The motive agencies of cultural diffusion are those concerned with these initiatives.

Communicative initiative manifests itself in two forms: *attention* and *elicitation*. Study of both animal and human interactions has revealed discrete and characteristic structures of behavior under which particular individuals in a group differentially command attention from their fellows under given circumstances. Other aspects of a social order generally tend to reflect subsisting attention patterns.[11] Not every individual may casually enter into dialog with any other. The familiar concepts of rank and dominance accord with this fact. Specific attributes of certain individuals, such as age, sex, bodily size, and strength, ornamentation, vitality, aggressiveness, and venturesomeness seem to predispose them to attract and hold attention.

Not only do some individuals in comparatively social species dominate attention, but they, or perhaps different individuals otherwise endowed with certain traits, enjoy the prerogative of setting the agenda for interactions, providing *cues* that frame the interlocutor's response within a given range of alternatives. This frame constitutes a feature of all communicative acts, for any sender automatically narrows the receiver's options to conform to a pattern imposed by the initial message and its terms. A question demands a relevant answer; an order calls for either compliance or defiance; a declaration evokes assent or dissent. Successive speech acts, and no doubt display acts as well, thus specify definite programs of articulating cues and responding choices.

But even apart from the initiative in opening such interactions, the privilege of dictating particular cues or formulating given options of response belongs in many cases, permanently or temporarily, to only one of the dyad partners. Not everyone, for instance, will command just any partner; certain kinds of questions may be posed, and even some sorts of declarations made, by one but not the other. Both the differential role in initiating and managing dialog, as well as the focusing of attention, depend on a potential in the individual that I shall call *Geltung*, using a German word signifying worthiness, respect, prestige, standing, importance, or validity, for which no close equivalent seems to occur in English; Habermas makes much of it.[12] *Geltung* contrasts differentiate and structure our societies and consequently help manage human interactions.

The qualities of individuals as registered on other persons, such as the primitive attributes mentioned above, all compelling attention, may further confer effective *Geltung*. But *Geltung*, a *control* employed in communication, may itself derive directly as well from communicative events. In fact, it appears reasonable to assume that an enormous portion of all human communication, and the provision made of means for it, revolves around *Geltung*, and represents attempts to secure, maintain, and continually test it. Hence one may assert that most human communication is *about* communication.

Communicative activity thus involves the capture of attention, the initiation of dialog, and the prescription of successive response options, and employs not only language but a host of bodily gestures and an infinity of artifactual devices. The social effects obtained necessarily involve, first, a reaching out of each person to others and, secondly, the exercise by individuals of some control over the form and import, although not the intrinsic content, of the discourse roles of others. These effects do not means quite the same as "power," as usually understood, and indeed may figure far more significantly in human relations than does actual compulsion or inescapable command. Yet in some circumstances hierarchical distinctions can result.

Among prescriptions governing performance of communicative acts may count a special class involving retransmission of a message. A speech act may of course enjoin another speech act or its counterpart in gesture or in artifactual manipulation. On such a basis, it becomes easy to envision genuine diffusion processes arising out of given interactions. The propagation, in this way or just spontaneously, of particular innovations over spatially dispersed populations may in addition both feed upon and foster *Geltung*, for proposers or sources of a message may both exploit and enhance their *Geltung* in transmitting it, and those receiving it in turn derive new *Geltung* from appropriation of the innovation, which thereafter they may similarly propagate. The network of encounters over which diffusion passes thus assumes, schematically, the form of a directed graph, with differential *Geltung* orienting flows. The progress of successive messages involved may in this case depend heavily on *Geltung* embodied in material, artifactual forms.

Effects of human communicative activity include a copious production of artifacts that may serve as code devices, and specifically as sources of *Geltung*, as well as the establishment of appropriate spatial and temporal arrangements, conjoined at times in ritual, to serve similar ends. As intimated above, one may suppose that such a motivation, rather than defensive and utilitarian productive ones, may best explain inveterate inventiveness and the accelerating modification of environments throughout the history of humankind. Even if our growing artificiality has so far proven tremendously advantageous ecologically, this may betoken nothing more than fortuitous, if fortunate, side effects ensuing from communicative elaborations. Granted, such a thesis rings more nearly true when taken as applying to an individual's life efforts than when measured against a general, impersonal, and aggregative summary of history. Today, a generation after the appearance of *Man's Role in Changing the Face of the Earth*,[13] one may permissibly conceive of the great transformation as serving other motivations than material production, and regard our ecological ascendancy as derivative of and dependent on developments in human communication—that is, cultural diffusion.

Models and Histories

Although cultural diffusion submits to profitable study as the realization of an idealized process,[14] it likewise necessarily deserves investigation as a long progression of concrete, unique, contingent episodes in human development. The ideal models necessarily confront a culture history. Culture history can reconstruct origins and dispersals, and discern the hearths of innovation and the pathways of diffusion.[15] It can even proffer insights into the mechanisms operating in these processes.[16] But, partaking of the character of history in general, it cannot provide formal process models or predictive universals.

The abstract models and the concrete record may converge, however, in some crucial moments in the history of the species, about which fruitful, possibly falsifiable, conjectures become feasible. The strongest evidence available for critiques of either the accounts of culture history or the propositions of the abstract formal process models, or both, must come from either human paleontology and archeology, on the one hand, or human biology and ecology, on the other. This situation authorizes reflection on some necessities and probabilities impinging on early human social development and especially communicative behavior.

In reconstructing the early stages of human communication, some degree of continuity with the communicative activities of higher animals deserves recognition. Notoriously, human beings employ gestural vocabularies only slightly more elaborate than and still homologous with those observable in many animals. Even more opposite, the particularly close and continual intercommunication and caretaking manifest in relationships between mother and offspring in humans, most other mammals, and even birds, merit notice. To anticipate a little, the hypothesis advanced herein will hold that parent-offspring interaction of a special, necessary kind has given rise to the entire pattern of social communication observable in later humankind—which underlies and essentially constitutes diffusion.

Caretaking

Begin with the brain. *Homo sapiens sapiens* takes longer to achieve cerebral maturity than any other species. The allometric ratios of brain-to-bodily-development are such that the human brain, growing and elaborating continuously for up to half a lifetime, much outstrips those of all other creatures in its final volume and complexity[17]—perhaps with an exception for some cetaceans. It does not suffice simply to assume that this enshrines a high intelligence, which thereupon takes over responsibility for whatever other advantages the species has acquired. That calls for too much special pleading for our "cognitive" endowments. Rather, certain other implications suggest themselves.

The protracted period of human brain development and, notably, of immaturity and partial incompetence, encompasses a time of rapid growth in body size, strength, and physical mobility. The young can wander freely and get into mischief long before they possess a fully ripened brain and nervous system that can process environmental information and respond to it properly. Humans are immensely vulnerable creatures for their first fifteen years.

In most mammals, intensive maternal caretaking, sometimes shared with other conspecifics, covers the interval until the young cerebroneural systems have matured, but this occurs in a very short time, even in most primates.[18] Human mothers confer the same sort of zealous care as other mothers, but they have to keep on doing so for many years, contending with increasingly inquisitive, agile, mobile, and elusive offspring. A human one-year-old can move around enough to get lost anywhere within a range of a few acres surrounding the home-based mother. A ten-year-old's locomotor aptitudes permits it to disappear anywhere within a range of some one or two thousand square miles, and a fifteen-year-old can vanish halfway around the world. Some reliable communication must come in if the young are to be protected!

Communication as a control on infant indiscretion, then, can provide an explanation for the survival of the young of a species like the human, so vulnerable because of protracted cerebral immaturity in the face of all the environmental hazards lurking within its extensive mobility range. The parent brain acts as surrogate for the deficient juvenile brain in the processing of information. Two key aspects of the communication that allows this require comment: the channels selected and the interactional framework of cues and choices controlling message traffic.

Evolutionary Steps

Intimate relationships between the very young and parent animals depend upon physical proximity. Olfactory or visual signs mobilize offspring to cluster near the mother, and auditory signals may maintain closeness. Similar sense-stimuli induce the mother to attend the young. The episode of caretaking tends to end after a short period of weeks or months, and then the young can operate competently on their own. As just explained, however, human offspring long continue in dependency because of their neurocerebral immaturity, and human parents go on furnishing attentive care for many years. Infants soon acquire locomotive skills and strength enabling them to venture out of sight and out of touch of mothers, and no form of "imprinting" in humans seems to endure long enough to inhibit this wandering after the first few years of life.[19] In environments replete with challenges, attractions, mysteries—and perils—mobility of offspring fosters learning but brings risks. The parent may monitor and to some extent control the offspring's activities at a distance if provided with a suitable communication link. Had the species no such faculty, its net survival probabilities would have sunk to zero in short order.

Communication must find channels not depending on proximity; tactile and kinesthetic modes do not avail. The olfactory mode does not facilitate messages, in the ordinary sense, at all, but carries only signs generated by spontaneous, physiological processes. It simply does not lend itself to syntactical ordering, and cannot formulate the needed kind of true communicative messages even though it carries over distance. Visual signals, on the other hand, offer an effective, codable, long-range mode, as long as the environment interposes no substantial obstacles. However, most of the environments of both early and modern humankind interfere with direct, protracted, visual monitoring. This leaves only the auditory mode to serve in caretaking at a distance. The vocal-aural channel, of necessity, becomes the vital link.

However speech arose—and countless speculations exist about its origins[20]—it seems reasonable to suppose that greater virtuosity and versatility in human vocalization became positively selected at some juncture when the very survival of the species demanded dramatic improvements in communication. As here conceived, that moment may well have coincided with the emergence of delayed cerebral maturation. This would, admittedly, project some form of language backward into very early times, a million or more years ago, perhaps by the era of *Homo erectus*.[21] Gestural, analog communication, well developed in the human species as in many others, goes along with vocalization, but the latter mode may gradually have assumed the full burden of transmission, and somehow in so doing acquired a lineal and programed digital structure—syntax. The partial shift from analog to digital would mark the crucial adaptive change—a shift, of course, by no means completed even yet. Only such an acquisition would safely permit the momentous further evolution of the brain.

Dependable two-way communication over distance, essential to the prolonged caretaking stage, demanded an additional evolutionary advance. The members of the species must, inevitably, operate under a program insuring (biologically) obligate participation in dialog exchange. Such a trait can rest on nothing else than an *innate* genetic basis. The well-known thesis of innate linguistic competence tacitly presupposes an even more fundamental underlying innate predisposition to linguistic activity as such, to continual communicative interaction.[22] As an innate behavioral program, the powerful urge to communicate, seek social integration, and *reach out* to others amounts to one of the most definitive sources of human motivation. It corresponds to the insights of poets, philosophers, and prophets, and figures as the prototypical instance of a pervading "altruism" contributing to inclusive fitness. It founds our social universe.

Social Evolution

Only populations bonded and coordinated in all habitual activities by communicative processes may count as true *societies*. This promotes the ants and bees and termites to such a distinction, alongside humankind. Colonial animals, although intimately bounded together in behavior, do not utilize communication, in its common sense, for bonding, but depend on physiological mechanisms for it. And even hymenopterans employ a very different, chemical mode of communicative exchange, akin almost to physiological control. So human beings present a most distinctive kind of sociality.

The comprehensive integration of societies in humankind appears to follow necessarily from innately obligate parent-offspring exchange using language, because if human individuals draw motivation from such programing, it must manifest itself not only in each child and present parent, but in anyone who could become a parent. And thus it must continue both before and throughout reproductive life, at least. Thus provided with an "urge" to interact communicatively, normal healthy human beings irrepressibly reach out to their fellows, and exceptions to this clearly constitute pathologies or sublimations.

The devices entering the human dialog have developed far beyond linguistic utterance to take in everything encodable. This fact, in view of what is here proposed, warrants an interpretation of the progress of humanity as advance in communicativeness, in sociality, instead of primarily as a march toward ecological dominance as such. It intimates that whatever adaptive advantages, technical virtuosities, or economic benefits ensued along our evolutionary path arose as secondary, though still fateful, consequences of the social and communicative developments in the species. Further, it identifies a motivation system still inspiring exploration and invention, yet not rooted in some supposed form of rational adaptive calculation or a "cognitive" appreciation of ecology and natural phenomena, now allegedly growing out of fortunate mythologies and superstitions and somehow leading to triumphant rationality and earthly mastery. Under the present interpretation, human beings became ecological dominants and economic managers in the course of evolving into uniquely social creatures, bonded in communication.

Diffusion represents a major aspect to this development, one that contributes to *worldwide species unity*—another striking biological peculiarity.

And Now Diffusion

The cultural diffusion process depends intrinsically upon communication episodes. Innovation, present in every given exchange, becomes propagated through repeated presentations and responses, serially extending out over space and time. The opportunity for transmitting an (always innovative) message with success depends upon the *Geltung* of its sender compared with that of the recipient. That *Geltung* quantum may in turn previously have accrued to the sender through the latter's acceptance of some other innovative message, through social learning. The receiver of a message may, in due course, harvest further *Geltung* from adoption of the innovation thus presented. The diffusion process, in other words, operates under the regulation of initiatives and elicitation by individual *Geltung*. Some previous writers, such as Rogers, have dimly perceived this principle but not generalized it;[23] and even Malinowski's observations of the Melanesian Kula Ring in a way epitomizes it.[24]

Both the sources and the manifestations of *Geltung* become very often concretized in certain spatial relationships. Much diffusion—of everyday innovations, to be sure; that is, of decision, judgment, working directives, definitions, and routine awards of exchange value—takes place under those relationships as instituted. The huge majority of diffusions are prosaic, predictable communications within institutional, usually hierarchical, social forms. Academics seem to cherish some sort of morbid interest in the more aberrant kind of diffusions, those gone a little wild, that jump the traces, as it were.

The conspicuous hierarchical structures of human societies appear to be almost entirely imposed by the spatial and temporal contexts of serial activities linked together in specific sequences through communication. Ritual, in the narrow sense, presents a case in point. Appraising any regular activity, circumstantially framed in a fixed space-time progression of steps, as subject to initiatives exercised by the preceding stages of the overall performance, a spontaneous construction of hierarchical relationships as spatio-temporal priorities becomes evident. If natural or artificial features of location, such as resources, dictate the order of the steps in a complex procedure, they will also tend to apportion control in the forms of initiative and elicitation prerogatives inherent in relative positions in the series.

As Marx pointed out, hierarchy in human life, although a highly complex matter, has to do with control of the means of production. This carries more conviction than does the hypothesis of its origin in aggression.[25] In order to grasp the implications of the insight fully, though, it behooves us to take heed of the fact that any step in production of any sort represents control of the means of production available to the operatives at the next and succeeding steps. Even more important, production should not refer primarily to goods and services in the sense of absolute material acts or objects, whether completed or being prepared, but rather to the communicative import of such acts and objects, and all dialog of any kind connected with them.

Hierarchy becomes, when thus assessed, an understandable property of a social system, reflecting natural and artificial space and time constraints. It works to differentiate human dialog, apportion and exploit *Geltung* and, among other things, generate and stabilize diffusion processes.

Although instances of intersocietal diffusion occur much less frequently than ordinary institutional transformations within societies, they are surely the more arresting and intriguing. In diffusions, too, normal communication processes play their usual role, if often under considerable impediments. Here, too, *Geltung* contrasts become no doubt decisive. Perhaps because such exceptional diffusion events amount to something like "great leaps" across cultural gaps, their role in history becomes portentous.

In the intersocietal case, but to a fair degree in the more routine episodes within societies as well, the spatio-temporal manifestations of the diffusion of innovations show logistical constraints other than those of hierarchy. Topographic barriers, linguistic incompatibilities, technological disparities, and so on, help to shape the patterns. There exist a multitude of obstructions and complications that partially frustrate and constrain their efforts but, biologically constituted through a long and special evolution to behave in a certain way, human beings *will* communicate and they *will* diffuse their messages among their fellows despite all hindrances.

Notes

1. See Colin Cherry, *On Human Communication: A Review, a Survey, and a Criticism* (Cambridge: MIT Press, 1957).
2. See John W. Smith, *The Behavior of Communication: An Ethological Approach* (Cambridge: Harvard University Press, 1956).
3. André Leroi-Gourhan, *Le geste et la parole*: vol. 1, *Technique et langage*; vol. 2, *La mémoire et les rhythmes* (Paris: Albin Michel, 1964–65).
4. See Anthony Wilden, *System and Structure: Essays in Communication and Exchange* (New York: Harper and Row, 1972).
5. Marshall D. Sahlins, *Culture and Practical Reason* (Chicago: University of Chicago Press, 1976); Mary T. Douglas, *The World of Goods: Towards an Anthropology of Consumption* (London: A. Lane, 1979); and especially Jean Baudrillard, *For a Critique of Political Economy of the Sign* (St. Louis: Telos, 1981).
6. Claude Lévi-Strauss, *Structural Anthropology* (New York: Basic Books, 1963); *The Raw and the Cooked* (New York: Harper and Row, 1969).
7. Smith, *Behavior of Communication*.
8. See four works by Erving Goffman: *The Presentation of Self in Everyday Life* (New York: Doubleday, 1959); *Interaction Ritual: Essays on Face-to-Face Behavior* (Chicago: Aldine, 1967); *Strategic Interaction* (Philadelphia: University of Pennsylvania Press, 1969); *Frame Analysis: An Essay on the Organization of Experience* (New York: Harper and Row, 1974).
9. See Martin Schwab, *Redehandeln: Eine institutionelle Sprechakttheorie* (Königstein, Taunus: Hain, 1980); John R. Searle, *Speech Acts: An Essay in the Philosophy of Language* (London: Cambridge University Press, 1969).
10. See Ray L. Birdwhistell, *Kinesics and Context: Essays on Body Motion Communication* (Philadelphia: University of Pennsylvania Press, 1970).
11. See Michael R. A. Chance, *Social Groups of Monkeys, Apes, and Men* (New York: Dutton, 1970).

12. Jürgen Habermas, *Theory and Practice* (Boston: Beacon, 1973).

13. William L. Thomas, ed., *Man's Role in Changing the Face of the Earth* (Chicago: University of Chicago Press, 1956).

14. See Torsten Hägerstrand, *Innovation Diffusion as a Spatial Process*, postscript and translation by Allan Pred (Chicago: University of Chicago Press, 1967).

15. See Carl O. Sauer, *Agricultural Origins and Dispersals* (New York: American Geographical Society, 1952).

16. See Alfred L. Kroeber, *The Nature of Culture* (Berkeley: University of California Press, 1952).

17. See John T. Bonner, *The Evolution of Culture in Animals* (Princeton, N.J.: Princeton University Press, 1980).

18. See Martin P. Richards, ed., *Integration of a Child into a Social World* (London: Cambridge University Press, 1974).

19. See Konrad Lorenz, *The Foundations of Ethology* (New York: Springer Verlag, 1981).

20. See Roger N. Wescott, ed., *Language Origins* (Silver Spring, Md.: Linstock, Hewes, Gordon, 1974).

21. See Harry J. Jerison, *Evolution of the Brain and Intelligence* (New York: Academic Press, 1973).

22. See Noam Chomsky, *Syntactic Structures* (The Hague: Mouton, 1957); Noam Chomsky, *Reflections on Language* (New York: Pantheon, 1975).

23. See Everett M. Rogers, *Diffusion of Innovations*, 3rd ed. (New York: Free Press, 1983).

24. See Bronislaw Malinowski, *Argonauts of the Western Pacific* (New York: Dutton, 1961).

25. See Lorenz, *Foundations of Ethology*.

CHAPTER TEN

Abilities, Skills, Competence
A SEARCH FOR ALTERNATIVES TO DIFFUSION

Joseph Sonnenfeld

Human behaviors have many sources. Some behaviors derive from abilities that are our genetic inheritance; others are based on skills that are more the product of culture and learning. Geographers have tended to focus on cultural behaviors, and, in a spatial context, to emphasize the importance of diffusion for understanding how these behaviors contribute to patterns of culture and development. Pursuit of the sources and routes of diffusion has helped us to understand these patterns better, but it has also restricted our thinking about culture change and the human talents that contribute to such change. It is as if we were all anxious to attribute the really important developments of a culture or people to diffusion from one or another center of innovation, the nature and sources of which are considered to be distinctive and few, respectively.

It is not my intention to deny the significance of diffusion, but I am concerned that we have so little to guide us in understanding what happens when equally creative and discerning minds attempt to solve problems for the sake of survival. For traditional populations, for example, the "conventional wisdom" is that those living on the margins of subsistence tend not to be especially innovative. They are considered to lack the sense of opportunity to innovate—meaning that marginal resources do not allow a people the luxury of experimenting with the possibility of failure, which is what one risks by using techniques not validated by tradition (or experience). This may explain varying degrees of conservatism among subsistence-level societies, but it does not seem as obviously applicable for understanding the behavior of individuals faced with the problem of having to improvise, to do what they have not been trained to do, when some new and unexpected threat to subsistence or survival arises.

Having worked among northern Alaska Eskimo in the prestatehood period, there is no question in my mind that many among them had the ability to improvise, in the materials they used, in the techniques they applied to specific tasks, and in the strategies they devised to resolve specific environmental and subsistence problems.[1] I have seen this same innovativeness among Tlingits in southeastern Alaska, and among Mexican villagers in the mountains of western Durango. I would assume such innovativeness to be universal; in other words, innovative and conservative tendencies can and do coexist, and constitute a persistent (and necessary) tension for a people having to contend with what to some degree is always an unpredictable subsistence environment. To innovate is not something (necessarily) that one is taught; rather, it is something an individual comes to realize that he or she does easily, or has talents for. And by the same token, neither is conservatism an attitude that one has to be taught (necessarily); it, too, is something that appears without effort; and, as with innovativeness, perhaps it comes more easily to some than to others, or is more common at certain periods of one's life than others.[2]

The talents that I have been recently concerned about relate mostly to wayfinding. The spatial abilities at issue seem to be almost universal. Most of us are able to make right or left turns at the correct time, given appropriate cues, and to remember the relevance of certain landmarks to where we are going or where we have come from. Also included among these talents is the ability to learn from experience. All of these contribute to the development of spatial skills, which are embellished as well by cultural learning, and individualized by one's own more or less distinctive personality. I am suggesting, in effect, the existence of an adaptive system—involving sensing, experiencing, learning—in which what is to be learned by diffusion from cultural sources outside one's own group, for the sake of either survival or comfort, may be no more important than what is learned or adopted from within one's group. The fact of diffusion, when it occurs, implies only the learning of that which is diffused, which is only one kind of learning, and not necessarily a different or more important kind of learning.

We know enough about how cultural groups differ, as well as about within-group variability, to realize that learning does not come equally easily to all; that what is learned is not simply a function of stimulus exposure and social conditioning: it is also a function of culture and personality, and also of "ability." I am not uncomfortable suggesting that there are things we do, of a rather complex nature, that involve the operation of "universal" abilities, or that involve the development of skills that one also finds almost universally, and that under other circumstances (of a more material nature) one would be tempted to ascribe to diffusion rather than to the operation of a universal mentality.[3] This implies that there are things that do and do not (or do not have to) diffuse, and more: that much of that which does get analyzed in terms of diffusion is only a small part of what is important for the well-being of a community.

I shall attempt to make the case for a more balanced treatment of culture change, which includes consideration of the nature and sources of traditional skills and capabilities, using wayfinding and associated spatial skills and travel behaviors as examples.

Wayfinding as Spatial Behavior

Wayfinding is a universally distributed skill. Everyone engages in it; but not everyone engages in the same forms of wayfinding, nor do all have the same talents for wayfinding. Many of the techniques of wayfinding are learned, both through formal and informal associations with others, as well as from personal experience. Some wayfinding elements are rather clearly the products of diffusion, in particular those involving the use of such navigational devices as the compass, the sextant, and the chronometer, all of which have complex histories.

Much of the navigational achievement we attribute to western Europe and the Mediterranean world had origins that preceded the Age of Discovery,[4] and there is evidence of Chinese and Arab influence westward into Europe as well as eastward into the Pacific.[5] If we include what was known about the stars and constellations, and the techniques and devices used for measuring them, the diffusion network is likely to have been broader still, to have extended through much of the New and Old Worlds.[6] The systems for identifying and representing cardinal directions and the orientation of ceremonial structures are sufficiently consistent, despite discontinuities in distribution, to also suggest diffusion effects.[7]

But there are also reasons for thinking that many of the similarities in the preinstrumental means for identifying locations and directions were other than the products of diffusion, considering, for example, the fact that all of humankind, as with almost all of those creatures that travel beyond the immediate range of "home," have the ability to find their way to distant places and subsequently to return home.

Rudiger Wehner, a neuroethologist whose specialty is insect navigation, compared the skylight compass used by the bee with the star or sidereal compass used by traditional Polynesian navigators.[8] Apart from the major difference between the two, that one utilizes skylight polarization and the other the horizon positions of rising and setting stars, Wehner noticed some interesting similarities. For example, by contrast with modern Western styles of navigation, neither the bees nor the Polynesians employ any kind of spherical geometry: the bees do not utilize great circle routes and the Polynesians do not "construct astronomical triangles by combining the horizon and celestial systems of coordinates."[9] Secondly, both the bees' and the Polynesians' compass systems are "approximate rather than exact solutions" to navigation, which Wehner suggests represents "an intellectual shortcut" for producing maps that are good enough rather than precise. Thirdly, both compass systems sacrifice "absolute precision . . . for functional simplicity"; they focus on a few limited aspects or features of the sky, which constitute "local solutions tailored to a specific environmental context"—meaning they are not easily applied to other areas. Finally, given the deficiencies of both systems of compass strategy, both use "backup systems" for reducing the likelihood of navigational errors. For Polynesians this means "drawing upon the sun, swell patterns, clouds, submerged coral reefs, or land-based birds," whereas the insect navigators "refer to the solar meridian (the sun's azimuth), which is centered in the less polarized half of the sky, and to noncelestial cues such as landmarks. Should they get lost they adopt an efficient searching strategy."[10]

This comparison suggests that there are certain principles of navigation or navigation strategy that seem appropriate to the navigating behaviors of mobile forms in an earth environment, even when these belong to groups as different as bees and Polynesians. Such strategies build on environmental regularities consistent with the sensory and information processing systems specific to each at a species level.

There is other evidence to support genetic control of wayfinding behaviors: we all engage in some form of cognitive mapping activity;[11] and we exhibit a drive to "competence,"[12] which is associated not only with play activities but also with exploration.[13] In addition, not only may there be a biogenetic basis for the structure of human language,[14] but there may also be an inherited neurostructural basis for the processing and organization of environmental information, which facilitates learning of certain kinds of environmental stimuli. This appears to be the reason why some migratory birds learn so easily to identify star patterns for orientation purposes.[15] All imply the existence of a more restricted or programed neural basis for learning than we normally associate with culture-controlled behavior of humans, meaning that we seem to be "prepared"[16] to learn certain things more easily or in a more consistent fashion than would be the case were culture alone in control of a tabula rasa brain.

This biopsychological theorizing suggests that there are certain basic aspects of wayfinding in humans that are the product of genetic inheritance. We focus on landmarks for orienting;[17] we think in terms of left and right for recalling travel routes;[18] we use time as a measure of distance;[19] and we are sensitive, generally, to elements of the geographic environment (especially structural consistencies), including wind and wave patterns, and diurnal and seasonal sky patterns, which we use widely as cues to direction and orientation.[20] To suggest that there is such biopsychological control over what we learn is to suggest also that wayfinding abilities and wayfinding styles can have a distribution not dependent on diffusion.

Clearly, wayfinding has been facilitated over time by new understandings of land and sky patterns, and by direction-enhancing and space-altering technologies; but the impact of these new developments is less clear. Has that which diffused from one culture group to another made any quantum difference in travel behavior; or did such new understanding or technique simply expand on the inventory of preexisting skills and techniques, permitting the substitution of one skill or technique for another?[21] Thus, did the compass permit travel of a kind that was not otherwise possible, or did it only make it easier for pilots or navigators to orient and maintain bearings; or for more persons to do so because the compass requires less skill than did the previous means for orienting and maintaining bearings?[22]

The diffusion issue is thus different for wayfinding than it is for agriculture, in which the development of domestication represented a technological revolution that made possible what we assume previously had not been possible. At least there is no reason to expect that there was any kind of genetic selection among early humans for an ability to domesticate plants or animals.[23] With wayfinding, by contrast, we are dealing with a trait that was selected for from the beginning.[24]

Sources of Spatial Skill

Wayfinding skills are among the earliest skills we associate with humans. How much of such skill is the result of biological inheritance, and how much is the product of more fertile than normal imagination, of the kind that represents distinctive innovation and thus qualifies for diffusionist treatment? Cognitive mapping is a universal ability, but how about the use of stars for navigation? The domicentric style of orientation, in which travelers retain their sense of relative location when moving away from sight of home,[25] is also probably natural; but how about skill in exploration of the kind that allows for travel far beyond the range of one's home space, beyond which domicentric orienting skills can be applied?

As a child, I could travel a fair distance from home, in urban or rural areas, and never worry about getting home safely. I assume that I used a natural orienting ability. I am not sure that I ever learned this from others, or that I even knew there was something to learn. By contrast, using my first compass did not come naturally to me. I had to be taught how to use it, and I have had to learn it over and over again. I know individuals who have never learned to use a compass, or who, if they do, do not feel secure in doing so. The use of a compass is obviously a learned ability, which depends on a more basic spatial and abstracting ability.

With increasing age, I became aware that in some circumstances I could become disoriented. This may be a vestibular dysfuncton associated with seasickness, or loss of some sensory capacity; or it may be related to lefthandedness and associated neural interference.[26] Whatever the cause, I have since had to learn conscious wayfinding skills in order to keep from becoming disoriented or lost in places where being lost might be inconvenient, or even dangerous.

I am making a distinction between conscious and nonconscious activities and skills.[27] Some things we are able to do almost unconsciously; our behavior "flows"; we do not have to think about our actions; we have never consciously had to learn how to do these things. There are other abilities and skills that are clearly more difficult, like reading a compass and reading a map were for me, that one has to learn consciously.[28]

Wayfinding abilities are mostly unconscious. We do not always know how we have acquired them; some of us may have learned them from others, whereas some seem to have developed these abilities on their own. Even in the absence of such "natural" aptitudes, we seem to be able to learn certain wayfinding behaviors to the point where these, too, become as if unconscious, requiring no additional effort to perform. The more complex skills involve much more conscious learning, but once developed, these also seem to operate at other than a fully conscious level. Consciousness—or awareness—of the skill that a task demands is probably inversely proportional to the level of development of the abilities that contribute to the relevant skill; the less proficient one is in a given ability, the more conscious one is of the need to work at developing and maintaining it.[29]

Abilities, Skills, Competence

The terms "ability" and "skill" have been used to distinguish between different behaviors or behavioral capacities; they are not intended to be viewed as equivalent. Unhappily, the literature often treats them as if they were the same;[30] and the issue of "competence" also helps confuse the distinction between the two.

The distinction between ability and skill is basic. Abilities are what we are born with, or they represent a potential that becomes manifest with development.[31] Spatial abilities or aptitudes generally develop early: the ability to judge distance and form, based on stereoscopic vision; the ability to use spatial context for recalling location;[32] and the ability to transform visual images to new perspectives.[33] The spatial memory that provides the basis for cognitive mapping can also be characterized as such an ability,[34] of the sort that we are genetically "prepared" to learn.

Skills, by contrast, build on abilities, but involve something more. They require the refinement of motor and sensory coordination, the addition of experiential knowledge, and also the existence of a certain discipline, including persistence. Skills require both the opportunity and the proper conditions for development. In a contemporary wayfinding context, this means having the right environmental exposures, supportive friends, parents, and teachers, and the motivation to attain such skills.[35] This last is based at least in part on personality, which itself is a complex of genetic endowment, personal experience, and cultural conditioning. Skills may be developed in spite of certain deficiencies in native ability—for example, when there is social expectation that particular skills be developed to at least some minimal level as a sign of maturity, which is defined culturally as well as genetically. Implicit is a capacity to learn; and although some are slower or have more difficulty in learning specific skills, most are able in time to

200

achieve what self and important social others define as desirable, or other-wise require for acceptance.

"Competence" emphasizes less the development of specific skills than the sense of being able to apply available skills—for example, to travel and explore. As with skills, it is also possible to develop competence in the absence of specific native abilities, thanks to our neural and behavioral plasticity.[36] And, conversely, it is possible to have the abilities without the opportunities or motivation to generate either the skills or competence that might otherwise have developed.[37]

Under normal circumstances, one would assume that abilities contrib-ute to skills and ultimately to competence, meaning that the one facilitates the learning that contributes to the development of the other(s); this has been referred to previously as "prepared learning,"[38] which occurs when that which has to be learned is "prepared" for by some form of facilitator intrinsic to the system. But extrinsic facilitators also contribute to the de-velopment of skills and competence, which is what culture is all about; if the proper support and training are lacking, competence simply may not develop.[39] Situational (extracultural) factors perform a similar function: they provide the necessary environmental or stimulus conditions for learn-ing, in the absence of which neither skills nor competence will develop.[40]

It is this mix of innate, cultural, and situational factors that confuses the issue of cultural diffusion. In the absence of clear indications of diffusion, are we to attribute distinctive spatial skills—such as involve, for example, knowledge of intricate sky features, or the use of a certain mnemonic system for enhancing spatial memory[41]—to the application of innate abili-ties that are universal? Or do we assume that these must be the product of uniquely innovative minds, and therefore also likely to be the product of more distinctive culture and diffusion?

The motivation to competence seems universal.[42] Exploration contrib-utes to the development of competence, even in the absence of rein-forcing rewards;[43] and the abilities that contribute to the development of wayfinding skill, including those involving orientation, visual search, and cognitive mapping, are also universal. With these as givens, any gap that we create between "natural" wayfinding and "innovative" wayfinding would seem inappropriate, as would interposing culture as a necessary and prior source of wayfinding technique and, by implication, diffusion as the expla-nation for subsequent distribution of such technique. In other words, when we evaluate the wayfinding achievements of different groups, we cannot ig-nore or downplay skills based on personal experiences in order to emphasize, in the context of what diffusion is supposed to be about, that some cultural introduction at a conceptual level has been instrumental in the subsequent travel achievements of the recipient group.[44]

The Learning-Creativity Gap

Innovations, whatever their source, may require little to sustain them once adopted. Knowledge of how to do something provides its own rewards, reinforcing behaviors, regardless of the source of the knowledge. Consider, for example, the insight that when sailing in rough waters one can avoid seasickness by focusing on the horizon. When boat movement becomes excessive, and the horizon begins to shift and sway, finding a means to "stabilize" that horizon is all that one may require to avoid seasickness, and to remain alert to surroundings in ways that can be critical not only for wayfinding but also for survival. This is a technique I learned from others rather late in life; it is easily adopted and requires practically no effort to sustain. It builds on a sense of bodily need for visual and vestibular equilibrium and requires only enough introspection to identify it as a preventive measure.

This is the kind of innovative experience that I would contend is universal. I do not mean that everyone experiences seasickness or that those who do are able to come upon the same cure; rather, that there are likely to be individuals among all populations who will experience seasickness under certain conditions who also have the capacity to identify this means of horizon control for mitigating its effects. In addition, this is the kind of knowledge that, once created, is easily understood and adopted because of the existence of a universal adopting mentality. How different is the use of a star compass for directing wayfinders,[45] or of an oral tradition that ritualizes ancestral travels in order to facilitate the reconstruction (recall) of difficult travel routes?[46] In both cases, one can imagine a gap between the insight that contributes to wayfinding and the cultural formalization of the insight that transforms it into a cultural trait more easily accessible to others.[47]

Granted that we all are able to learn from others' insights, and that we are borrowers and imitators in much that we do; the issue with wayfinding is not so much that of seeking sources of innovation, but rather of using native talents to perform rather fundamental "organic" functions essential for the survival of mobile beings. That wayfinding builds on knowledge generally taught or obtained from others does not mean that it does not develop otherwise, given the appropriate experiences (environmental exposures) and the time for these to mature into insights of utility, if not also of understanding. Generally, we should expect the threshold of discovery of the critical environmental patterns and relationships useful for wayfinding to be lowered as experience increases, consistent with what has been referred to as the "Pasteur principle,"[48] according to which, the making of chance discoveries "favors the prepared mind. Some special receptivity born from past experience permits [an individual] to discern a new fact or to perceive ideas in a new relationship." All that is needed is a "background of knowledge, based on . . . abilities to observe, remember, and quickly form significant new associations."[49]

I am not suggesting that we are universal orienters, or that we have some unerring "sixth sense" for direction.[50] Indeed, the wayfinding skills of traditional populations in territories other than their own has often been remarked on in negative terms, and this includes even the highly skilled Eskimo and Australian aborigines.[51] But there are few who do not also remark on how finely attuned these populations are to almost all the elements that can contribute to wayfinding in their own territories,[52] and none that I know of ever speaks of any contribution to such skill from external sources. This suggests locally developed understanding, and further suggests that although there may be individual differences in the capacity for discovery of the patterns and relationships critical for wayfinding, these do not apply for the group at-large.

I am not really uncomfortable with the position that there are differentials, generally, in the creativity of individuals and groups, or that the gap between creativity and learning has to do more with creativity than it does with learning ability. There are probably many who do not achieve adequate understanding of wayfinding on their own, and who, therefore, are required to learn this from others—meaning that they have to be taught how to be effective in wayfinding. Yet, for most, the process is "painless." All it takes is for someone to point out a pattern, to identify a relationship, to convey an insight, and the rest of us are also able to see and experience it (as with the vertigo-horizon relationship); and we subsequently retain the new insight and apply it as if it were our own. That some are able to discover critical relationships, to "create" wayfinding knowledge, and that others who appear less creative are able easily to assimilate such knowledge, suggests that there is no necessary relationship between easy learning and creativity.[53] But I would also suggest that the gap between the two is less critical because of the existence of a universal learning capacity.

To return to an earlier theme, we come into this world "prepared" to learn at least certain things important for survival, and spatial orientation is included among them.[54] The kind of learning we appear to be programed for includes both the more genetically-controlled learning of appropriate behaviors in more predictable environmental situations (for example, how to orient), and the more open-ended learning of behaviors that vary according to experiences in the various conditioning environments that we are exposed to at an early age. James Austin, a neurophysiologist who has written perceptively on the subject of creativity, has characterized the difference between these two kinds of learning as the equivalent of what in computer terms is referred to as hard-wiring and soft-wiring.[55] The hard-wired portions of our brain provide for behaviors that are part of the original human design, responsible for the operational nervous system that we have inherited. This system provides us with at least the essentials for survival, including the ability to find our way about. The soft-wiring, by contrast, has responsibility for the open-ended portion of the brain's neural circuitry, providing us with a less directed behavioral potential that we presume was also part of the original human design. It is the soft-wiring that permits the programing of new learning into our brains, and is what keeps us changeable, flexible, and as variable as we are as a species. In a somewhat different sense, this soft-wiring also allows us to become less flexible, to be susceptible to environmental and cultural conditioning that narrows the range of our behaviors.

As an example of such soft-wire conditioning, I would briefly mention a trait referred to as "field dependence." The psychologists who have developed and applied this concept have found that different cultural groups appear to perform differently on certain psychophysical tests of field dependence.[56] The more field-dependent have greater difficulty than the less field-dependent in dealing objectively with visual field elements when these occur within a distorting visual field. The level of field dependence seems to generalize to a variety of traits or behaviors. For example, the more field-dependent individuals, in social terms, are more amenable to authority and to persuasion by influential social others; and in environmental terms, they are more likely to become spatially disoriented in complexly structured travel environments.[57] Hunting populations typically are characterized as among the less field-dependent of populations, and peasant farmers among the more field-dependent.

It has been suggested that part of the reason for this variation in field dependence relates to child-training practices, more or less permissive in nature, which are prescribed by socio-economic systems that differently value individual initiative and independent decision-making.[58] Field-dependence measures distinguish not only the more and less field-dependent societies, but also the more and less field-dependent individuals and groups within societies. The primary variables among the more complex contemporary societies include age, sex, place of residence (urban, rural), level of education, ethnicity, and religious affiliation.

Here, then, is a trait—field dependence—that varies between and within populations, in ways that do not obviously implicate diffusion as the cause. Instead, field dependence seems to exist as a kind of structural demand of the social or cultural system, eliciting a consistency of training logic (conditioning) that has psychophysical as well as social significance, and with the ability to influence the direction of learning that we are prepared for, in spatial if not also in social terms.

There are factors other than culturally prescribed child-training practices that also influence the level of an individual's field dependence,[59] just as there are many reasons for child-training practices. But the point is that this kind of effort to probe an underlying cognitive structure, which seems to exist across societies and environments, goes far beyond what one looks for when seeking evidence for diffusion as the source of the similarities in cultural traits that are widely distributed.

There is no question that diffusion studies in geography and the related social sciences have legitimate motivations and goals; yet these occasionally seem limited in both the understanding they seek, and in the understanding of culture process that they provide, relating to cultural development and cultural achievements in general. Diffusion simply is the means by which information is conveyed from innovators to adopters, many of whom are themselves also innovators. Evidence for diffusion is only evidence for diffusion, and has little to do with innovativeness, ability, or skill.

Conclusions

I have attempted to make a case for a kind of behavior that, in its distributional features, lends itself to other than a diffusionist explanation. There is a biological basis for the similarities in distributional characteristics of certain basic abilities that contribute to wayfinding and related spatial behaviors. This implies genetic control, either of the abilities directly, or of the neural circuitry that "prepares" us for learning appropriate behaviors. These ability-based behaviors are "environmentally labile," meaning that they depend on environmental exposure (experience) to become manifest, and thus they are also liable to modification by the environment.[60]

I have suggested a difference between abilities and skills, the former a genetic function and the latter, in addition, a product of learning and experience. Skills are necessary for the individual to succeed in those behaviors for which native abilities alone are inadequate; in the context of wayfinding, humankind may be distinctive in this sense. Abilities contribute to skill development, but by themselves are not sufficient for its development.

Environmental competence builds on the abilities and skills that contribute to the sense of being able to adapt to, control, manipulate, or otherwise accommodate to the environment. Competence depends on behavioral plasticity in order to compensate for inadequate skill development, which, in turn, may relate to deficiencies in the abilities on which these build. Such plasticity implies a built-in flexibility, which allows the brain to assume a diversity of alternate functions.

Diffusion of skills undoubtedly occurs, most characteristically within groups. Skills are transmitted from individual to individual and across generations, typically through family ties, but involving also the operation of more and less formal institutions that a culture "provides" for preserving, enhancing, and transmitting the skills it considers essential. However, inasmuch as universal abilities contribute to skill development, it may be difficult to identify those skills that are a product of diffusion from outside one's group, short of evidence that renders the probability of independent invention or development unlikely. Linguistic evidence is one such, if only because of the low probability that similar terms for similar phenomena will develop independently in different linguistic groups. Wayfinding skill and related spatial and environmental knowledge, for which linguistic or other symbolic evidence of a common source is lacking, cannot otherwise be attributed to diffusion, regardless of the sophistication of noninstrumental understanding that we assume such skill and knowledge to require. The universality of a drive for competence, and the presence of what is perceived to be a demanding wayfinding environment, should be sufficient justification for assuming at least the potential for similar, independent solutions to wayfinding problems in a universally shared environment. The interesting question may be not *why* so many have equivalent wayfinding skills, but rather why wayfinding skills are only minimally developed among others.[61]

Diffusion and development are a function of behavioral processes, the specifics of which are not accessible to the investigators of cultures whose members no longer survive—meaning that our understanding is based on "evidence which is both dumb and ambiguous."[62] The fact of diffusion, and of the change that appears to follow diffusion, of the sort that archeology is able to establish, cannot be used to draw conclusions about either the innovative capacities or the cognitive skills of the adopting cultures. Both innovativeness and skill are implicit in the blending of new and old traditions, which is what diffusion usually requires if adopting cultures are to survive the change. Paradoxically, more skill may have been required to sustain that which was lost or replaced by technological introductions than was or is needed to operate and maintain the introduced technology.[63] This may be part of the reason for the success of certain diffusions, as well as the occasional resistance to diffusion: simply, not all that is new and adopted is more productive or demanding than that which is replaced. And just as diffusion implies "preparation" for adoption, a lack of diffusion may imply resistance to or interference with adoption, the effective reasons for which may be either cultural or cognitive in nature.

Acknowledging the fact of diffusion is only the first step in understanding the diffusion process. The critical elements of diffusion are behavioral and situational in nature, and imply the operation of talents that have long been with us; and the same can be said of the innovations that lead to diffusion.

Notes

1. See J. Sonnenfeld, "Changes in Subsistence Among Barrow Eskimo," doctoral dissertation, Department of Geography, Johns Hopkins University, 1957.

2. Social or cultural conditioning is among the major sources of conservatism, which includes the tendency to conformity (vs. autonomy) and a concern with tradition; but there may also be a more "normal" developmental dimension to such tendencies. See, for example, J. L. M. Dawson, "Ecology, Cultural Pressure to

Conformity, and Lefthandedness: A Biosocial Psychological Approach," in J. L. M. Dawson and W. J. Lanner, eds., *Readings in Cross-Cultural Psychology* (Hong Kong: Hong Kong University Press, 1974), pp. 124–49; E. H. Erikson, "Growth and Crises of the 'Healthy Personality,'" in C. Kluckhohn et al., eds., *Personality in Nature, Society, and Culture* (New York: Knopf, 1964), pp. 185–225; J. Piaget, *Intelligence and Affectivity: Their Relationship During Child Development* (Palo Alto: Annual Reviews, 1981).

3. Or do we not normally so consider the fabrication and use of knives, axes, skin scrapers, and grinding stones? See, for example, W. H. Holmes, *Handbook of Aboriginal American Antiquities*, part 1, *Introduction, The Lithic Industries*, Smithsonian Institution, Bureau of American Ethnology, Bulletin 60 (Washington, D.C.: U.S. Government Printing Office, 1919). Jett states this even more strongly by suggesting that "on the whole, the more general, important, or basic a trait is, the less useful it is as evidence of diffusion . . . because it may plausibly have been elicited by innate qualities of the human psyche, environment, economy, or social structure" (S. C. Jett, comment on B. Lunkur's "The Bicephalous 'Animal Style' in Northern Eurasian Religious Art and Its Eastern Hemisphere Analogies," *Current Anthropology* 25 [1974]: 474).

4. See C. Singer et al., "Cartography, Survey, and Navigation to 1400," in C. Singer et al., eds., *History of Technology*, vol. 3 (New York: Oxford University Press, 1957), pp. 501–29.

5. See D. Lewis, *The Voyaging Stars* (New York: Norton, 1978); R. K. Johnson and J. K. Mahelona, *Na Inoa Koku: A Catalogue of Hawaiian and Pacific Star Names* (Honolulu: Topgalant Publishing Company, 1975).

6. See A. F. Aveni and G. Urton, eds., "Ethnoastronomy and Archaeoastronomy in the American Tropics," *Annals of the New York Academy of Sciences* 385 (1982); E. C. Baity, "Archaeoastronomy and Ethnoastronomy So Far," *Current Anthropology* 14 (1973): 384–449; Johnson and Mahelona, *Na Inoa Koku*; G. de Santillana and G. H. von Dechend, *Hamlet's Mill: An Essay on Myth and the Frame of Time* (Boston: Gambit, 1969).

7. See Baity, "Archaeoastronomy and Ethnoastronomy."

8. R. Wehner, "Celestial and Terrestrial Navigation: Human Strategies—Insect Strategies," in F. Huber and H. Markl, eds., *Neuroethology and Behavioural Physiology* (Berlin: Springer-Verlag, 1983), pp. 366–81.

9. Ibid., p. 374.

10. Ibid.

11. See J. O'Keefe and L. Nadel, *The Hippocampus as a Cognitive Map* (Oxford: Clarendon Press, 1978).

12. See R. W. White, "Motivation Reconsidered: The Concept of Competence," *Psychological Review* 66 (1959): 297–333.

13. See I. R. Inglis, "Towards a Cognitive Theory of Exploratory Behavior," in J. Archer and L. Burke, eds., *Exploration in Animals and Humans* (Wokingham, Berkshire: Van Nostrand Reinhold, 1983), pp. 72–117.

14. See E. H. Lenneberg, *Biological Foundations of Language* (New York: Wiley, 1967).

15. See C. D. Laughlin, Jr., and E. G. D'Aquili, *Biogenetic Structuralism* (New York: Columbia University Press, 1974), p. 107.

16. Ibid., pp. 110–14; see also M. E. P. Seligman, "On the Generality of the Laws of Learning," *Psychological Review* 77 (1970): 406–18.

17. See R. G. Golledge, "Learning about Urban Environments," in T. Carlstein

et al., eds., *Timing Space and Spacing Time*, vol. 1 (London: Edward Arnold, 1978), pp. 76–98.

18. See O'Keefe and Nadel, *Hippocampus*; J. Money, *A Standardized Road Map Test of Direction Sense* (San Raphael, Calif.: Academic Therapy Publications, 1976).

19. See H. Gatty, *Finding Your Way on Land or Sea* (Brattleboro, Vt.: Stephen Greene, 1983), pp. 39–40 (originally published as *Nature Is Your Guide*, 1958).

20. See R. R. Baker, *Human Navigation and the Sixth Sense* (London: Hodder and Stoughton, 1981); Gatty, *Finding Your Way*.

21. For example, analogous to implement and material replacements among traditional populations. See J. Sonnenfeld, "Changes in an Eskimo Hunting Technology, an Introduction to Implement Geography," *Annals*, Association of American Geographers, 50 (1960): 172–86.

22. See Gatty, *Finding Your Way*; T. Gladwin, *East Is a Big Bird: Navigation and Logic on Puluwat Atoll* (Cambridge: Harvard University Press, 1970); Lewis, *Voyaging Stars*.

23. Nurturance "abilities," however, may have contributed to the success of the process of domestication.

24. As with language, art, and religion, the development of which, if not quite from the earliest of human beginnings, I do not consider to have required the stimulus of diffusion in order to have evolved, though *specific* languages, art, and religious forms obviously did diffuse.

25. See Gatty, *Finding Your Way*; J. Sonnenfeld, "Egocentric Perspectives on Geographic Orientation," *Annals*, Association of American Geographers, 72 (1982): 68–76.

26. See J. Sonnenfeld, "The Communication of Environmental Meaning: Hemispheres in Conflict," in Mary Ritchie Key, ed., *Non-Verbal Communication Today: Current Research* (Berlin: Mouton, 1982), pp. 17–29.

27. See K. R. Popper and J. C. Eccles, *The Self and Its Brain* (Berlin: Springer International, 1977).

28. There are also other abilities or skills, like orienting unaligned radar imagery or making the mental calculations required for "dead reckoning," which some persons appear not to be able to learn; and some may not be able to learn even the "simpler" behaviors I have mentioned, like reading a map or using a compass. There are, in fact, individuals with such spatial disabilities that they do not engage in certain kinds of wayfinding behavior for lack of a conscious sense that they can do what they want to do: get to certain places alone, or without having to ask directions, or travel at night, or to places where they have not been before, for fear of not getting back (J. Sonnenfeld, unpublished data from study of spatial skills in a southeast Alaskan community).

29. In the inverse case, more talented performers may have to force themselves to think consciously about what it is that they seem to be able to do without "thinking" in order to explain their skill to others less blessed with the appropriate talents.

30. There are exceptions; for example, D. R. Olson and E. Bialystok, *Spatial Cognition* (Hillsdale, N.J.: Lawrence Erlbaum Associates, 1983).

31. See J. Piaget, *Biology and Knowledge* (Chicago: University of Chicago Press, 1971).

32. See N. Foreman et al., "Spatial Memory in Preschool Infants," *Developmental Psychobiology* 17 (1984): 129–37.

33. See J. Blaut et al., "Environmental Mapping in Young Children," *Environment and Behavior* 2 (1970): 335–49.

34. See O'Keefe and Nadel, *Hippocampus*.
35. See J. Sonnenfeld, "Tests of Spatial Skill: A Validation Problem," in *Man-Environment Systems* 15 (1985).
36. See R. Held, "Plasticity in Sensory-Motor Systems," *Scientific American* 213 (1965): 84–94; R. Walsh, *Toward an Ecology of Brain* (Jamaica, N.Y.: Spectrum Publications, 1981).
37. See M. Cole and J. S. Bruner, "Preliminaries to a Theory of Cultural Differences," in I. J. Gordon, ed., *Early Childhood Education* (Chicago: University of Chicago Press, 1972), pp. 161–79. It should be equally obvious that there may also be limits in the ability to accommodate for certain deficiencies. For example, having certain skills (hunting) in the absence of other skills (wayfinding) may not be enough to ensure one's survival (ultimate measure of competence) within stressful environmental settings.
38. Laughlin and d'Aquili, *Biogenetic Structuralism*, p. 110.
39. See Cole and Bruner, "Preliminaries to a Theory."
40. A false sense of competence, based on inadequate experience, is less likely to survive a test of the skills that contribute to it, though there is never really any guarantee that human competence is ever sufficient to ensure successful performance in the absence of complete control over environment.
41. See M. J. Meggitt, "Gadjari among the Walbiri Aborigines of Central Australia," *Oceania* 36 (1966): 173–213; Lewis, *Voyaging Stars*.
42. See White, "Motivation Reconsidered."
43. See Inglis, "Towards a Cognitive Theory."
44. To hypothesize that many wayfinding skills are capable of being developed independently does not mean that diffusion of wayfinding and navigation techniques did not occur or was unimportant: clearly they did diffuse and were significant: see Singer, "Cartography, Survey, and Navigation"; Lewis, *Voyaging Stars*. The problem is in distinguishing between what specifically was diffused and what was developed independently. What does one look for in order to make a case for diffusion? Probably techniques that were inappropriate to a local travel landscape, which would suggest that they were introduced from (or developed) elsewhere; also linguistic evidence for other-culture influences, such as the use of similar terms for directions, or similarities in the identification and characterization of key constellations; and perhaps also similar mnemonic techniques for facilitating the memorization of travel routes. For these, one studies the deictic lexicons of traditional populations (J. P. Denny, "Locating the Universals in the Lexical Systems for Spatial Deixis," in *Papers from the Parasession on the Lexicon* (Chicago: University of Chicago Press, Chicago Linguistic Society, 1978, pp. 71–84; S. Einarson, "Terms of Direction in Old Icelandic," *Journal of English and German Philology* 43 [1944]: 265–85); also, the star inventories collected by ethnoastronomers (Baity, "Archaeoastronomy and Ethnoastronomy"; Johnson and Mahelona, *Na Inoa Koku*); and the preserved accounts of ancestral travels (Meggitt, "Gadjari"; F. deLaguna, *The Story of a Tlingit Community*, Smithsonian Institution, Bureau of American Ethnology, Bulletin 172 [Washington, D.C.: U.S. Government Printing Office, 1960]; not to mention also the Old and New Testaments of the Bible). However, occasional problems may arise in the determination of what is or is not appropriate to a specific setting, particularly when dealing with the analysis of sky features that are used for orientation and navigation. For example, how does one deal with the error in star maps that derive from antiquity, considering the fact that star positions do change over time? Although star maps were updated for navigation purposes in

areas of Polynesia and Melanesia (C. O. Kursh and T. C. Kreps, "Star Paths: Linear Constellations in Tropical Navigation," *Current Anthropology* 15 [1974]: 334–37), Baity ("Archaeoastronomy and Ethnoastronomy," p. 407) indicates that in ancient Greece, at least, obsolete maps continued to be used—meaning that they would have been innappropriate to contemporaneous conditions, but not obviously because of diffusion from a place with a different sky condition. In addition, how is one to interpret occasional similarities in constellation inventory, given that constellation figures (imagery) also differ from place to place (J. B. Needham, *Science and Civilization in China*, vol. 3, *Mathematics and the Science of the Heavens and the Earth* [London: Cambridge University Press, 1959]; de Santillana and von Dechend, *Hamlet's Mill*)? Such variable imagery may be the product of independent attempts to perceive structure in sky features, a closure function (F. H. Allport, *Theories of Perception and the Concept of Structure* [New York: Wiley, 1955], p. 117). Alternatively it may be an example of stimulus diffusion as modified by a more locally relevant imagery. Because knowledge of sky features may be associated with subsistence activities as well as with ritual practice (G. Reichel-Dolmatoff, "Astronomical Models of Social Behavior among Some Indians of Colombia," *Annals of the New York Academy of Sciences* 385 [1982]: 165–80), even when a case can be made for a diffusion of sky knowledge as part of a sky-based ritual system (de Santillana and von Dechend, *Hamlet's Mill*), we have no easy way of knowing whether such diffusion was also tied to the use of sky data for wayfinding, or whether, instead, it was a local innovator who transformed the use of such knowledge to navigational use. This is analogous to the suggestion that animal domestication had ritualistic origins unrelated to subsistence needs (E. Isaac, *Geography of Domestication* [Englewood Cliffs, N.J.: Prentice-Hall, 1970], chap. 6). Indeed, the same has been proposed (early use of lodestone for "magico-ritual" purposes) for the development of the magnetic compass (J. B. Needham, *Science and Civilization in China*, vol. 4, *Physics and Physical Technology*, part 1 [London: Cambridge University Press, 1962]).

45. See M. D. Halpern, "The Origins of the Carolinian Sidereal Compass," Master's thesis, Department of Anthropology, Texas A&M University, 1985.

46. See Meggitt, "Gadjari."

47. The gap between an individual's insight (invention) and the cultural adoption (internal diffusion) of the invention is the difference between unique skills and culturally distinctive skills and, ultimately, between what came to be known as innovative and noninnovative cultures. However, such characterization is based not on the presence or absence of innovativeness, but rather on evidence for the formalization or cultural adoption of innovations. Barnett's description of every human being as an innovator expresses this distinction rather nicely, as does his reference to the ubiquity of inventions; these, he suggests, are often "unpredictable, and innumerable others are both unplanned and unwanted." He refers to innovation by "impulse" and perceptively includes among human innovations the "multitudes [that] go unnoticed by either their creators or anyone else" (H. G. Barnett, *Innovation: The Basis of Cultural Change* [New York: McGraw-Hill, 1953], p. 16).

48. J. H. Austin, *Chase, Chance, and Creativity* (New York: Columbia University Press, 1978).

49. Ibid., p. 78.

50. See Baker, *Human Navigation*.

51. For example, V. Stefansson, *My Life with the Eskimo* (New York: Macmillan, 1913); also Gatty, *Finding Your Way*.

52. See E. Carpenter, "Space Concepts of the Aivilik Eskimos," *Explorations* (Studies in Culture and Communication), 5 (1955): 131–45.

53. See, for example, M. Wallach, "Creativity," in P. Mussen, ed., *Manual of Child Psychology*, vol. 1 (New York: Wiley, 1969), pp. 1211–72.

54. See Foreman, "Spatial Memory."

55. See Austin, *Chase*.

56. See H. A. Witkin and J. W. Berry, "Psychological Differentiation in Cross-Cultural Perspective," *Journal of Cross-Cultural Psychology* 6 (1975): 4–87; Dawson, "Ecology."

57. To be more field-independent generally means to be able more easily to identify specific field elements as clues to the structure of an area, free of such distortion as might be caused by unusual lighting effects, or weather, or surface conditions. The ability to identify sky features, including constellation figures, should also be an easier task for those who are more field-independent. Success in identifying figures embedded in a concealing matrix of competing stimulus elements (the Embedded Figures Test) is one of the basic measures of field (in)dependence: see H. A. Witkin and D. R. Goodenough, *Cognitive Styles: Essence and Origins* (New York: International Universities Press, 1981), pp. 14–15.

58. See Dawson, "Ecology"; H. Barry et al., "The Relation of Child Training to Subsistence Economy," *American Anthropologist* 61 (1959): 51–63.

59. See Witkin and Berry, "Psychological Differentiation."

60. See J. H. Barkow, "Darwinian Psychological Anthropology: A Biosocial Approach," *Current Anthropology* 14 (1977): 373–87.

61. There are a number of good reasons—relating to other than innate ability or innovative capacities—for not finding a more consistent distribution of spatial skills. For example, (1) there may be a lack of appropriately demanding situations or opportunities for either the specific abilities to become manifest or for the related spatial skills to develop (e.g., the difference between travel on the open plains and travel in wooded mountain terrain, or through a variably structured city; similarly the difference between the travel habits of sedentary and nomadic folk); (2) there may be cultural constraints on skill development, or on the experience-producing exposures that contribute to the development of such skills (e.g., restrictions on female travel, or a demand for cultural isolation); or (3) cultural or technological developments may be sufficiently sophisticated so as to no longer require individuals to retain traditional abilities and skills in order to feel competent to travel about. Indeed, some may even become insensitive to the demands of spatial skill for travel, considering that well-conditioned urban travelers hardly have to make conscious travel decisions in order to satisfy most of their travel needs. Even in the presence of opportunities to learn spatial skills relevant to more demanding travel, many resist (for many reasons) and seem satisfied to depend instead on simple spatial mnemonics and "intuitions." These are often enough sufficient not to require more (see J. Sonnenfeld, "Travel Patterns and Wayfinding—Waykeeping Relationships," paper presented at the annual meeting of the Association of American Geographers, Washington, D.C., 1984). The permissiveness of our society—in terms of what it requires of its members to feel spatially competent—and the security of most of our travel environments (though a real sense of fear may develop in the absence of appropriate social skills in certain environments) do little to encourage otherwise, so that in time the distribution of spatial skills becomes almost a random function, in cases consistent with native abilities and personal preferences, and in others a product of voluntary associations, of the sort that pressure for compliance: for

example, the military and paramilitary groups whose members are expected to develop specified skills, whether or not native abilities are conducive to their development. In time, spatial disorientation rather than spatial skill becomes a sufficiently common trait for designers to attempt to accommodate it in the designs of the complex spatial settings that they create: see K. Lynch, *The Image of the City* (Cambridge: MIT Press, 1960); R. E. Passini, "Wayfinding: A Study of Spatial Problem-Solving with Implications for Physical Design," Ph.D. dissertation, Department of Man-Environment Relations, Pennsylvania State University, 1977.

62. R. J. C. Atkinson, "Aspects of the Archaeoastronomy of Stonehenge," in D. C. Heggie, ed., *Archaeoastronomy in the Old World* (London: Cambridge University Press, 1982), p. 115.

63. See Sonnenfeld, "Changes."

PART FOUR

Methods and Models in Diffusion Studies

CHAPTER ELEVEN

Some Unexplored Problems in the Modeling of Culture Transfer and Transformation

Torsten Hägerstrand

The study of the diffusion of innovations is the study of how initially small events may develop into landslides that may well erase their own beginnings. In this respect invention and diffusion are like mutation and drift in biology. As a result we have to a large extent applied natural science techniques to such studies. Although this may be well motivated, we have reason to move beyond this format.

For most of the development of human culture we have been unable to observe the processes of diffusion as a continuous succession of events, developing from minute beginnings in temporal, spatial, and social dimensions. We can never reconstruct long-past events year by year, place by place, and group by group. Friedrich Ratzel, whose "science of movement" (*Bewegungslehre*) came to inspire Frobenius's "science of cultural realms" (*Kulturkreislehre*), inferred diffusion from maps of the static distribution of selected ethnographical items. When he said "space is the face of a gigantic clock and the things that move across this space are its hands," he had even seen that clock in motion by watching the considerable changes that occurred during his own lifetime.[1]

Reasonable documentation on the origin and dissemination of innovatory ideas and things was not available for research until sometime during the eighteenth century, and then only for selected items and groups in the general population. Even today, when we stand in the middle of incessant change, the empirical problem is formidable. My professor in statistics, Carl-Erik Quensel, who was also a demographer, used to say about causes of death that "we know when a person has died but not when he began to be taken ill." Innovations are analogous. Sometimes we may state immediately and with precision that a certain person or organization has adopted a new item. This still does not mean that we know when the innovator began to think about the innovation or where it was picked up.

Let us, for example, assume that an amply funded and well-staffed research institute noted by careful reading of newspaper texts the first appearance and subsequent spread of a new word. This material would represent a very interesting body of information. It would still not show if the first user of a word in print had invented it or had picked it up on the streets, in which case a widespread oral use might have been the fact before printed documentation began to reflect the diffusion.

On the one hand we need more data, on the other our data are not always appropriate. Historical data, whether travelers' tales or the findings of archeologists, are accidental samples of an unknown nature. They can be interpreted but not influenced. In the modern period, with superficially abundant data, things are not too different. Administrative interests, not consciously posed scientific questions, normally determine the form and scope of documentation. Census takers do not include items until they are already rather widespread. Students of weather and climate have managed to get society to pay for large-scale and systematic collection of data that is both scientifically relevant and practically useful. Students of cultural change have not been able—perhaps have not even tried—to make a similar impact. We therefore have to rely on proxies for much of our work.

We must therefore continue to construct hypothetical models of the course of events to improve our understanding of past, present, and future. It is always risky to develop such models because it is easy to criticize the many aspects that have been left out. In part this is because models are too often taken as statements of truth instead of questions concerning the direction of further research. Only theoretical constructs will enable us to influence the future collection of information in such directions that obscure points in our reasoning become better elucidated. Such conceptual structures may take the shape of mathematical formulas, simulation programs, or verbal arguments depending upon the taste and ability of the researcher. They are, in any case, only more or less helpful images of a reality that will never be fully accessible. Part of the reason is the spatially distributed nature of critical events. Part of the reason is that the workings of the human mind are so deeply hidden that personal perspectives and motivations can be inferred only indirectly and with great uncertainty.

Nevertheless, students of the human and social sciences have one advantage that natural scientists lack: they are themselves part of the universe of their investigations and therefore know much about it by reason of their own experiences and actions. It has not been considered appropriate to admit the importance of this source of knowledge. In reality we cannot avoid some dependence upon it and I can see no reason why we should not make open use of this circumstance, with care and criticism. I believe that, like Ratzel, one can infer things of general interest for the understanding of culture transfer and transformation by extrapolation from one's own biography.

I should like to suggest some directions in which further model-building might move. Some arise from work begun in the 1950s but never pursued. They might seem outdated, but the purpose of bringing them up is to stimulate new questions. The final suggestion is related to the work that occupies me presently. But *one* theme connects them all: the general nature of cultural change rather than the more traditional concern with the spread of single items.

This unifying theme is well illustrated by personal experience. When I read texts in Swedish that I wrote in the 1930s and 1940s, I find the style strikingly old-fashioned. At that time the plural endings of verbs were still used. Today the plural endings have disappeared in my own texts as well as in most others'. I am not conscious of a decision to change but a change has nevertheless occurred. If I had the time and energy, I could scan the whole period and make a statistical time-series of the disappearance of an old usage and the emergence of a new one. What is important is that the change, whether it happened in one step at a certain point in time or gradually, did not take place in a free realm of options. It was constrained by the general structure of the Swedish language. The "choice space" in this particular case offered only three possibilities if one wanted to remain comprehensible. The first would have been to stubbornly adhere to traditional forms of singular and plural despite social pressure. The second would have been to give up the singular form and use the plural everywhere, a stance that would have given a text a kind of majestic flavor. The third would have been to follow the principle of least effort and use singular forms all over, as the majority of writers came to do.

The Principle of Limited Possibilities

The list of alternatives provides an example of Goldenweiser's "principle of limited possibilities in the development of culture."[2] This was brought into the anthropological debate to support the antidiffusionist stance. If a problem of widespread nature had few practical solutions, similar forms might well be invented at geographically widespread locations. Similarity was thus no proof of imitation through diffusion. In 1912 Lowie asked, "How many ways of fastening a skin membrane to a drum are conceivable?"[3] Haberlandt added that there are limited possibilities in the development of arrow-points or of sword-handles.[4] These are straightforward microscale examples, not very different from my observation of linguistic change. System-wide applications of the principle were considered in the same period, such as Dilthey's belief in a logical limitation of possible systems of philosophy.[5]

A short quotation from Goldenweiser illustrates his reasoning: "When a special form of social organization, style of art or mythology, develops in an area, not only does it tend to perpetuate itself, but it also becomes operative in checking other developments in the same sphere of culture."[6] The statement has a considerable resemblance to arguments about structuration currently being developed by Giddens, according to which human action normally re-creates existing structures but also gradually transforms them.[7] According to the principle of limited possibilities, this transformation is a stepwise process. In each immediate step only a restricted number of options are available. Not only cognitive and social processes, which were Goldenweiser's major concern, but also solutions to technical problems are fenced in by the momentary availability of choice space. That the intended function of a tool and the material at hand for making it largely determines its form is obvious. More interesting when thinking about diffusion is that a complex construction or constellation of items cannot come into being until more elementary ones have been made available.

Although the principle of limited possibilities was observed a long time ago and commented upon by leading students of culture, it does not seem to have played any more important role in the development of theories of cultural change. Perhaps the reason is that our Western belief in unlimited possibilities and eternal progress forbids us to think in terms of constraints. However that may be, to my mind much could be done around limitations as an organizing theoretical principle.

The evolution of technological hardware would be a suitable area to move into to begin with: in this case it is rather obvious how limitations come about, because different inventions presuppose each other over time. Charles Babbage, the British mathematician, constructed in principle the first computer in the 1830s.[8] He could not make it work at the large scale he had in mind because he had only mechanical components at his disposal and the friction in the system was simply too great. His ideas could not be applied until the electrical relay had come into being. The vacuum tube and then the transistor made the computer even more possible. The micro-chip made it an everyday item of technology. In a similar fashion the telephone had to be available before skyscrapers were feasible.[9] The telephone did not cause the skyscraper, but it removed the limitation that the need to hand-carry messages imposed. Skyscrapers would have needed huge numbers of elevators to accommodate messengers, thus reducing space for offices. These are crude and modern examples of the workings of limitations but clearly also of the consequences of the transcendence of them. Technology has concentrated its efforts on trying first to transgress the physical boundaries defined by our biological capabilities and later the boundaries of our inherited technologies. This had taken place only step by step. A corresponding cumulative development has occurred in realms other than technology: in law, language, the arts, and in institutional organization. Small adjustments are probably more characteristic of cultural change than are sudden breakthroughs. That the cumulation of adjustments might then lead to very divergent aggregates is also part of the general picture.

This idea of change in small steps, each contained in frames of limited possibilities, does not relegate spatial diffusion to an insignificant position in the theory of cultural transformation. It invites us rather to view independent problem-solving and imitative transfer from place to place as connected facets of the total process of evolution. This, however, requires us to adopt some postulates that presently might be difficult to prove but at least seem highly plausible.

A first fundamental postulate is that the human being is a satisficer, not an optimizer. Even given a small set of possibilities, not all will be investigated in any systematic fashion when some local problem needs to be solved. To find just one workable solution is probably enough. This is then likely to be imitated by the usual working of the neighborhood effect. In some place, remote from the first, the same problem might be solved either in the identical fashion or differently. Viewed over a very wide area, such as one or two continents, a small number of solutions might well fill out the whole possibility space.

Secondly, one must postulate that there are first-, second-, and third-order, etc. problems to solve, depending on the "distance" of their possibility space from inputs derived straight from nature. To measure length in steps or with a rod is a low-order problem, just as in measuring time with a mark for each day. Measuring velocity is a higher-order problem in the sequence, because a rather precise clock is needed, which itself requires a series of inventions more and more remote from what can be picked up from the ground anywhere. A rather advanced theoretical knowledge must be present to solve still higher-order problems. So, even if the logic of a solution is straightforward and easy enough to be realized by persons in many places, the practical possibilities depend on the availability of useful inputs. Unless we believe that everything can be thought out and fabricated independently by every small population group—which clearly is impossible—then diffusion and its sibling, trade, is a necessity for cultural evolution to take off beyond the prime orders of problem-solving.

Geographic Consequences

What are the major geographic consequences of the combination of widely scattered problem-solving at first and the subsequent spatial diffusion of solutions? This question lends itself to investigation by simulation. Assume a long island, evenly populated and, to begin with, inhabited exclusively by pedestrians (Fig. 11.1). Assume further that we are able to record the place and time of elementary innovations that are offered straight from nature, such as the art of catching prey in a pitfall. Let us call this innovation (a). Inasmuch as direct observation or face-to-face conversation are the only ways of spreading knowledge about inventions, and inasmuch as mobility is low, sideward diffusion over time will be very slow.

At a later point in time a second innovation, (b), is invented at some other place on our island. It also spreads in the same very slow fashion. At a certain time, however, knowledge of both (a) and (b) will be available in the same area. If it is logically possible and practically useful, (a) and (b) may be combined in this one area into something entirely new (c). The stress is on the word "may." If the combination is made, then a new invention has come into being, which in its turn will also spread slowly outward.

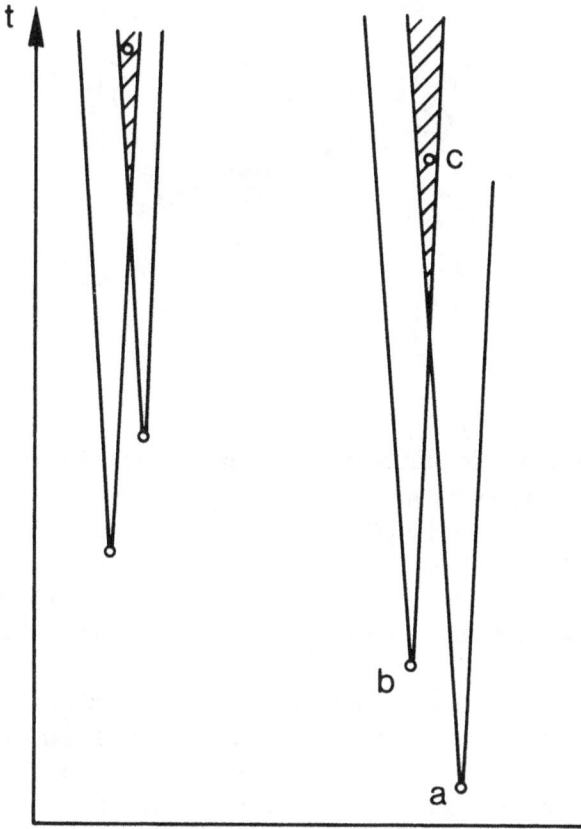

Figure 11.1

Every human being has to be a problem-solver and many have constructive ideas. Therefore one would assume that at least simple inventions appear wherever human beings live. This would mean that several forms of (a) and (b) would exist, although in somewhat different shapes. The inputs for more complex combinations would not, however, be present with the same likelihood everywhere. In my example the center of the island would be the area where the richest variety of simple solutions become known, if only after a very long time. This would lead both to the likelihood of more unusual combinations and to problems not encountered in less rich environments. New problems would produce a new and different need to step up the complexity of combinations.

On the world map, given coastal trade and the effect of certain topo-

Figure 11.2

graphical barriers, such a simulation would point to the Middle East and to Middle America[10] as the most likely peak areas for the accumulation of knowledge (Fig. 11.2). Carl Sauer also gave southeastern Asia the same central status, a conclusion requiring that waterways be given considerable weight.[11] Many archeological and anthropological findings suggest we have underestimated the ability of humankind to move on the waters of the world.

These peak areas of accumulated knowledge would in their turn gradually establish themselves as very visible centers for advanced innovations. Step by step these innovations would move out toward the peripheries. This would both enrich the cognitive environments of the peripheries and give rise to new kinds of problems.

Let us proceed further through historical time (Fig. 11.3). Over several thousands of years faster and more powerful means of transportation became available, first at sea and somewhat later by land. The new physical mobility established in the middle of the nineteenth century provided the conditions for a correspondingly increased mobility of technical ideas. It also created a host of new problems to be solved. Advanced combinations of more elementary ideas became possible over much wider areas and much faster than before. England, France, Germany, and the United States competed to invent new and complex technologies. The same ideas seem to have been advanced simultaneously in, as it seems, widely scattered places although the printed word and low-level electronic communication suggest at least the possibility of massive diffusion. Large areas of the world were still left in realms of very limited and low-level possibilities.

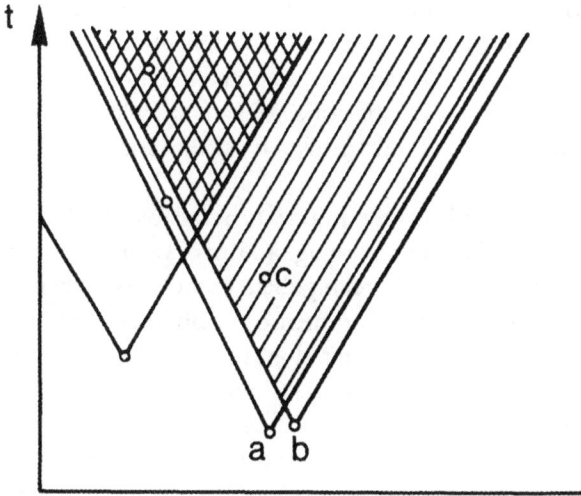

Figure 11.3

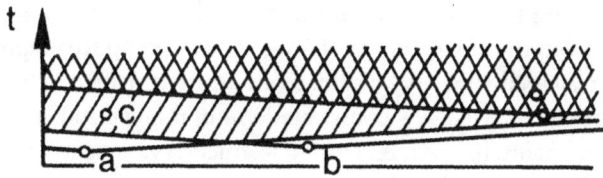

Figure 11.4

After World War II we have seen the explosive growth of long-distance air transportation, of sophisticated forms of electronic communication, and of printed sources. Knowledge of new ideas is hardly limited by distance any more, especially in the industrial world (Figure 11.4). From a crude geographic perspective, new inventions can be expected almost anywhere, except in Third World countries, which never had a chance to participate in the step-by-step learning process. Seen at a finer scale and in higher spatial dimensions, we shall probably find other limitations than remoteness from inputs that make cumulative growth more or less likely in various areas and places. Some companies take steps to keep their development work secret. In the sciences and professions the high degree of specialization provides for very quick communications inside existing groupings, but creates barriers for the transfer of ideas between them. The sheer mass of information tends to cause congestion. The difficulty all of us have giving up one pattern of thought for another is also a limitation of possibilities. So, despite the tremendous amount of aggregate knowledge, the principle of limited possibilities is still at work in every locality and over every short span of time.

On the whole I think this condition is unavoidable and therefore a helpful tool for understanding what is going on. But developments have made the simple geographical map less telling than it used to be, when low mobility was the overriding limitation for intense human interaction. In order to be able to identify all the hidden limitations that constrain the world of today, we would have to develop additional techniques for description and analysis. People and their knowledge, and space and time, would still matter, but we would have to understand internal and external structures more like the maze of channels in an anthill than a flat network of interconnecting highways.

The general model is in fact only a modern variation of a very old metaphor, according to which a cultural center is like a big tree. The roots suck up matter from the environment. This is then lifted up to a higher level in the stem, reshaped, and finally spread out again as refined fruits. If such a circular process is what has constituted cultural evolution, then it seems essential to maintain a vital, even if elementary, inventiveness among human beings in general. Otherwise matter to work on might cease to flow into the centers where the more advanced contributions are worked out.

Let me now bring up a different line of thought. I go back again to my first example of the changing use of Swedish grammar. In principle the options were three, but in reality only two—namely, to stick to tradition or to take part in an ongoing wave of change. A systematic analysis of a large set of biographical sources would indicate to what extent the precise dating of the adoption of an innovation of this kind is an oversimplification. When and where somebody acquires a new *thing* can be taken to be a point event in time and space. Sometimes we can find data that help us to pin down the succession of such events from place to place with great precision. In the work carried out by geographers so far, the mapping of adoptions as point events has been a common procedure.

From our own experience we know it is rather unlikely that adoption of innovation happens without mental preparation. In my own simulation models from the 1950s I tried to provide for this preparatory process by assuming that nonadopters needed repeated exposures to adopters before they made their own decisions to adopt.[12] This part of the modeling has been rather overlooked in subsequent work. That it should be overlooked is not very surprising, for it complicates computations, and the psychological assumptions made were purely hypothetical and rather arbitrary. They were not well supported by empirical data other than by some interview findings in rural sociology that there was a time-lag between an individual's being informed about a new item and then adopting it. The period between the two events may be one of reflection and calculation, or one of increasing social pressure, or possibly both. I believe this is an entirely open question and something we ought to look deeper into.

One way of approaching the matter is to try to separate the study of the gradual transformation of small, everyday events from the more dramatic, nonrecurrent adoption of things and behaviors that require bigger investments and corresponding reorganizations of life. The change of grammatical style over a longer period of time is clearly an example of the first kind of process. So is the gradual transformation of manners over time, so entertainingly described by Norbert Elias.[13] In the same category fall changing tastes concerning such things as the visual arts, music, dress, and interior decoration. All these are things we have to deal with without being entirely aware of why we take a certain stand or why we change as time goes on.

By focusing on this kind of change we perhaps come closer to fundamental psychological and social processes than we do when asking questions about "more important" matters. We cannot entirely remove economic considerations, but we can shift them to the background. There they constitute just one among many other problems, rather than overriding problems that must be solved before adoption can take place. I save very little ink or time by using the singular form of verbs instead of the plural when I write. From the point of view of monetary cost or time-use, it does not matter if I choose to listen to a record of a Mozart symphony instead of an electronic exercise by John Cage. But how I have come to prefer one alternative to another is indicative of my place as receiver and sender in the transfer and transformation of culture.

The German philosopher and musicologist Adorno has put forward an illustration of the kind of reasoning required to understand the process of diffusion as well as the resistance to diffusion.[14] He asked why eighteenth- and nineteenth-century audiences were able to gradually accept what for them was contemporary music, whereas today most concert-goers refuse to listen to the "serious" compositions of our own time. The concert programs of earlier times always included a mixture of well-known and new pieces and this (probably unintended) strategy gradually made the unfamiliar familiar and finally wanted. People could hear ensemble music only by going to concerts, which strictly limited the possibilities. Then came recorded music. People could choose what they wanted to listen to. Clearly the majority spent their money on the familiar. Planners of concert programs, finding themselves in a new, competitive situation, no longer dared discourage their potential audience by including modern music. Previously limited channels of communication between composers and the public were transcended. Freedom of choice fossilized general musical taste and serious contemporary composers appear now as an isolated caste, creating for its own internal edification.

Adorno's analysis of musical innovation brings a different perspective from what we have usually tried to model. Here there is no question of a clear-cut diffusion across a population of one isolated element at a time, but instead a gradual erosion and accumulation of habits taking place within a framework of continued social and technological change. Face-to-face communication is undoubtedly still part of the process, because humans like to talk about their experiences. But also present is a chain of private and institutional reactions to the new environmental conditions brought on by the technical change of recorded music.

Going back to my first example of the changing use of Swedish grammar, a closer analysis would likewise reveal a background of slowly working institutional and even ideological forces. A direct influence was the decision by publishers and newspapers, in particular in Stockholm, to give up traditional forms in favor of new ones. Reading probably influences writing much more than talking does. In the background lay the displacement of German influences by English-American ones after 1945. In the even more distant background operated the anti-elitist sentiments of the dominating Swedish social-democratic ideology. Traditional grammar may have been one of the symbols that were hard to tolerate as Swedes strove for a classless society.

Whatever the motivations, my example has *one normative center* that favors one of *two options*. This situation is rather common. It is striking to see how one center can be the source of wave after wave of innovations over long periods of time. We also commonly encounter situations where *two options* compete more strongly, because each is supported by its *own normative center*. This is an interesting case for modeling efforts, in part because models could elucidate an old question in human geography.

Cultural boundaries, like those between languages, religions, or traits in material culture, are frequently rather sharp and are maintained over very long periods of time. A classic explanation is to view such boundaries as the effect of barriers to communication. Barriers may be topographic or simply invisible breaks in a social network. Sometimes, however, sharp cultural boundaries run through open country and the reference to barriers does not seem right, because there can be abundant human interaction. A case in point would be the boundary between the Finnish and Swedish languages in southwestern Finland. In such cases the explanation could be the existence of distant normative centers, which continuously send out impulses recommending behaviors that mutually exclude each other. A diffusion model that allows receptors to pressure alternately from one side and then the other would give some insight into processes that produce a very sharp and stable boundary between competing options, those that produce a more blurred, but still stable, boundary zone and, finally, those that lead to a displacement of the boundary in one or the other direction.[15]

A similar mechanism of thrust and counterthrust can be assumed to work behind affiliation to political parties. But inasmuch as most political parties work out of the capital of a nation, factors other than the location of normative centers must come to dominate the resulting pattern on the map. Clearly, it is necessary to build upon well-founded psychological assumptions about how persons react when caught in a crossfire of messages concerning mutually exclusive choices.

Corporeality, Possibility Spaces, and Denovations

The third application of the principle of limited possibilities is more difficult to give substance to in a few sentences. It moves the focus from invention and its geographic spread to the problem of incorporating innovations into preexisting patterns of life, work, and environment. So far I have discussed the principle of limited possibilities as a perspective on inventions and innovations at the moments when they happen. Change is like the growth of a coral reef, where additions at the water surface are conditioned by the forms that have come into being before. The obverse is that the way in which choices are made within the framework of possibilities tends to determine the form of the possibility space in the next round. In order to understand which way the system may be moving, we also need to consider how present choices define future possibility spaces. Such understanding would be as relevant for the study of history as for arguments about the future.

No well-elaborated theory or methodology is available for the purpose. The human, social, and technical sciences have elaborated their worldviews too far apart from each other. And yet it is in the interaction of the human, social, and technical realms that possibility spaces emerge. A direction I think might lead to new insights would be to seriously introduce the *corporeality of humankind and society* into the reasoning process, something the human and social sciences have neglected.[16] In such a "tangible" perspective the whole population of an area, together with its equipment and territory, would form a huge aggregate possibility space in which some combinations would be feasible simultaneously, and others would not be.

Let me illustrate using an example from developmental psychology. A three-year-old child given a piece of paper filled with pictures printed on both sides will believe they can cut out all of them as if the two sides were totally independent. After a try the child would find that the real outcome would depend upon the order in which the pictures were cut out. One choice is destructive in one way and another choice is destructive in some other way. Nothing can save the whole and initial pattern of open possibilities. If several children were to cut out from the same piece of paper, the fastest or most aggressive would have theirs first. Whatever the case, unusable leftovers would be unavoidable.

The problem of choice and the problem of power sound familiar to the student of history and society. What is perhaps not so familiar is to see the course of events in terms of *the budgeting of a limited, tangible, basic resource*. Bringing the child development analogy up to the societal level, what would correspond to the paper and what would correspond to the figures to be cut out?

My co-workers and I have tried to find an answer in a world-picture based on the conception of *a fiber surface* made up of the unbroken and indivisible biographies of human beings, localities, and tools. Human projects, such as the pictures of the child above, whether initiated by individuals or institutions, can then be viewed as space/time shapes to be cut out from the limited surface. A "morphological" approach of this kind has the advantage that one can identify conflicts caused by overlapping demands upon time and space emanating from both the same and different actors. It also depicts the leftovers in terms of persons, times, and places as soon as some new dominating pattern of allocation has established itself.

In this perspective the adoption of any tangible innovation can be seen as the fitting in of a new pattern of time-use over the lifelines of persons, things, and localities. Every innovation requires specific persons and things to be present at particular places in time and space. But because persons and things are indivisible, the solution simultaneously creates specific absences. If everybody drives a car, streets cease to be social meeting places. In order to make any innovation possible, some preexisting time-uses involving persons, things, and space may have to be abandoned. One can easily appreciate this by just considering the unemployed workers and derelict factories around us these days. At the microscale, those who believe that they gain in wealth or comfort by adopting some innovation frequently find they have to give up something else of value, at least in the long run. As is well known, innovations nearly always have some unintended, and frequently deplorable, consequences.

The view that society at every moment has limited capacity to accommodate human projects opens up a large and almost totally neglected area for research. I am referring to the shadow-side of innovations. It follows from the condition of limited possibilities that innovations imply *de-novations* or *ex-novations*. The sad thing is that those who lose are frequently quite different groups of persons from those who gain. But it is also clear that those who gain in the short run may also lose in the long run—for example, because the increased number of fellow adopters gradually changes the overall pattern of possibility spaces.

To conclude, I do not think we shall have a mature science of cultural transfer and transformation until we are able to view both the constructive and destructive side of the process. The principle of limited possibilities might be a helpful device in this undertaking.

Notes

1. Friedrich Ratzel, *Anthropogeographie: Zweiter Teil: Die geographische Verbreitung des Menschen* (Stuttgart: J. Engelhorn Nachf., 1912), p. 411.

2. A. A. Goldenweiser, "The Principle of Limited Possibilities in the Development of Culture," *Journal of American Folklore* 26 (1913): 259–90.

3. Robert H. Lowie, "On the Principle of Convergence in Ethnology," *Journal of American Folklore* 25 (1912): 24–42.

4. A. Haberlandt, "Prähistorisch-ethnographische Parallelen," *Archiv für Anthropologie* 12 (1913): 1–25.

5. Wilhelm Dilthey, *Dilthey's Philosophy of Existence: Introduction to Weltanschauungslehre* (London: Vision Press, 1957), pp. 28–29.

6. Goldenweiser, "Principle," p. 279.

7. Anthony Giddens, *Central Problems in Social Theory: Action, Structure and Contradiction in Social Analysis* (Berkeley: University of California Press, 1979).

8. See Bertram V. Bowden, ed., *Faster Than Thought: A Symposium on Digital Computing Machines* (London: Pitman, 1953), pp. 7–18.

9. Ithiel de Sola Pool, *Forecasting the Telephone: A Retrospective Technology Assessment of the Telephone* (Norwood, N.J.: Ablex, 1983), p. 43.

10. See Carl O. Sauer, "Middle America as a Cultural Historical Location," in P. L. Wagner and M. W. Mikesell, eds., *Readings in Cultural Geography* (Chicago: University of Chicago Press, 1962), pp. 195–201.

11. Carl O. Sauer, *Agricultural Origins and Dispersals* (New York: American Geographical Society, 1952).

12. Torsten Hägerstrand, *Innovation Diffusion as a Spatial Process* (1953; English trans., Chicago: University of Chicago Press, 1967), pp. 264–66.

13. Norbert Elias, *The Civilizing Process: The History of Manners* (New York: Pantheon, 1978).

14. Theodor W. Adorno, "Schwierigkeiten in der Auffassung neuer Musik," in Wolfgang Burde, ed., *Aspekte der neuen Musik* (Kassel: Bahrenreiter, 1968).

15. See Keisuke Suzuki, "An Analysis of Change of Spatial Distribution of Information by Simulations Based on Diffusion Models," *Discussion Paper Series*, no. 12 (Tokyo: Asia University, Institute for Economic and Social Research, 1984). This study simulates the propagation of competing information from two centers.

16. See Chr. Van Paassen, "Human Geography in Terms of Existential Anthropology," *Tijdschrift voor Economische en Sociale Geografie* 67 (1976): 324–41.

CHAPTER TWELVE

Adoption Environment and Environmental Diffusion Processes
MERGING POSITIVISTIC AND HUMANISTIC PERSPECTIVES

Avinoam Meir

Modern spatial diffusion theory relies primarily on the external notion of information flow and the role of innovation propagators. Its neglect of an "insider" view of agents and actors, characteristic of positivist theories in general, has led me to search for an alternative approach that attempts to merge positivist notions of spatial diffusion theory with humanism.[1] This chapter seeks to expand the notion of adoption environment, its conceptualization and identification. I first review the alternative approach through a discussion of the basic tenets and shortcomings of both spatial diffusion theory and the humanistic approach, arguing for their complementarity and for an integrated approach. I then describe the notion of adoption environment using the example of adoption of modern educational services among Bedouin nomads of Israel. This example serves as a second stage in the clarification and conceptualization of the alternative approach.

Spatial Diffusion Theory: A Review

The theory of spatial diffusion processes, according to Hägerstrand, is structured around two major forces: the neighborhood and hierarchical

The author gratefully acknowledges suggestions and comments by Nick Entrikin on an early version of this chapter.

effects.[2] The key notion underlying these effects is the spatial flow of information. The nature of information flow has been characterized according to the distance decay mechanisms and spatial interaction models. Remoteness and a lower hierarchical position within a spatial system would cause smaller volumes of information flow, weaker awareness of the innovation and, consequently, its later or less intense adoption.

More recently, new directions of research have emerged; they have been termed the market and infrastructure model and the resources model.[3] These developments have significantly expanded the domain of the basic theory suggested by Hägerstrand.

Spatial diffusion theory, emphasizing the role of information flow on the neighborhood and hierarchical models, is regarded here as a partial explanation of real spatial diffusion processes. It is questionable whether the recent market and infrastructure and resources models provide the relevant and more complete expansion of theory necessary for understanding the diffusion of *all* types of innovations. In fact, the domain of the market and infrastructure school in diffusion research is limited to the diffusion of propagator-supported, material innovations.[4] Diffusion processes that involve such nonmaterial innovations as ideas, norms, or organizational structures present a problem. These nonmaterial innovations may not conform to the expanded market and infrastructure scheme, because the presence or absence of diffusion agencies may be irrelevant to this situation.

Furthermore, although the problem of the personal/cultural complex of potential adopters is relevant to all types of innovations, the market and infrastructure model pays relatively little attention to it. Characteristic of this model is its hypothesis that demand for an innovation is a function of the amount of information disseminated from the diffusion agency and the potential adopter's financial ability to purchase the innovation.[5] This means that the diffusion agent views all individuals within a given social or areal context as potential adopters who, subject to resource availability, only lack sufficient information to induce demand for the innovation.

These assumptions raise several questions. Can the amount of information per se induce demand for the innovation? Can resources and the availability of the innovation be considered sufficient conditions for adoption? Can all individuals be automatically considered as potential adopters? A positivist view of these questions would mean accepting the notion of the "rational man," whose decision to adopt an innovation is conditioned by information only, and whose adoption act is solely determined by innovation availability and resources. By such an acceptance the particular value of "economic man" is imposed on actors without examining whether this value holds in reality.

The notion of information inherent in diffusion theory is also the subject of Blaut's criticism that information is separated from the material world and given a space of its own.[6] Blaut further amplifies the argument made above concerning the ability of information alone to induce demand for an innovation. He treats this notion as a theoretical bias stemming from a disturbingly elitist theory concerning the causal efficacy of knowledge as against the role of such other cultural elements as value, social structure, and economic conditions.

Thus, it appears that spatial diffusion students have been isolating their research domain from the internal context of the innovation adoption situation. Clearly, then, our understanding of spatial diffusion processes cannot be improved if we maintain this isolation and continue to employ external notions indifferently and without taking a broader view. Such a broader view inevitably requires an examination of the internal context of the adoption situation, which can be approached through notions of the "humanistic alternative" in human geography.

The Humanistic Approach in Human Geography

The rise of the humanistic school in geography in recent years is attributed primarily to the growing discontent with the notion of objective space that underlies the positivist, physical-science oriented approach.[7] The objective space notion has emerged through the tendency to remove religious, metaphysical, and social elements from the thoughts of the individual. Consequently, different individuals are thought to perceive one objective world. This unidimensional abstraction of the world and humankind has led to an attempt to formulate universal laws and theories of human spatial processes and patterns.

The universal validity of such laws and theories of human spatial behavior has been seriously questioned. Critiques of the objective space idea have raised the argument that its unidimensional nature does not allow individual perception of the world to vary according to different personality backgrounds, or according to different environmental characteristics of places in the world.[8] By imposing their own values and conceptual frameworks in explaining human behavior, geographers have neglected the meanings that peoples and places have for each other, and therefore lack reflexivity in their explanations.[9]

Discontent with positivist spatial geography has led human geographers to challenge the dictatorship of positivist scientific thought through the introduction of humanistic philosophy as an alternative explanation of human spatial behavior. Most writers emphasize the *intentionality* of human behavior. Human intentions are determined by individual sets of aspirations, symbols, and values. Consequently, the range of goals is different from the profit maximization or cost minimization dichotomy. Furthermore, actions taken by individuals have to be framed within their specific situations—that is, human *awareness* of, and *experience* with, current and historical environments, and the societal *contexts* of activity. In other words, grasping the sum total of a person's experience with his or her milieu is a crucial element in understanding a person's actions and involvement in that milieu. Any research attempt in this direction has to take into account the different *meanings* attached to different *essences* by different human beings.

Given this view of humanity, humanistic geographers have found it necessary to put aside theories and models about persons and phenomena. They advocate an analysis of human perception of a particular phenomenon without presuppositions. Consequently, the number of subjective worlds influencing individual behavior depends upon the attitudes and intentions of human beings. Therefore, in studying human spatial behavior the humanistic geographer first investigates these different worlds, rather than starting, as does the positivist, with simplifying assumptions about them.[10] Thus the imposition of researchers' own concepts and values on their understanding of human behavior should be avoided.

Several lines of criticism have been raised concerning this humanistic approach. The first relates to individual thoughts. In order to understand one's perception of and attitude toward a phenomenon, it is necessary to reconstruct one's thoughts about it. This involves two problems. First, the private nature of individual thoughts makes them, at least in part, inaccessible to an outsider. Secondly, observed agents encounter difficulties in reconstructing their own thoughts regarding particular contemporary issues; for an uncontemporaneous or detached observer attempting to reconstruct an agent's thoughts regarding past events, the problem is that much greater. Thus, the observer's own thougths are being called upon, and it is difficult to separate them from those of the investigated subject. In other words, it is impossible for social scientists to totally neutralize their own values in the framework of explaining human behavior.[11]

236

The second line of criticism relates to intentions. An individual's behavior is not independent of the behavior of other individuals in the same environment. Similar as well as conflicting intentions exist, both of which make full attainment of the individual's intention difficult.[12] The possible consequence is a compromising of personal values and intentions. Their perceptions of a problem or phenomenon, originally quite different, become less polarized. Consequently, a much more common view of the environment and the world emerges than that implied in Relph's statement that there are as many worlds as there are individuals and the attitudes they can assume.[13]

Another criticism of the humanistic approach in geography was raised by Talarchek. Humanistic geography, he argues, has failed to develop any coherent methodology. Whatever methodology it uses is vague and unstandardized, lacks criteria of precision, and is therefore impractical in its approach to prediction. In addition, a mechanistic adoption of the phenomenological approach would necessitate abandonment of all the substantial achievements of geography during the scientific revolution of the 1960s, and therefore the loss of much of the discipline's expertise, particular viewpoint, and position among the social sciences.[14]

Humanistic-Positivistic Complementarity in Geography

In fact, humanistic geographers have become aware of some of the difficulties involved with their approach. One critical issue concerns the notion of plurality of worlds. The contention has been made that some elements of common view or generality regarding phenomena are inevitably shared by individuals. Thus, Guelke has raised the proposition of rational thinking, in which different individuals understand a certain situation in a similar way due to their adoption of a certain theory of the situation.[15] Relph has contended that individuals share some consensual view of the world because they are part of the same real world from which their experience and therefore perceptions are taken.[16] Hägerstrand has spoken of a twilight zone between aggregate behavior and individual behavior.[17] Thus, humanistic geographers have not totally denied the possibility of approaching some generalizations about human perception of phenomena.

Another issue is the notion of pure consciousness inherent in humanism. Ley has claimed that consciousness is meaningless without attaching it to the relevant temporal and spatial context.[18] He argues that without such an attachment the notion of pure consciousness becomes as much an abstraction from human experience as does the notion of the isotropic plain.

These issues have brought humanistic geographers to seek a perspective on their approach and to attempt to reduce the polarization between it and the positivist approach. Representative of this trend is Buttimer's contention that direction is to be found within the spirit of phenomenological purpose, rather than in the practice of phenomenological procedures.[19] In fact, some humanistic geographers have maintained that both approaches are relevant to each other to various degrees. Tuan has regarded positivist and humanist geography as two edges of a continuum. In no case can an explanation of human behavior be situated on any extreme edge of the continuum. On the one hand, humanistic geographers draw critically from scientific knowledge, but on the other hand they make positivist geographers aware of facts and ideas to which, because of their conceptual framework, the positivists have no access.[20]

In other words, humanistic geographers do not necessarily advocate a total overthrow of theories and models, and the scientific method in general. Rather, they recognize their importance in exposing order on earth insofar as the framework of understanding humankind is expanded toward a geographical synthesis to include personal values and experience within the physical environment and within a particular political, social, economic, and ideological context.[21]

The apparent complementarity between positivist and humanist approaches is thus capable of providing geography with a valuable path that may increase understanding of geographical problems. It is important to recognize the notion of a consensual perception regarding personal values and environmental experience as well as accepted positivist concepts. This notion facilitates generalizations leading to the formulation of theories and models. The notion of consensual perception should not, however, be taken for granted nor should it be determined from above. The formulation of its specific nature should start from below, similar to Guelke's "Idealistic Alternative,"[22] and only then be put to the scrutiny of formal scientific methods.

This does not imply, however, that a search for universal laws is advocated here as the only goal, or that the humanistic approach should be adopted in its entirety. The goal should be to expand the understanding of human behavior by grasping the ongoing dialectic of milieu and civilization,[23] while recognizing the divisibility of the universal geographic system into differing cultural subsystems. This implies that we recognize the notions of cultural relativism, context, synthesis, and holism and, therefore, our inability to apply flatly positivist theories. Within subsystems, however, the complementarity between positivist and humanist notions should be employed by combining external positivist theories with internal humanist viewpoints that reflect existing environmental contexts. Specifically, these viewpoints should be framed as intrasubsystemic forces that do not necessarily have to be derived through phenomenological procedures but rather through the "spirit of the phenomenological purpose." Emphasis should be given to the formulation of the consensual view representing the insider perception of the phenomenon within the particular context of the action.

Thus, on the one hand, positivist concepts of space and spatial organization represent external theories. On the other hand, human intentionality and experience, and environmental settings and contexts, represent humanistic internal viewpoints. Both sets of theories must be employed to explain human *environmental behavior*. *Spatial behavior* considers external theories alone. This view is similar to Gregory's that "theories which are external to the life-world under investigation" are "legitimate prejudices which furnish the *necessary* conditions for any understanding: they must not be bracketed."[24]

Spatial Diffusion Processes: An Environmental Approach

I am calling for a merger between positivistic spatial diffusion theory using models as external (or outsider) notions and humanistic internal (or insider) notions pertaining to the contextual situation of the individual adopter. I am suggesting that the internal view be incorporated through the concept of the innovation adoption environment or environment effect.[25]

The underlying assumption of the concept of adoption environment is that each innovation has a set of particular conditions that must be fulfilled if it is to be adopted. Information about the innovation and its availability is necessary but not a sufficient condition for adoption. Other sets of factors related to the particular innovation must be taken into account in order for it to be adopted. These are the individual's experience, norms, values, and intentions regarding the particular object, the individual's socio-economic status, and the public and institutional organizational frameworks within which the individual is situated, and which represent cultural, societal, political, and geographical contexts pertaining to the particular innovation.

Individual adopters are not acting within a vacuum or on an isotropic plain. Rather, their actions are conducted within an environmental context that assumes a multidimensional nature, each dimension exerting varying degrees of influence on the actions of different individuals.[26]

The adoption environment should include all identifiable factors related to the interface between the potential adopter and a particular innovation, with the exception of information about it and its availability. Buttimer has suggested a holistic framework for understanding human experience, which may be also be relevant for understanding the adopter/innovation interface.[27] The framework consists of three distinct spheres: the noosphere (features of consciousness that influence *genre de vie*), the biosphere (organic and territorial milieu), and the socio-technosphere (operational environment). These factors represent the internal (or insider) view of the interaction between the potential adopter and the innovation, a view that humanistic geographers claim is missing from the current context of positivist spatial geography. The individual thus develops a perception of the innovation that is the outcome of the mutual interplay between specific factors. This perception provides the ground for the decision to act—that is, to adopt, delay adoption, or reject the innovation.

An understanding of the perception of an innovation by the potential adopter (individual or group of individuals), as derived from these environmental factors, involves an investigation of the situation in a way similar to that suggested by the humanist geographers reviewed earlier. By knowing the goals of individuals, it is possible to identify their intentions regarding the innovation, and whether or not it is suited to a particular need. Personal suitability of the innovation for an individual, its adoptability, can be understood from the individual's socio-cultural values and norms regarding the change in lifestyle involved with adoption of the innovation, economic ability to obtain it, direct experience with successful adoptions by members of his or her cultural or social group, and perception of the overall compatibility of the innovation with the cultural, social, political, and geographical environmental contexts within which activities are conducted. In other words, the meaning attached to an innovation by the potential adopter within the adopted milieu and *genre de vie* is reconstructed and is reflected in the nature of the decision regarding adoption of the innovation.

From these notions it is possible to develop a consensual view that serves as an overall validation of an individual's perceptions of the innovation—that is, a generalized understanding of the common components of the various adoption situations through which the environmental effect can be constructed and verified. As Gregory has put it, culturally defined structures of meaning are incorporated into sets of typical (community) responses to changes in the external or phenomenal environment,[28] which is similar to Guelke's approach in which individuals perceive an object according to a particular rational theory they develop about it.[29]

Regarding the consensual view, it is not argued here that all individuals perceive the innovation uniformly. Based on the assumption that each innovation has a particular set of conditions necessary for its adoption, this set composes the environmental effect for most potential adopters, but each condition has a different relevance for different individuals. These conditions can be identified only from below: namely, an examination of the adoption situation for each potential adopter or representative segment of potential adopters within a cultural subsystem, avoiding, as far as possible, any presuppositions about them. Only in the next stage of research will these conditions be summarized and crystalized into the particular adoption environment. With this it is possible to develop a generalized understanding of the adoption situation that serves as a comprehensive framework for understanding such situations for the entire population in question.

However, the construction of the adoption environment should not follow a strict, idealistic-type procedure, because it is impossible to fully reconstruct the potential adopter's thoughts and, therefore, pure consciousness about an innovation. Rather, the attempt is made to state what these thoughts might have been under certain conditions—that is, to reconstruct the actors's (insider) view of the life world from an observer's (outsider) position. These views, as suggested by Gregory,[30] are not incompatible with each other.

The Adoption Environment of Education among Bedouin Nomads: An Example

The introduction of modern formal education into a nomadic population serves as an illustration of searching the adoption environment and its usefulness for understanding diffusion processes. In a study of the diffusion of modern schooling among the Israeli Negev Bedouin nomads,[31] an attempt was made to apply the neighborhood and hierarchical effects of diffusion theory. The results have revealed the importance of information flow, although this was not overwhelmingly strong. The need arose to reconstruct the adoption environment for modern formal educational services among the Bedouin. As a first stage, the problem had to be put within the general framework of development, rather than the traditional framework of modernization.[32] The basic argument is that the ideologies of nomadic tribal societies are generally in conflict with those of state authorities, resulting in reluctance by the former to accept education.

Western education and schools are generally regarded as incompatible with and even detrimental to the nomadic way of life. Nomads prefer their children to be taught environmental and moral senses by nature and the tribe. Economically, nomadic children early assume an important role in the family and tribal labor force, which also defers schooling.

Nomadism further serves as a strategy to preserve tribal units and avoid intertribal conflict. Through the process of education, and thus exposure to modernization effects, individualistic ideas are introduced, social status becomes acquired rather than inherited, and the cohesion of tribal and extended family units is threatened. Under such circumstances, intertribal mix, as a consequence of children attending schools, is strongly objected to on the grounds that it can be detrimental to tribal existence. Despite this general objection to modern education, there are variations among nomadic societies in their willingness to accept it. These variations stem from the situation of the particular society along the nomadism-sedentarism continuum. The closer they are to sedentarization, the more familiar they become with modern education and schooling.

The crux of the problem is whether the familiarity of nomads with modern education can be equated with its acceptance. Evidence from various countries suggests that this is not necessarily the case, and the example of the Israeli Negev Bedouin may serve as an illustration.[33] Over the past four decades the Negev Bedouin have led an increasingly sedentary life. About 40 percent of the fifty five thousand persons are now living in four towns planned by the Israeli government. Another 40 percent are living in dispersed rural communities established during a spontaneous sedentarization process. The rest are still semi nomadic.

In recent decades Bedouin contacts with the surrounding modern environment have intensified considerably, and information about modern education and its impact within Israeli society has been disseminating among the Bedouin. Yet, despite free public education, Bedouin acceptance of the innovation has been rather slow and is incomplete even in the mid-1980s.

Two issues can be identified here as an illustration of the problem of searching the adoption environment for diffusion processes. The first refers to the ideology of tribalism. Given differential tribal status and dormant and active intertribal conflict among the Bedouin, each tribe wishes to have its own educational facilities. Such demands conflict with governmental policy constraints aimed at economic efficiency. Consequently, not all tribes have been granted permission for a separate school. By 1978, the educational system had been operating for at least two decades, yet only six of thirty tribes had a separate school, whereas twenty tribes had to share their schools with three or more additional tribes. This has had an impact upon the spatial distribution of schools. Eleven tribes and about 20 percent of all school children are located more than seven kilometers away from the closest school. Consequently, two barriers stand in the way: intertribal mix and long commuting distances. These imply lowered social and physical welfare for a significant proportion of Bedouin children and therefore reluctance on the part of many parents of certain tribes to send their children to school at all.

This situation is further aggravated by the cultural values of nomadism. Even partially or completely sedentary nomads regard their children, especially the girls, as a major labor force. The Israeli Bedouin, who are more modernized than most nomadic societies in the Middle East and Africa, still maintain a strict value system concerning the social and economic role of girls, and resist educating them. As late as 1976, in thirteen out of sixteen Bedouin elementary schools, less than 25 percent of the students were girls. The situation improved considerably by 1982, by which time girls accounted for more than 30 percent of the students in seventeen out of twenty-four schools. Even this turnaround, however, does not imply overall acceptance of modern education. In 1978, only about 18 percent of Bedouin girls had attended seventh grade, compared with 61 percent of boys. Girls drop out, beginning in the sixth grade, which reflects the still strict social norms of their status within Bedouin society.

These two examples reflect the complexity of constructing the adoption environment in order to understand the adoption of modern education among pastoral nomads within the context of diffusion. The availability of public education, as well as information about schools, could not sufficiently balance the fear of involvement in mixed schools, of detachment of children from the tribal milieu due to school remoteness, or of exposing girls to outsiders and detracting them from the family labor force. In other words nomadic children and parents have been exposed to the benefits of

243

modern education, yet until recently they regarded it as irrelevant and even detrimental to their *genre de vie*.

In a study of the diffusion of modern education among nomads, information about the hierarchical and neighborhood effects of this innovation should be considered. However, the process of reconstructing the innovation adoption environment specific to this innovation within this particular societal and environmental context requires an intersubjective familiarity of the outsider with the individuals and groups under study in an attempt to look into the problem from the inside. The purpose should be to identify the insider view of education and its relevance.

Such an attempt would possibly but not necessarily involve an understanding of values, intentions, experience, and norms about such issues as the status of females within nomadic society, intertribal conflict structure, the role of tribal leaders, the interaction of individuals and groups with general governmental development policy, as well as a multitude of other relevant contextual issues.[34] Yet, in conducting diffusion studies, students should not commit themselves to any of these issues from the outsider viewpoint, however relevant it may seem. Rather, relevance should originate from the people themselves, and it is the task of the researcher to identify and illuminate it.

Conclusions

Approaching the potential adopter under the notion of adoption environment reintroduces the idea of cultural man into spatial diffusion research, representing the insider view of a particular situation. Cultural man cannot, however, be separated from the positivist rational man, whose adoption behavior is determined solely by information flow. It is only by combining the positivist spatial diffusion model, which provides an external view of the general dynamics of the situation, with humanistic contextual notions of individual potential adopters, that our traditional references to spatial diffusion processes can be expanded toward *environmental diffusion processes*. That such incorporation is possible and even desirable in human geography in general is also made clear by Gregory, who calls for an interplay between subjective intentionality and the universe of external objective social relationships, and argues that these frames of explanation are of necessity mediated by one another.[35]

The approach hereby suggested thus calls for a merger of the information effect (the neighborhood and hierarchical effects) with the environment effect to yield an explanatory scheme of environmental diffusion processes. Within this scheme an interplay between information elements and components constituting the adoption environment takes place, revealing variations in their relative strength among potential adopters. The behavior of a potential adopter as derived from information effects may be altered by the environmental effect, which may change the time of adoption or the innovation adoption intensity at any time period. Thus, the geographical pattern of diffusion processes, which differs significantly from that postulated by traditional models, comes to be better understood.

The incorporation of the environmental and information effects in analyzing environmental innovation diffusion processes implies that the amount of unexplained facts about the process is reduced. The understanding of the geographical pattern established by the environmental diffusion process is thus increased beyond what could have been achieved by positivistic models alone. The suggested approach may be regarded as theoretically and empirically progressive; compared with traditional spatial diffusion theory, it increases the amount of empirical content related to the diffusion process.

Notes

1. Avinoam Meir, "A Spatial-Humanistic Perspective of Innovation Diffusion Processes," *Geoforum* 13 (1982): 57–68.

2. Torsten Hägerstrand, *Innovation Diffusion as a Spatial Process* (Chicago: University of Chicago Press, 1967); see also Peter Gould, *Spatial Diffusion*, Commission on College Geography, Resource Paper no. 4 (Washington, D.C.: Association of American Geographers, 1969); Lawrence A. Brown, *Diffusion Processes and Location: A Conceptual Framework and Bibliography*, Bibliography Series no. 4 (Philadelphia: Regional Science Association, 1968).

3. See Lawrence A. Brown and Kevin R. Cox, "Empirical Regularities in the Diffusion of Innovation," *Annals*, Association of American Geographers, 61 (1971): 551–59; L. A. Brown et al., "The Diffusion of Cable Television in Ohio: A Case Study of Diffusion Agency Location Patterns and Processes of the Polynuclear Type," *Economic Geography* 50 (1974): 228–29; L. A. Brown, "The Market and Infrastructure Context of Adoption: A Spatial Perspective on the Diffusion of Innovation," *Economic Geography* 51 (1975): 185–216; L. A. Brown, "Diffusion Research in Geography: A Thematic Account," *Studies in the Diffusion of Innovation*, Discussion Paper Series, no. 53 (Columbus: Ohio State University, Department of Geography, 1978); L. S. Yapa, "Innovation Diffusion and Economic Involution: An

Essay," *Studies in the Diffusion of Innovation*, Discussion Paper Series, no. 40 (Columbus: Ohio State University, Department of Geography, 1976).

4. See Brown, "Diffusion Research."

5. Ibid.

6. James M. Blaut, "Two Views of Diffusion," *Annals*, Association of American Geographers, 67 (1977): 343–49.

7. See Gunnar Olsson, "Explanation, Prediction and Meaning Variance: An Assessment of Distance Interaction Models," *Economic Geography* 46 (1970): 223–33; Wilbur Zelinsky, "The Demigod's Dilemma," *Annals*, Association of American Geographers, 65 (1975): 123–43; L. King, "Alternatives to Positive Economic Geography," *Annals*, Association of American Geographers, 66 (1976): 293–308; D. J. Walmsley, "Positivism and Phenomenology in Human Geography," *Canadian Geographer* 28 (1984): 95–107; Nicholas J. Entrikin, "Contemporary Humanism in Geography," *Annals*, Association of American Geographers, 66 (1976): 615–32.

8. See Edward Relph, *Place and Placelessness* (London: Pion, 1976).

9. See David Ley and Marwyn Samuels, eds., *Humanistic Geography: Prospect and Problems* (Chicago: Maaroufa Press, 1978).

10. See Relph, *Place and Placelessness*.

11. See Gary M. Talarchek, *Phenomenology as a New Paradigm in Human Geography*, Discussion Paper no. 39 (Syracuse, N.Y.: Syracuse University, Department of Geography, 1977).

12. See Sheldon J. Watts and Susan J. Watts, "On the Idealist Alternative in Geography and History," *Professional Geographer* 30 (1978): 123–27.

13. Relph, *Place and Placelessness*; see also Anne Buttimer, "Charism and Context: The Challenge of *la géographie humaine*," in Ley and Samuels, *Humanistic Geography*, pp. 58–76.

14. Talarchek, *Phenomenology*.

15. Leonard Guelke, "An Idealist Alternative in Human Geography," *Annals*, Association of American Geographers, 64 (1974): 193–202.

16. Relph, *Place and Placelessness*.

17. Torsten Hägerstrand, "What about People in Regional Science?," *Papers*, Regional Science Association, 24 (1974): 7–24.

18. David Ley, "Social Geography and Social Action," in Ley and Samuels, *Humanistic Geography*, pp. 22–40.

19. Anne Buttimer, "Grasping the Dynamism of Lifeworld," *Annals*, Association of American Geographers, 66 (1976): 277–92.

20. Yi-Fu Tuan, "Humanistic Geography," *Annals*, Association of American Geographers, 66 (1976): 266–76.

21. See Cole Harris, "Theory and Synthesis in Historical Geography," *Canadian Geographer* 15 (1971): 147–72; Cole Harris, "The Historical Mind and the Practice of Geography," in Ley and Samuels, *Humanistic Geography*, pp. 123–37; Annette Buttimer, *Values in Geography*, Commission on College Geography, Resource Paper no. 24 (Washington, D.C.: Association of American Geographers, 1974).

22. Guelke, "Idealist Alternative."

23. See Buttimer, "Charism."

24. Derek Gregory, *Ideology, Science and Human Geography* (London: Hutchinson, 1978).

25. See Avinoam Meir, "Diffusion Spread and Spatial Innovation Transmission

Processes: The Adoption of Industry by Kibbutzim in Israel," Ph.D. dissertation, Department of Geography, University of Cincinnatti, 1977.

26. See Ley, "Social Geography."

27. Buttimer, "Charism."

28. Gregory, *Ideology.*

29. Guelke, "Idealist Alternative."

30. Gregory, *Ideology.*

31. Avinoam Meir, "Diffusion of Modernization among Bedouins of the Israel Negev Desert," *Ekistics* 50 (1983): 451–59.

32. See Avinoam Meir, "Delivering Essential Public Services for Desert Nomads," in Y. Gradus, ed., *Resources and Development in Sparsely Populated Arid Environments* (Boulder, Colo.: Westview Press, 1985), pp. 132–49.

33. See Avinoam Meir, "Pastoral Nomads and the Dialectics of Modernization and Development: Delivering Public Educational Services to the Israeli Negev Bedouin," *Environment and Planning D: Society and Space* (1986), vol. 4, pp. 85–95.

34. Ibid.

35. Gregory, *Ideology*; see also Marvin W. Mikesell, "Tradition and Innovation in Cultural Geography," *Annals*, Association of American Geographers, 68 (1978): 1–16.

CHAPTER THIRTEEN

The Diffusion of Public Assistance
POLITICAL CONSTRAINTS ON AFDC PARTICIPATION

Janet E. Kodras

Diffusion theory places a political innovation in an evolving historical and geographic context, which enables the researcher to understand the situation in which the program developed and reasons for its variable adoption. This analysis uses supply-side and demand-side diffusion conceptualizations to examine forces affecting the adoption of public welfare policies in the United States. Although public assistance programs are rarely studied from these perspectives, it is contended here that diffusion theory, with its spatial and temporal dimensions and its focus upon causal forces of provision and demand, serves as an appropriate conceptual foundation.

This chapter has three sections. First is a discussion of the applicability of diffusion theory to political innovations. Drawing upon this general framework, the second section presents an empirical analysis of participation in the Aid to Families with Dependent Children program (AFDC), one of the largest and most costly welfare policies in the U.S.A. A final section summarizes the substantive findings in terms of their methodological, theoretical, and political implications.

Application of Diffusion Theory to Political Innovations

Two dimensions of diffusion theory are instrumental in conceptualizing the variable adoption of political innovations, such as public assistance programs. This section first summarizes the general perspectives and then provides a framework for analyzing the diffusion of government policies.

One of the major traditions of diffusion research is the "adoption perspective," which focuses upon the potential adopter as the principal actor in the diffusion process.[1] In examining the decision to adopt, researchers working within this tradition are concerned with the level of awareness about the innovation, which is a function of the type and extent of information dissemination. A second concern is the potential adopter's receptivity or resistance to the innovation, which is a function of the need for the innovation as well as the individual's innovativeness, a social-psychological trait influencing demand for the innovation.

In focusing upon the decision strategies made by the potential adopter, the adoption perspective tends to shortchange conditions beyond the individual's control, which affect accessibility to, or availability of, the innovation. This dimension of diffusion is the primary concern of the "market and infrastructure perspective."[2] Researchers working within the tradition emphasize the way in which the innovation is supplied to potential adopters. One concern is the establishment and relative location of the diffusion agency, the outlet through which the innovation is distributed. A second concern is the set of strategies implemented by each agency to induce adoption in its service area.

Considering the adoption together with the market and infrastructure perspectives, it is evident that unless the innovation is made available at or near the location of the potential adopter, through the establishment of a diffusion agency, the individual will not have the option to adopt in the first place. Even in the presence of a diffusion agency, however, dissemination strategies may focus on some segments of the population in lieu of others. Even in this case, access to the innovation does not itself guarantee adoption. The innovation may not be congruent with the potential adopter's needs, or psychological disposition toward acceptance may not be present.

Paralleling the large body of diffusion research, work dealing with public programs has tended to take an adoption perspective. For example, the "American states" literature attributes differences in the timing of policy initiation by states to their relative innovativeness, and cross-national diffusion studies attribute adoption of new programs, such as Social Security, to national innovativeness.[3]

Drawing upon the preceding discussion, I contend that the study of public sector innovations requires the combined strengths of the adoption perspective and the market and infrastructure perspective. In the case of public assistance programs, of which AFDC is an example, at least four aspects of diffusion require examination:

1. the motivation underlying program availability;
2. the character and structural organization of government entities serving as diffusion agencies;
3. the strategies by which the program is diffused;
4. the need/demand for government assistance on the part of the population.

The first three elements are components of the supply of an innovation, and thus accord with the market and infrastructure perspective. The fourth element represents demand for the innovation, as articulated in the adoption perspective. A discussion of each point follows.

Motivation refers to the philosophy and broad guiding principles underlying the initiation, maintenance, and alteration of government programs. Whereas private sector innovations are generally driven by profit criteria, providing a single goal with a fairly clear-cut set of rules, public innovations often entail a complex set of purposes, which may, in fact, be contradictory. Although the stated intention of policy may be service provision, the set of underlying objectives may differ considerably. For example, the stated purpose of the U.S. food stamp program was to assist low-income households in the purchase of a basic need, whereas the underlying intention was originally to assist agricultural interests by increasing demand for domestic food products.[4] More generally, there are always differing attitudes about the rights and responsibilities of the state to provide public assistance as well as the appropriateness of different types of social and economic aid. It is necessary, therefore, to study the variety of actors at all levels of the government bureaucracy, whose attitudes toward public assistance in general, and the individual program specifically, influence its design, organization, operation, and effectiveness.

The impact of these differential attitudes is influenced by the character and organizational structure of the *diffusion agency*. In public sector diffusions, the structure, or control, of these entities is often decentralized, with the national government acting as overall coordinator, and state and local units responsible for day-to-day administration.[5] As diffusion proceeds down the federal hierarchy, there is considerable latitude for national, regional, and local interests to prevail, and thus the nature of the program may vary considerably from level to level of the bureaucracy and, within each level, from place to place. This is illustrated by the location of diffusion agencies. According to service provision criteria, the other with which these are established should reflect the degree of need among the population. In fact, however, this concern may be overridden by broader political interests. Further, the local character of diffusion agencies may vary considerably even if blanket coverage is mandated. Welfare offices, for example, are found in every U.S. county, but they differ in locational proximity to the eligible population, size and quality of staff, convenience in application procedures, and so forth.

Differences in interpretation of the purpose of the program are also evident in the agency *dissemination strategies*. Broad outlines of this diffusion are often specified at high levels of government and might include decision-making powers associated with each level of the program bureaucracy, such as market selection criteria based on whom the program is designed to serve, and the means of targeting that market, such as promotional campaigns, service infrastructures, and user costs.[6] Once again, however, local attitudes will affect implementation, particularly because subnational units are often given considerable discretion in program administration. For example, with regard to voter registration and school desegregation, local jurisdictions in the southern U.S.A. resisted new program guidelines long after the programs had been established. Even more egregious examples are found in programs where eligibility criteria are left largely to local or state governments, as in AFDC.

The preceding aspects of entitlement program availability not only reflect *need/demand* for assistance, as indicated in several examples above, but also influence it. Potential user awareness of entitlement and willingness to adopt are affected by diffusion agency actions and local, regional, and national attitudes toward public assistance. An example of this is the moral authority of the U.S. presidency, which has represented social welfare programs as either a haven for fraud or, alternatively, as a safety net for the deserving poor, and thus has profoundly affected societal values.

Even when a program is effectively supplied, however, individuals may nevertheless resist. Examples include opposition to early collectivization schemes in the Soviet Union and the prohibition era in the United States, both of which ran counter to deep-seated values and traditions. Accordingly, a "cultural fit" between public programs and potential users is an additional element of importance. In the case of public assistance programs, resistance is seen in the form of stigmas attached to the use of welfare.

In summary, the diffusion of political innovations occurs when the state, a complexly structured diffusion agency working with a variety of motivations and purposes, devises a set of strategies to provide the program, and when potential adopters decide whether or not to accept the program. These events are dependent upon the needs of potential adopters, the extent to which the policy identifies with their attitudes, and the influence of societal norms.

To further illustrate the applicability of diffusion theory to political innovations, I turn now to an empirical analysis of the AFDC program. This case study demonstrates that the market and infrastructure perspective and the more commonly utilized adoption perspective are both essential for understanding the diffusion of this public policy.

Participation in the AFDC Program

AFDC is one of the largest, costliest, and oldest of U.S. public assistance programs.[7] Established by the Social Security Act of 1935, it provides federal grants to the states to help defray the costs of providing financial assistance to households with a single head and needy children. The size of the federal grant depends on state median income, with wealthier states paying a larger portion of program costs.

Although the national government does provide guidelines, the states are given considerable discretion in the operation of AFDC. The state legislature and welfare bureaucracies determine eligibility criteria and benefit levels, both of which vary considerably throughout the country.[8] States have the option to provide payments to households where two parents are present but unemployed (AFDC-UP). Approximately half of the states have elected to participate in the AFDC-UP option. These and other aspects of decentralized control result in substantial interstate disparities in program supply, which may influence its adoption rate.

The preceding framework of public policy diffusion has identified two important forces influencing program adoption: the level of need/demand for assistance and the strategies of implementation through which the program is provided. The purpose of this analysis is to examine the extent to which spatial variations in the growth of AFDC participation are related to the distribution of demand versus interstate differentials in program provision, given decentralized control. To operationalize this question, a dynamic model of AFDC participation rates was specified and estimated for the states during the 1970s:

$$P_{80} - P_{70} = f(P_{70}, D, S) \tag{Eq. 1}$$

P_{80} is the percentage of families in a state participating in AFDC in 1980, P_{70} is the equivalent for 1970, and D and S are sets of independent variables representing program demand and supply respectively. D includes decade changes in the state unemployment rate (D_1); percentage of families below the poverty level (D_2); female labor force participation (D_3); divorce rates (D_4); and percent of female-headed families below the poverty level (D_5). These variables represent various aspects of demand, because the program is targeted toward low-income, and primarily female-headed, families. It is anticipated that participation growth will be positively related to growth in each of these conditions, with the exception of female labor force participation.

The supply matrix, S, includes decade changes in the cash benefit paid to a family of four with no other income (S_1); the ratio of poor families to the total number of state and local welfare employees (S_2); and an index of administrative restrictiveness (S_3). A fourth supply measure is a dummy variable indicating the existence of the unemployed parent program in 1975 (S_4). States offering this optional program were coded with a unit score on the variable. These supply variables represent elements of state administration and, as such, they reflect the underlying motivations, strategies, and support (or the lack of it) for AFDC by different state welfare bureaucracies.

The rationale for selecting the supply variables warrants a brief comment. Growth in the benefit level (S_1) is included to test the proposition that program adoption is greater where monetary incentives to participate are higher. Growth in the ratio of poor families to welfare employees (S_2) measures the increase in a state's welfare caseload.[9] The burden of heavy caseloads may deter participation due to delays, confusion, and frustration. Change in program restrictiveness (S_3) is calculated by taking the difference between standardized indices of administrative regulations for 1970 and 1979.[10] State variations in administrative restrictiveness represent the relative difficulty of applying and participating, and should therefore influence the adoption rate. The AFDC-UP dummy variable, (S_4), has been employed to represent the variable presence of this optional program rider and its possible effect in raising program participation.

The model was estimated for the 48 conterminous states using ordinary least squares regression. The stepwise procedure, which was terminated when variables not in the model failed to achieve a 95 percent confidence level, yielded the following model (with t-values shown in parentheses):

$$P_{80} - P_{70} = 1.55 - 0.25P_{70} + 0.54D_1 + 0.09D_s \qquad \text{(Eq. 2)}$$
$$\phantom{P_{80} - P_{70} = 1.55}\; (-2.2) \qquad (4.8) \qquad (2.7)$$

$$R^2 = 0.49$$

The model indicates that AFDC participation growth during the 1970s was most highly associated with growth in unemployment rates (D_1) and with growth in the number of poor, female-headed families (D_s), and that states with higher initial participation (P_{70}) experienced less growth. The negative parameter for the initial level variable suggests that AFDC dynamics during the decade were characterized by "saturation," rather than "explosive growth," an interpretation that would have held if the parameter had been positive.[11]

This finding is very much in accordance with our conceptualizations of the diffusion process. Early in the dissemination of an innovation, we expect certain individuals or areas to emerge as leaders in the adoption. As the diffusion process matures, the original areas may well reach saturation level and, as the innovation diffuses elsewhere, the newer areas experience their greatest growth in acceptance. This saturation is certainly to be expected in the case of a mature program, such as AFDC, and is substantiated by the results of the analysis.

In addition, note that none of the supply variables are significant. The results suggest that program use is a simple response to growing need, such as unemployment and female poverty, and not subject to political constraints in program provision. Thus it appears that adoption is not subject to the principle of limited possibilities—in this case, the very different political contexts in which eligible recipients find themselves.

Given the decentralized nature of program provision, these findings are problematic, requiring us to reexamine the initial model. By specifying a set of demand and supply factors as independent variables, the model does not accord with the complexities of the American welfare system. Rather than pose the question, "Is program adoption a function of demand *or* supply?" and viewing demand and supply as independent variables operating as separate forces, the model should be used to estimate to what extent program adoption reflects demand for assistance *within* different political contexts. Demand and supply do not operate independently. Rather, they interact *in place* as influences upon adoption. To address this issue the initial model was respecified, using the expansion method, a testing framework that examines whether relationships vary across contexts.[12]

Beginning with the significant elements of the initial model,

$$P_{80} - P_{70} = a + bP_{70} + cD_1 + dD_5 \qquad \text{(Eq. 3)}$$

The constant parameters, a, b, c, and d, represent the national average in the relationship between program adoption and its determinants. To test whether the response of program adoption to need *varies* across political contexts, these parameters were "expanded" from constants to functions of program supply characteristics: benefit levels (S_1), caseloads (S_2), administrative restrictiveness (S_3), and presence or absence of AFDC-UP (S_4):

$$
\begin{aligned}
a &= a_0 + a_1S_1 + a_2S_2 + a_3S_3 + a_4S_4 & \text{(Eq. 4)} \\
b &= b_0 + b_1S_1 + b_2S_2 + b_3S_3 + b_4S_4 & \text{(Eq. 5)} \\
c &= c_0 + c_1S_1 + c_2S_2 + c_3S_3 + c_4S_4 & \text{(Eq. 6)} \\
d &= d_0 + d_1S_1 + d_2S_2 + d_3S_3 + d_4S_4 & \text{(Eq. 7)}
\end{aligned}
$$

These supply variables are now expressed as levels in 1975, rather than changes over the decade, to represent the political context of the program. Equations 4–7 were substituted for the constant parameters in equation 3. The final model was estimated, again using a stepwise procedure, with the result:

$$P_{80} - P_{70} = 1.46194 - 0.35823P_{70} + 0.89154S_4 + 0.00142D_1S_1$$
$$(-3.4) \qquad (2.5) \qquad (3.7)$$
$$+ 0.00055D_5S_1 - 0.00322D_5S_2$$
$$(3.1) \qquad (-3.1)$$
$$R^2 = 0.61 \qquad \text{(Eq. 8)}$$

The results indicate that AFDC participation growth during the 1970s was related to its initial level (P_{70}), the presence of AFDC-UP (S_4) unemployment growth interacting with benefit levels (D_1S_1), and growth in poor, female-headed families interacting with benefit levels (D_5S_1) and caseloads (D_5S_2).

First, note that none of the dynamic demand variables operate independently of the welfare context measures. The unemployment parameter, which measures the response of participation growth to growth in unemployment (D_1), is a positive function of support levels (S_1). In other words, in states where benefits are higher, unemployment growth more readily translates into growth in AFDC participation.

In the case of female poverty growth (D_5), the parameter is also a positive function of benefits (S_1). This allows us to draw a similar conclusion to that presented for unemployment growth. That is, in states where benefits are higher, growth in female poverty more readily translates into growth in AFDC participation. Additionally, the parameter for poor, famale-headed families is found to vary with the size of the welfare caseload (S_2). Thus, the size of the welfare system relative to state needs, determines, in part, the extent to which poverty feminization is addressed by the program. Other things being constant, poverty feminization results in less participation growth in states with a smaller welfare bureaucracy.

The remaining significant variables include the initial level (P_{70}), which by virtue of the significantly negative parameter, must again be taken as evidence of saturation. Finally, the unemployed-parent program (S_4) is found to have a positive, significant, and independent effect upon growth in the AFDC program. This is to be expected, inasmuch as the AFDC-UP program increases the number of eligible recipients. This is the only supply variable that operates independently of demand growth, a result which suggests that participation growth is not immediately responsive to benefits, but to characteristics of program operation. Benefits, as noted, only have an effect through their interaction with unemployment growth and poverty feminization.

To further explore the effect of program supply characteristics upon the operation of demand variables, the state parameters for unemployment and poor female-headed families growth can be computed. This involves substituting the significant estimates obtained in equation 8 back into their respective locations in equations 6 and 7. For growth in unemployment (c) and poor female-headed families (d), the parameters are found by:

$$c = f(S_1) = 0.00142S_1 \qquad \text{(Eq. 9)}$$
$$d = f(S_1, S_2) = 0.00055S_1 - 0.00322S_2 \qquad \text{(Eq. 10)}$$

Estimating individual state effects involves multiplying parameter estimates by their benefits (S_1) and caseloads (S_2), as shown in equations 9 and 10. The results are state estimates of the overall effect of unemployment growth and poor female-headed family growth upon AFDC adoption during the 1970s. These parameters are mapped in Figures 13.1 and 13.2.

Due to interstate disparities in benefits, unemployment growth has the largest impact upon AFDC dynamics in lower New England and the Middle Atlantic states, the upper Midwest, and Washington and California. The lowest response to growth in unemployment is found in a broad band of southern states from South Carolina to Texas. A similar pattern emerges from the map of the poverty feminization parameter, which incorporates the effects of state variations in both benefits and caseloads. An important feature of Figure 13.2 is the presence of negative values for the poverty feminization parameter in some southern states. This is attributable to the relatively low benefits and higher caseloads found in the South and suggests that poor female-headed families are finding welfare programs in the South extremely restrictive.

The maps illustrate the extent to which program participation responds to changing need (growth in unemployment and female poverty) across different policy contexts (variation in benefit levels and caseload size). For a given growth in need, participation increases are greatest where the benefit incentive is strongest and, in the case of poverty feminization, where the welfare bureaucracy is sufficient to meet potential demand.

The response of program adoption to changing need varies by states because they are the physical manifestations of a federalized welfare system. The decentralized provision of welfare allows for variations in benefit levels and caseload size, which has impacts upon the response to need. The maps illustrate that the southeastern states, with the greatest demonstrated need for public assistance, exhibit the lowest sensitivity of program adoption to that need.

Summary

The results of my analysis have methodological, theoretical, and substantive implications for the diffusion of political innovations. First, the reason for presenting both the initial and the reformulated models was to make a methodological point. The standard regression model, utilizing

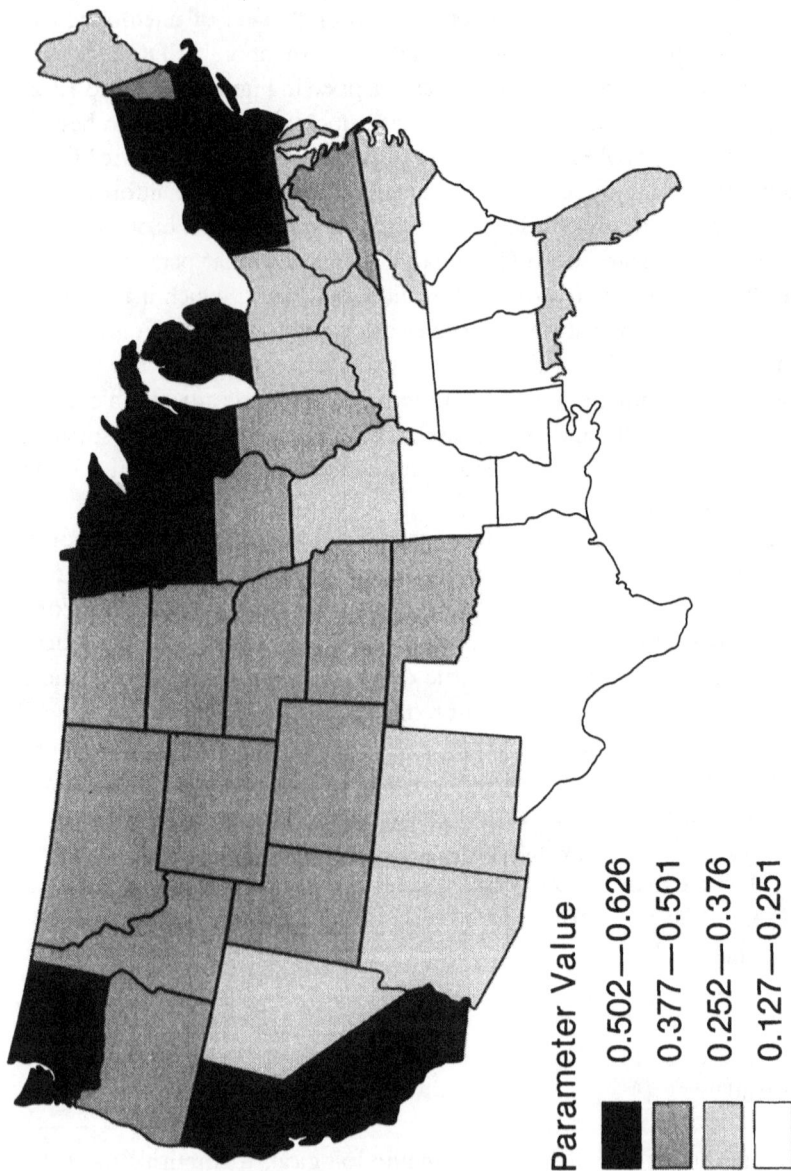

Figure 13.1. State Estimates of Effects of Unemployment on AFDC Adoption, 1970s

Parameter Value

0.502—0.626

0.377—0.501

0.252—0.376

0.127—0.251

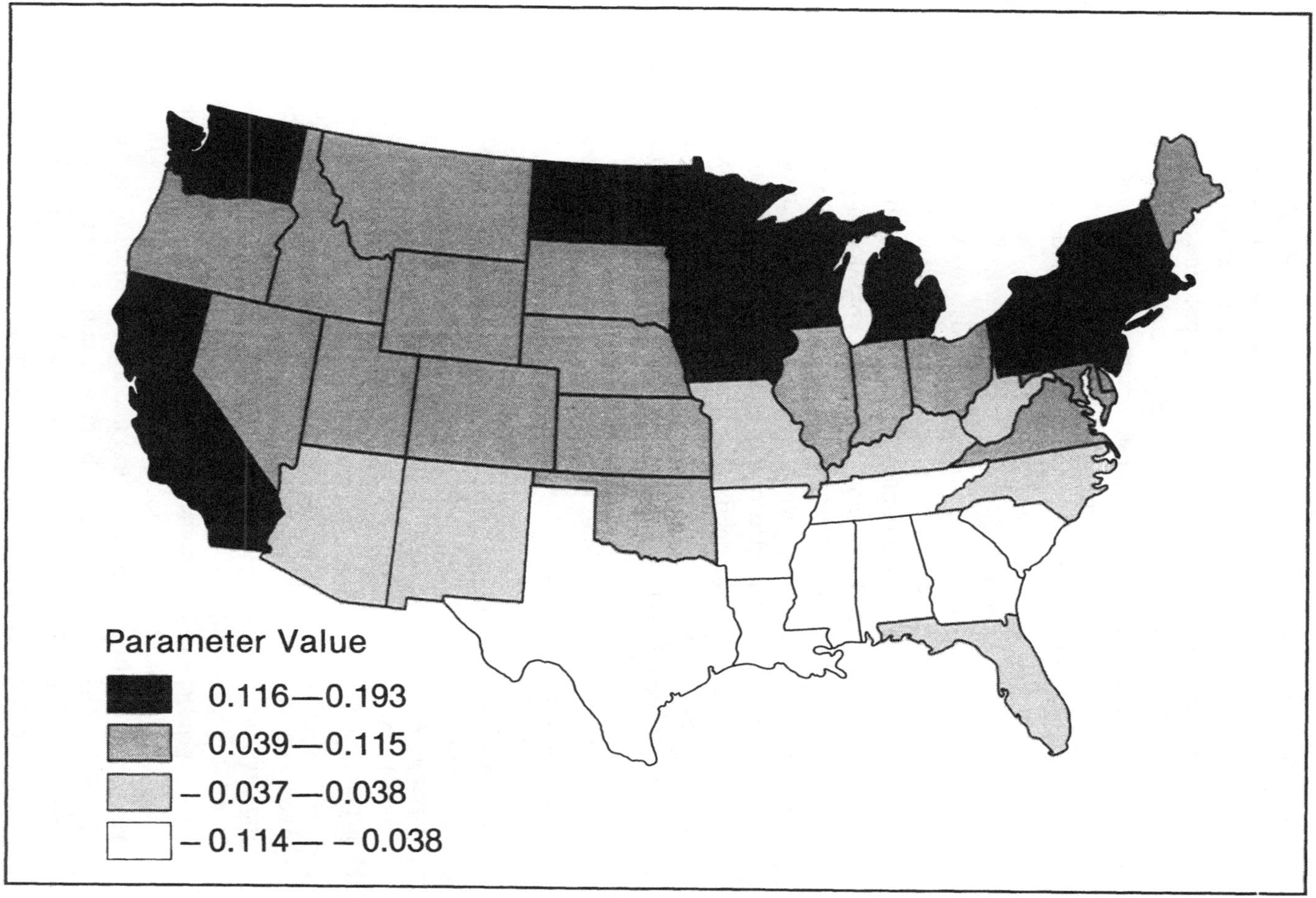

Figure 13.2. State Estimates of Effects of Poverty Feminization on AFDC Adoption, 1970s

Parameter Value

0.116—0.193

0.039—0.115

−0.037—0.038

−0.114—−0.038

constant parameters, is often an inappropriate technique for diffusion research. Rather than assuming that the processes are nomothetic, everywhere and at all times the same, the purpose of diffusion research is to explicitly examine *changing* relationships across space and time, and as embedded in different contexts. For quantifiable studies of diffusion, we require techniques—such as the expansion method—that are more flexible than the standard nomothetic approaches and allow us to more fully identify the complexities of the diffusion process. The initial model indicated that program adoption was simply a response to need. The expansion method, which provides a testing framework to examine whether relationships vary across contexts, was used in the reformulated models to identify the impact of decentralized administration on program response to need.

Turning to the theoretical implications, my analysis has shown that demand effects are driven by program supply characteristics. Specifically, unemployment growth and poverty feminization generate more growth in welfare participation in high benefit states than in those that offer lower benefits. Additionally, the effect of growth in the number of poor, female-headed families upon participation dynamics is diminished in states with relatively small welfare bureaucracies. Both the adoption perspective and the market and infrastructure perspective are instrumental in allowing us to identify these demand and supply effects in the continued diffusion of a mature program. They would also serve as a foundation for an analysis of the origin and initial spread of a new public policy, inasmuch as both the original governmental motivations and strategies, and potential adopters' growing awareness and demand for assistance, would influence its early adoption. The conceptualizations would also be appropriate in studying the reverse diffusion of welfare programs in the U.S.A. due to budget cuts. At issue would be the way in which program withdrawal has caused spatial variations in decreasing participation.

Finally, the analysis addresses a substantive issue long contemplated by researchers examining welfare participation determinants: Is program use more responsive to socio-economic conditions of need or to political conditions of program supply? The findings show that these forces do not operate independently of one another. Instead, welfare participation adequately reflects the demand for assistance only in those jurisdictions where the program is effectively supplied. These findings accord with the complexities of the American welfare system, demonstrating political constraints upon adoption, rather than assuming that eligibles are able to exhibit rational, free choice in the decision to use welfare.

260

The findings, in turn, have ramifications for another current debate, which concerns the level of the government hierarchy most appropriate to provide welfare assistance. Further decentralization of control, known as the New Federalism, by granting the individual states greater responsibility in program design and administration, portends increasing spatial inequities in the response of public assistance to need.

Notes

1. See E. M. Rogers, *Modernization among Peasants: The Impact of Communication* (New York: Holt, Rinehart, and Winston, 1969); E. M. Rogers and F. F. Shoemaker, *Communication of Innovations: A Cross Cultural Approach* (New York: Free Press, 1971).

2. See L. A. Brown, *Innovation Diffusion: A New Perspective* (New York: Methuen, 1981).

3. See D. Collier and R. E. Messick, "Prerequisites versus Diffusion: Testing Alternative Explanations of Social Security Adoption," *American Political Science Review* 69 (1975): 1299–1315; V. Gray, "Innovation in the States: A Diffusion Study," *American Political Science Review* 67 (1973): 174–85; M. H. Ross and E. Homer, "Galton's Problem in Cross-National Research," *World Politics* 29 (1976): 1–28; J. Walker, "The Diffusion of Innovations among the American States," *American Political Science Review* 63 (1969): 880–99.

4. See J. E. Kodras, "The Geographic Perspective in Social Policy Evaluation: A Conceptual Approach with Application to the U.S. Food Stamp Program," Ph.D. dissertation, Department of Geography, Ohio State University, 1982, chap. 4.

5. Brown (*Innovation*, chap. 3) has identified three organizational modes within which diffusion agencies operate: a centralized decision-making structure, a decentralized decision-making structure, and a decentralized structure with a coordinating propagator. As noted, most public assistance policies fall into this last category.

6. More generally, Brown (*Innovation*, chap. 4) notes four elements of diffusion strategies, all of which have corollaries in public sector diffusion: the development of infrastructure and organizational capabilities, pricing, promotional communications, and market selection/segmentation. The orchestration of these into a diffusion agency strategy depends upon innovation characteristics, agency characteristics, innovation life cycle, and the spatial extent of diffusion.

7. See L. Platky, "Aid to Families with Dependent Children: An Overview, October, 1977," *Social Security Bulletin* 40 (1977): 17–22.

8. See E. Wohlenberg, "Interstate Variations in AFDC Programs," *Economic Geography* 52 (1976): 254–66.

9. The caseload variable is based on all welfare employees, not caseworkers only, and the total poverty population, not all of which is served by welfare.

10. The 1970 index is reported in E. Wohlenberg, "An Index of Eligibility Standards for Welfare Benefits," *Professional Geographer* 28 (1976): 381–84. Data for the 1979 index were derived from E. Chief, "Need Determination in the AFDC Program," *Social Security Bulletin* 42 (1979): 11–21.

11. See G. I. Thrall, "Regional Dynamics of Local Government Welfare Expenditures," *Urban Geography* 2 (1981): 255–68.

12. See E. Casetti, "Generating Models by the Expansion Method: Applications to Geographic Research," *Geographical Analysis* 4 (1972): 81–91; E. Casetti, "Mathematical Modelling and the Expansion Method," in R. B. Mandal, ed., *Statistics for Geographers and Social Scientists* (New Delhi: Concept Publishing, 1982), chap. 4; E. Casetti, "The Dual Expansions Method: An Application to Evaluating the Effects of Population Growth on Development," in *IEEE Transactions on Systems, Man, and Cybernetics*, vol. 16-SMC (1986): 29–39.

Summation

CONTEMPORARY DIFFUSION RESEARCH

The diffusion process involves the physical transfer of things or artifacts (pots, plants, plans, books, or automobiles); the transfer of techniques for constructing or replicating such artifacts; the transfer of institutionalized systems of relationships (be they ecclesiastical, managerial, ceremonial, military, or economic); and the transfer of ideas or complexes of ideas including religious beliefs and political ideologies. Consequently, it is a phenomenon confronted by a host of disciplines besides geography and anthropology. Diffusion figures importantly in the study of history, economics, political science, and sociology. Given this broad relevance, it is surprising that a critical examination from a multidisciplinary perspective of both the concept and the phenomenon of diffusion does not exist.

This volume, like the conference upon which it was based, had four major aims: (1) to assess the successes and shortcomings of the diffusion model of culture change in explaining the transfer and transformation of ideas and material culture over space and time; (2) to foster an interchange between scholars from the major disciplines concerned with such spatial and temporal change; (3) to map future directions for inquiry; and (4) to disseminate the results of the interchange. In the main, the chapters in this volume therefore offer theoretical and programmatic perspectives rather than new data.

As Peter Haggett has remarked, "in general language the term 'diffusion' means simply to spread out, to disperse, or to intermingle, but in its scientific usage it has acquired more precise meanings."[1] In that scientific sense, diffusion means the transfer or transmission of objects, processes, ideas, and information from one population or region to another. Few scholars would deny that cultural diffusion has occurred throughout world prehistory and history. However, opinions as to the importance of diffusion in culture change vary enormously. Some scholars have elevated diffusion to the status of an "ism" or a "supposed universal and exclusive historical process";[2] others have largely dismissed diffusion, ignored it, or been unwilling to grant it any causal primacy whatever in the process of culture change. Nonetheless, if for no other reason than the ubiquitousness of the process, the determination of the role of diffusion in culture change remains of central importance in a number of the social sciences and humanities.

Although there are a number of academic disputes that center on the validity of the "diffusionist" paradigm, this volume has concentrated on four broad areas of interest (agreement and disagreement): diffusion in prehistory; diffusion in history; the history and theory of diffusion; and the methods and models in diffusion studies.

Diffusion in Prehistory

This section has been concerned with accounting for the origins and spread of cultural traits and processes in the more remote past. The radically contrasting perspectives of cultural geography, anthropology, and the "New Archeology" have been brought to bear upon these questions. Particular attention has been paid to the role of diffusion in the development and spread of food production and associated elements of Neolithic culture.

The determination of the role of diffusion in this worldwide development is a key question in prehistory: if agriculture and complex society can be shown to have emerged independently in the Old and New Worlds, then the similar trajectories that these developments followed in each region suggest that the processes of cultural transformation were governed by some universal regularity of cultural evolution. On the other hand, if these regions can be shown to have been linked by culture contact over time, the independence of the various historical "trials" disappears. Under the latter circumstances, the rise of agriculture in the two hemispheres would have to be viewed as events whose similarities were due largely to diffusion rather than to the independent operation of specifiable laws of cultural development. The problem remains far from resolution.

George F. Carter has pursued a twofold purpose in his chapter: (1) to provide a defense of "cultural historical diffusionism" and (2) to do so by reviewing the evidence of transoceanic contact between the Old and New Worlds before A.D. 1500. In the process, he has also provided a spirited account of his emergence as an unreconstructed diffusionist. Throughout his paper Carter has applied what he elsewhere calls "Kilmer's Law": "Only God can make a tree." This being so, any demonstrable pre-Columbian parallels between the domesticated plant and animal repertories of the Old and New Worlds must be taken as proof of transoceanic diffusion: they cannot be dismissed as due to "independent invention" by peoples never in contact with one another. With this observation in hand, Carter has mustered diverse—and often fragmentary—evidence of the possible presence of Old World plants and animals (including the chicken, the elephant, cotton, and the bottle gourd) in the New World in pre-Columbian times. He has also reversed the question and cited possible examples of the pre-Columbian diffusion of New World species (including corn, the sweet potato, the peanut, and the hibiscus) to Asia, Pacific islands, Africa, and Europe. He has expanded his discussion to include some elements of culture not governed by Kilmer's law, including coins, cylinder stamp seals, writing, and carved inscriptions.

Alan Osborn's chapter has approached the problem from a very different perspective. Although willing to admit that inventions occur at a specific time and place and spread by diffusion, Osborn has contended that the study of "origins and dispersals," in Sauer's memorable phrase,[3] is mere description. One does not explain a cultural trait by tracing its diffusion. To do that, one must understand what part the trait plays in the cultural system in which it is found and thus the way the trait contributes to the "adaptive fitness" of the population that bears that culture. Traits will spread only where they are useful; they do not simply diffuse, they are selected in the Darwinian sense. Thus, Osborn has concerned himself chiefly with what is called the "adoption environment" in diffusion studies.

Osborn's argument has focused on the use of ground shell in the tempering of ceramic vessels by Native American peoples after about A.D. 1000 in eastern North America. The appearance and distribution of this cultural trait has been explained as due to the simple spread of an idea over space and time. Osborn has contended, however, that the emergence and current distribution of this cultural complex could be understood only by examining precisely how it "fit" into the cultural systems of which it was a part and how it contributed to the environmental adaptation of that system.

In chapter 3, D. Bruce Dickson has wished a plague on the intellectual houses of both Carter and Osborn. He has identified—and rejected—two general classes of scientific explanation of cultural change: the "utopian" and the "epidemic." Dickson has suggested that the former class of explanation tends to be found in the work of anthropologically trained prehistorians who have been heavily influenced by functionalism or structural functionalism, general systems theory, and neoclassical economics. Utopian explanations emphasize the holistic nature of cultures, focus on the intercommunication between their parts, and see them as self-maintaining systems that tend toward equilibrium. In contrast, Dickson has asserted that "epidemic" theories tend to be found in the tool kits of cultural geographers and culture historians. In this class of explanation the emphasis is placed on the simple distribution of culture traits as a means of reconstructing culture process. As in an epidemic disease, continuous distribution of these phenomena are taken as prima facie evidence of contact between cultures. *Contact* is regarded as a universal historical process that, in itself, can account for culture change. Such theories tend to emphasize the cumulative, even "accumulative," nature of cultures and their susceptibility to novelty and change.

Dickson has illustrated the differences between these two rival classes of explanation by examining their contrastive interpretations of the evidence for the emergence of agriculture. Each of these classes of explanation is really a way of thinking about the problem of cultural tansformation, and each brings different facets of culture to the forefront and structures their examination in a particular manner. Dickson has concluded that both explanatory forms have proven inadequate to the task of accounting for the emergence of agriculture. He has suggested four "dimensions" that any comprehensive future alternative explanation of the problem of agricultural origins must address.

Diffusion in History

Chapters in part 2 have concentrated on diffusion within and between Europe, America and, to a lesser extent, Japan, during recorded time. For the most part, authors have focused on the transfer and transformation of political, social, economic, and legal ideas and institutions since the beginning of the Christian era. A largely unstated agenda in some of these chapters is examination of the concept of an emerging "modern world system" as postulated by Wallerstein,[4] Nash,[5] Wolf,[6] Frank,[7] and others. Scholars dealing in historical time are able to assess the role of diffusion and the utility of "diffusionism" as a school of historical explanation using the rich documentation available for the processes of culture change and transformation during the last two thousand years. Here too, a variety of perspectives and approaches, including history, geography, and archeology, have been brought together.

In chapter 4 William H. McNeill has argued the general case for the primacy of diffusion in history. He has noted that, for a variety of reasons (not the least of which are ethnic, national, and religious pride), the importance of the diffusion process is often neglected in historiography. McNeill has made the point that early humankind had greater mobility on sea and land than we tend to credit. Particularly after about 1700 B.C., mobility on land was usually impeded by the polities of the nomadic peoples of Central Asia. Technology and organization seesawed with politics thereafter. Camel caravans and standardized packing systems facilitated trade; aggressive, disunited nomadic polities discouraged it. On occasion, a single polity, such as that established under Ghengis Khan, unified the nomads and rendered land movement across Central Asia particularly easy for a time. Sea transport circumvented such problems, and nomadic sea raiding of trade vessels was put down by European cannon-armed merchant shipping after A.D. 1500.

McNeill has also raised an important point in the history of diffusionism. Flushed with the success of their expansive, industrial culture in the nineteenth century, Europeans began to selectively forget that many of their ideas and much of their material culture had come from other parts of the world, in particular Islamic countries and China.

Karl W. Butzer's chapter bridges the sections on prehistory and history. Archeological and archival sources are used to demonstrate the functional integration of eastern Spain into a developing Mediterranean trading system from preclassical times to those of Islam. Butzer has argued persuasively the importance of studying adoption environments. Roman and pre-Roman irrigation systems in eastern Spain created a cultural preadaption in favor of the more extensive irrigation systems brought into the area by the Islamic invaders. None of this could have happened, however, without the well-developed transport and trade network that connected eastern Spain to the major urban centers of the western Mediterranean.

The richness of the documentary record available to the student of the diffusion of contemporary culture is apparent in the chapter by Peter J. Hugill. Using this record, Hugill has contended that most of the early technical developments in the world automobile industry originated within a small area in northwestern Europe. Production and management systems were added in North America and the resulting technological complexes diffused globally. Diffusion paths are obscured by unwillingness on the part of producing companies to admit that copying is the norm in the industry, but Hugill has asserted that a voluminous popular and technical literature attests to the primacy of diffusion. Hugill has argued strongly for the importance of the specific adoption environment in the initial adoption phase of any revolutionary new technological paradigms.

Bruce Seely's chapter also concerns recent history and the automobile, although his focus is on the diffusion of the scientific method—or perhaps of "scientism"—into highway engineering during the development of hard-surfaced roads in the United States. Engineers in the federal Bureau of Public Roads attempted to adopt what they saw as scientific methods to resolve road construction problems after the First World War. Seely has found their signal lack of success instructive. Engineers of the period had inadequate understanding of the limitations of the scientific method. They attempted to solve complex, multidimensional problems with insufficient theory and experiments that restricted them to single variables. The problems were eventually solved pragmatically by highway engineers working chiefly in state highway departments. These engineers did not attempt to adopt the rigorous deductive methods of science but instead continued to approach the problems of road construction in a practical, case-by-case manner. Seely has thus presented an example of the diffusion and adoption of a set of ideas and procedures inappropriate to their adoption environment. Such a subject is rare in the diffusion literature, but one wonders how often situations such as he has described can be met with in the real world.

The History and Theory Diffusion

Chapters in part 3 concentrate on the intellectual history of the doctrine of diffusionism and its utility (or inutility) in cultural studies. J. Nicholas Entrikin (chap. 8) has placed diffusion studies in the context of the larger conceptual or paradigmatic shifts that have taken place within the discipline of geography during the twentieth century. Entrikin has identified the sequence of paradigms that have characterized geography in the modern era as: "environmentalism to regional synthesis to spatial analysis and finally into the present, pluralistic stage best described as post-spatial analysis." He has then examined the differing roles assigned to the diffusion process and the varying emphases placed upon diffusionism within each of these successive paradigms.

Following Entrikin's historical survey of diffusion as a concept within the discipline of geography, Philip L. Wagner (chap. 9) has provided an examination of diffusion as a process of human communication. Using the model of culture emerging in modern information science as his point of departure, Wagner has viewed diffusion as a subset of the communication process in general. He has noted that communication always occurs in conformity to "'codes' or sets of prescriptive or at least interpretable *rules*," and that these rules divide communicators into one of two functions: initiator or attendee, communicator or receptor. Wagner has suggested that the impact of subsequent communication is governed in large measure by the *Geltung*—the worthiness or prestige—of the individual communicator. Communication, and therefore diffusion, occur in a social context in which the success of an innovative message "depends upon the *Geltung* of its sender compared with that of the recipient." The notion of *Geltung* provides a means of explaining, and perhaps predicting, the path of diffusion within and between societies. Wagner has ended his chapter with an emphatic affirmation of the universality of the diffusion process: inasmuch as human beings are "biologically constituted through a long and special evolution to behave in a certain way, human beings *will* communicate, they *will* diffuse their messages among their fellows despite all hindrances."

Joseph Sonnenfeld (chap. 10) has offered an interesting counterpoint to Wagner's use of the universal characteristics of our species to demonstrate the inevitability of diffusion. Like Wagner, Sonnenfeld has begun his script with a discussion of a basic human characteristic: "innate abilities"—aptitudes and talents that, in part at least, are a product of the genetic inheritance of our species. The specific example used is "wayfinding," or the ability to orient and guide oneself through strange surroundings. Such ability is, to a greater or lesser degree, part of our genetic baggage as a species, yet the manifestation of such native human ability in practical navigation in the various cultures of the world is generally interpreted by geographers as due to the diffusion of learned techniques. By his example, Sonnenfeld has offered the possibility that at least the most basic techniques of wayfinding and other "inborn abilities" are universal to the species and therefore not prima facie evidence of historical contacts between separate peoples.

Methods and Models in Diffusion Studies

Torsten Hägerstrand (chap. 11) has emphasized the multifaceted nature of the diffusion process and has suggested a number of unresolved problems encountered in gauging and assessing it. Hägerstrand begins with a discussion of the principle of limited possibilities and turns that key intellectual weapon of the antidiffusionists to good account in his analysis of diffusion. Central to his argument is the notion that contemporary technical change may be radically changing the nature of the diffusion process itself. Cities have been seen as centers of innovation. Hägerstrand has suggested that, in the past, cities may in fact have collected and concentrated the innovations occurring in the areas surrounding them, rather than acting as their original source or stimulus. The advent of sophisticated communication networks in the contemporary era may be altering the role of cities by decentralizing the innovation and diffusion process. Other chapters in part 4 have followed similar themes by dealing with a number of theoretical and practical problems in the study of diffusion posed by contemporary technical and infrastructural change.

Avinoam Meir (chap. 12) has made a case for leavening the positivist social science found in diffusion studies done in economic geography with the humanism traditionally found in cultural geography. Meir's chief objection to positivist studies has focused on their neglect of the actors involved in the process. He has suggested that this neglect may be rectified if future positivist studies of the adoption environment are undertaken from the standpoint of the adopter. As an example of the utility of such an approach, Meir has examined the diffusion of modern educational services among Israel's Bedouin population from the perspective of the people themselves. Meir's chapter is thus in the tradition of the symbolic interactionist critique of positivist sociology; Blumer,[8] Goffman,[9] and Strauss[10] have make a similar case for focusing on the actor in social analysis. Meir has also argued forcefully for a more intensive study of the adoption environment by positivist social scientists.

Janet E. Kodras's study (chap. 13) treats public sector innovation and diffusion, and is a major corrective to excessive concern with adoption environments. She has analyzed the state itself as a "complexly structured diffusion agency" and has considered the importance of potential adopters' needs and attitudes. She has applied this complex view of innovation diffusion to the federal-supported, state-administered AFDC program. Kodras has concluded that supply and demand forces are both important to the spread of innovation, but that a "supply-side" view is an important contribution to the "enabling infrastructure" that allows innovations to diffuse. This is a refinement of the market and infrastructure approach initially developed by Lawrence Brown.[11] In contrast to Meir, Kodras has contended that previous diffusion studies have been most concerned with the adopter, or the "demand-side" of innovation. She has mustered convincing evidence to suggest that this distorts our understanding of the diffusion process, that such innovations do not operate in a "free market," and that the availability of public sector innovations has little to do with demand for them. Kodras has demonstrated the necessity for merging demand- and supply-side perspectives to properly predict the diffusion of public sector innovations. Some states choose to adopt specific innovations, some do not. Among those states that chose to adopt them, provision for supplying the innovation varies in the pattern of funding, in both space and time, as competing interest groups successively substitute their definitions of the market and appropriate supply level for the innovation.

A clear general conclusion of this volume is that the nature of the adoption environment is central to the diffusion process. Sometimes diffusion is encouraged and sometimes not. What defines the adoption environment is highly complex. The level of technology at the time of diffusion, the institutional framework, and the ideational background are clearly the three key variables, although they are not of equal force in all examples. Most of the substantive work presented here deals with successful examples of diffusion, although it is instructive from a theoretical perspective to have Seely's case study of a failure of diffusion. The theoretical work is not refined enough to offer any overall theory to predict diffusion in all situations under study by social scientists. There clearly are areas where predictive modeling can offer more accurate understanding of cases limited carefully as to technologies, institutions, and ideas. There is also a need for broad, interpretive, humanistic, inferential studies to point the way toward improved theoretical understanding.

Notes

1. Peter Haggett, *Geography: A Modern Synthesis* (New York, Harper and Row, 1972), p. 348.

2. Murray J. Leaf, *Man, Mind, and Science; A History of Anthropology* (New York: Columbia University Press, 1979), p. 164.

3. Carl O. Sauer, *Agricultural Origins and Dispersals* (New York: American Geographics Society, 1952).

4. Immanuel Wallerstein, *The Modern World-System* (New York: Academic Press, 1974).

5. June Nash, "Ethnographic Aspects of the World Capitalist System," *Annual Review of Anthropology* 10 (1981): 393–423.

6. Eric Wolf, *Europe and the People without History* (Berkeley: University of California Press, 1982).

7. André Gunder Frank, *World Accumulation, 1492–1789* (New York: Monthly Review Press, 1978).

8. Herbert Blumer, *Symbolic Interactionism* (Englewood Cliffs, N.J.: Prentice-Hall, 1969).

9. Erving Goffman, *The Presentation of Self in Everyday Life* (Garden City, N.Y.: Doubleday, 1959).

10. Anselm Strauss, *Mirrors and Masks* (San Francisco: Sociology Press, 1969).

11. Lawrence A. Brown, *Innovation Diffusion: A New Perspective* (New York: Methuen, 1981).

List of Contributors

Karl W. Butzer, Dickson Centennial Professor of Liberal Arts
Department of Geography, University of Texas at Austin

George F. Carter, Professor Emeritus
Department of Geography, Texas A&M University

D. Bruce Dickson, Associate Professor
Department of Anthropology, Texas A&M University

J. Nicholas Entrikin, Professor
Department of Geography, University of California, Los Angeles

Torsten Hägerstrand, Professor
Department of Social and Economic Geography, University of Lund, Sweden

Peter J. Hugill, Associate Professor
Department of Geography, Texas A&M University

Janet E. Kodras, Assistant Professor
Department of Geography, Florida State University

LIST OF CONTRIBUTORS

William H. McNeill, Distinguished Service Professor of History
Department of History, University of Chicago

Avinoam Meir, Professor
Department of Geography, Ben Gurion University of the Negev, Israel

Alan Osborn, Assistant Professor
Department of Anthropology, University of Nebraska

Bruce Seely, Assistant Professor of History and Science, Technology
and Society
Department of Social Science, Michigan Technological University

Joseph Sonnenfeld, Professor
Department of Geography, Texas A&M University

Philip L. Wagner, Professor
Department of Geography, Simon Fraser University, Canada

Index

The Transfer and Transformation of Ideas and Material Culture was composed into type on a Linotron 202 phototypesetter in ten point Galliard with three-point spacing between the lines. Galliard and Galliard Italic were selected for display. The book was designed by Jim Billingsley, typeset by Vera-Reyes, Inc., printed offset by Thomson-Shore, Inc., and bound by John H. Dekker & Sons, Inc. The paper on which this book is printed bears acid-free characteristics for an effective life of at least three hundred years.

TEXAS A&M UNIVERSITY PRESS : COLLEGE STATION